Studies in Polar Law

VOLUME 4

The titles published in this series are listed at *brill.com/splw*

Arctic Policies of Non-Arctic States

Arctic Policies of Non-Arctic States

Edited by

Medy Dervovic, Laura Ulatowski and Stefan Kirchner

BRILL | NIJHOFF

LEIDEN | BOSTON

Library of Congress Cataloging-in-Publication Data

Names: Dervovic, Medy editor | Ulatowski, Laura editor | Kirchner, Stefan, 1976- editor
Title: Arctic policies of non-arctic states / edited by Medy Dervovic, Laura Ulatowski, and Stefan Kirchner.
Description: Leiden ; Boston : Brill Academic Publishers, Inc, 2025. | Series: Studies in polar law, 2589-6822 ; volume 4 | Includes bibliographical references and index.
Identifiers: LCCN 2025031986 (print) | LCCN 2025031987 (ebook) | ISBN 9789004734678 hardback | ISBN 9789004734685 pdf
Subjects: LCSH: International law--Arctic regions | Arctic regions--International status | Polar regions--International status | Arctic regions--Strategic aspects
Classification: LCC KZ4110.P65 A739 2025 (print) | LCC KZ4110.P65 (ebook) | DDC 341.2/9--DC23/eng/20250723
LC record available at https://lccn.loc.gov/2025031986
LC ebook record available at https://lccn.loc.gov/2025031987

Typeface for the Latin, Greek, and Cyrillic scripts: "Brill". See and download: brill.com/brill-typeface.

ISSN 2589-6822
ISBN 978-90-04-73467-8 (hardback)
ISBN 978-90-04-73468-5 (e-book)
DOI 10.1163/9789004734685

Contents

Foreword

Arctic Policies of Non-Arctic States is a welcoming addition to the existing studies on the engagement in the Arctic governance of those nations that do not have land territories above the Arctic Circle, the non-Arctic States. This volume has its distinct added values. First, it includes examination of the impacts or otherwise of the February 2022 and ongoing Russian invasion of Ukraine on the Arctic policies of 10 nations covered (three Asian States added from Chapter 1). Second, it provides detailed examination of the policies of those non-Arctic States less prominent in previous studies: Belgium, Greece, and Latvia. Finally, this volume is ably edited as well as many of its chapters written by early to mid-career scholars, providing fresh insights into the subject matter.

According to the editors, this volume tries to provide "a snapshot" of different perspectives of the Arctic being retrieved from the Arctic-related policies and activities of 10 non-Arctic States from Europe and Asia (*Preface*, p. VIII). This editorial policy is well reflected in its ordering of its chapters based on the alphabetical order of the names of non-Arctic States being examined; and the book has succeeded in achieving this modest objective. An in-depth and panoramic reading of this book, however, will enable the reader to tease out a few recurring and intersecting themes: a historically and strategically defined relationship of each of those non-Arctic States with the Russian Federation *and* the United States, the two giants in Arctic governance; and the relative dependencies on the resources and their trade, both marine living and mineral, from the wider Arctic region including those areas under the jurisdiction of the eight Arctic States.

This insight gained from this book unavoidably leads to an academic appetite to analyze the potential impact of a more recent challenge coming from the other Arctic giant, the United States, under the second Trump administration on the Arctic policies of non-Arctic States. This, of course, must await the follow-up volume, hopefully from the same editors, in this Brill's Studies in Polar Law series.

Akiho Shibata
Cherry blossoming Kobe, Japan, 1 April 2025

Preface

Because of climate change, the Arctic has gained significant attention from policy actors from beyond the circumpolar north. This increased attention in the first two decades of the 21st century has been reflected by an increasing number of non-Arctic observer States at the Arctic Council. Since the escalation of Russia's war against Ukraine, the cooperation across political divides that had characterized the international governance of the Arctic since the end of the Cold War has been replaced by a clear separation between Russia and the seven Western Arctic States. The outside interest in the Arctic, however, remains high.

The idea behind this book is to provide readers with insights into perceptions that exist in non-Arctic States and their impact on policymaking. This volume collects chapters from emerging and established voices in Arctic policy research. While most authors come from or work outside the Arctic region, they are connected to the Arctic in different ways. The picture provided here is necessarily incomplete and will focus on Europe and Asia. At the same time, this collection brings together different perspectives because the authors represent a range of different disciplines.

The chapters brought together in this book provide academics' views from national perspectives rather than a complete and coherent picture. This collection is an attempt to capture the way other States look at the Arctic region and its governance at a time of multi-dimensional change. The Arctic changes, as do the political conditions in which its international governance operates.

While the Arctic Council's relevance has decreased dramatically in recent years, it remains the most important international forum focused on the Arctic region. It therefore seems fitting to begin this collection with a look at the five Asian States that have gained observer status with the Arctic Council: the People's Republic of China, India, Japan, Singapore, and the Republic of Korea. *Julie Auffret-Cariou* and *Rashmi Ramesh* show that, while Asia is not speaking on Arctic issues with a single voice, there is potential for cooperation between Asian and Arctic States – especially in the area of scientific cooperation. However, the authors also show differences and rift potentials between the different Asian States. It, therefore, does not come as a surprise that Asia is far less unified in its policy approach than Europe. In relation to Russia, the authors identify China and India as potential advocates for a return to including Russia in Arctic cooperation, highlighting the risk that the desire for a return to the old normal, while Russia continues its illegal war against Ukraine, might trump the value-based concerns of all other Arctic States besides Russia.

Belgium's connection to the Arctic region is based primarily on a rich history of scientific research. *Romain Chuffart* and *Karen van Loon* show that the Arctic is an object of policy-interest that has gained more and more attention in recent years. Even though Belgium did not engage in official Arctic policy activities until a few years ago, there is a wide interest in Arctic-related issues among different policy actors in the country. The example of Belgium is interesting in particular due to the multi-level nature of governance in the tri-lingual country.

China's interest in the Arctic has long garnered attention in the Arctic region. While there have been examples of cooperation, there are also concerns about China's intentions in the region. Unlike the Member States of the European Union and Japan, the People's Republic of China (PRC) is inherently unfree. The Beijing government is pursuing aggressive policies towards their maritime neighbours and has a highly negative track record when it comes to dealing with workers' rights elsewhere. The official disregard for human rights, democracy, fundamental freedoms, and international law put the PRC at odds with the shared values that provide the fundament for international cooperation across the Arctic, with the notable exception of Russia. China actively supports the Russian Federation in its illegal war of aggression against Ukraine, thereby deepening the rift with the West, including the other Arctic States. The positive outlook that might have existed in the past when it comes to cooperation with China in the Arctic has proven to not have been justified. In recent years, China appears to have pivoted clearly towards Russia. This cooperation between undemocratic powers in the Arctic poses a threat to peace and security in the region. *Marco Volpe*'s chapter shows that China is also an active player in the field of scientific exploration in the Arctic region. Given that scientific engagement has been a door-opener to policy roles in the Arctic, Beijing's approach appears to deserve more caution than becomes immediately clear from *Volpe*'s chapter. The promise of scientific advancements that is included in the official policies described by *Volpe* is inseparably intertwined with the threat posed by the very nature of the government of the PRC. International cooperation in the Arctic accelerated after the end of the Cold War in the 1990s, when it was hoped that Russia would move along a path to eventual democratization. This hope has been shattered, as has been the hope that China would reform based on outside influences through international trade. Instead, the West's offers for cooperation have been used by both Russia and China for their own interests. Russia has seriously damaged the Arctic Council and China has the potential to further disrupt the international governance of the Arctic. Both countries, one Arctic, governing about half of the Arctic land territory and population, and one claiming a (legally non-existent) "near-Arctic" status, pose threats to Arctic governance. *Volpe*'s chapter might help readers to better understand China's approach and its own interests and capabilities in scientific research in the Arctic. It is to be hoped that the seven Western Arctic States have not forgotten that Laocoön's famous words are not limited to Greeks. In the Arctic, they also apply to the enticing promise of future scientific research. Given the importance of scientific research for those who are involved in Arctic governance and diplomacy, the promise of Chinese scientific research has to be seen for what it is.

In terms of ship operations, the Mediterranean country of Greece, with a population of just over ten million people, continues to punch far above its weight. Compared to other countries from Europe's Mediterranean region, Greece is trailing in terms of Arctic policy development. *Apostolos Tsiouvalas* and *Konstantinos Deligiannis-Virvos* put the Hellenic Republic's Arctic-related policy into a wider political and historical context with a particular view to maritime issues and scientific research, and they provide the outlines of the potential future Arctic policy of Greece.

Japan, on the other hand, has long played an important role in Arctic affairs as a non-Arctic State. Unlike China, Japan has a clear claim to being almost Arctic: not only is Japan located at the south of the Sea of Okhotsk, which, similar to the Bay of Bothnia, experiences Arctic-like sea conditions in the winter months, similar to the Arctic States it is also home to a marginalized Indigenous people, the Ainu. In addition, Japanese institutions, such as in Sapporo and Kobe, make important contributions to interdisciplinary Arctic research, including in the fields of international law and Arctic governance. Forming an international team based in Japan, *Juha Saunavaara, Marina Lomaeva, Hiroki Takakura*, and *Fujio Ohnishi* investigate recent developments in Japan's Arctic policy in the wake of the 2022 escalation of the invasion of Ukraine by Russia, which has severely disrupted international cooperation in the Arctic, especially in the Arctic Council, of which Japan is an observer. Their chapter shows that Japanese institutions have taken pragmatic steps that are aimed at safeguarding scientific research in the Arctic without betraying the values that have underpinned Arctic cooperation and that have been abandoned by the Russian Federation.

Like the other European countries discussed in this book, Latvia is a member of both the European Union and the North Atlantic Treaty Organization (NATO). The Baltic nation's Arctic policy activities are seen primarily through these lenses. In light of current security developments in Europe, it is hardly surprising that security matters are given particular prominence in the chapter written by *Gints Jegermanis* and *Pavel Tkach*. The authors also look at the possibility of Arctic Council observer status for Latvia. For the moment, this seems to be only a hypothetical question as approval of observer status obligations requires the consent of all Arctic Council members. Given Estonia's negative experience and the overall political situation, it seems unlikely that new observer applications would be approved anytime soon.

Eline Lüschen looks at a country with a long history of exploration in the Arctic, the Netherlands. Ranging from the 16th-century era of exploration to modern-day scientific and economic activities, including the Arctic Council and the challenge of climate change, the author sets the stage for a treatment of the Arctic policy of the Netherlands today. In doing so, she connects history and the present with a view to the future and provides an update on the current state of affairs when it comes to international policy cooperation in the Arctic.

From Southern Europe, the Arctic might at times seem distant, but there are factors that connect communities and cultures, such as food. Such a connection, specifically fish, is the starting point for *Ana Belén López Tárraga*'s chapter on Spain's interests in the Arctic. From there, the author expands the view to other natural resources and tourism, an area which is important for several Arctic States as well as for Spain, before turning to Spain's Polar Strategy, the country's interaction with the Arctic Council, and the potential future of Spain's Arctic policies.

It is our hope that through these chapters, readers inside and outside of the Arctic will get an understanding of different perceptions of the Arctic and how these perceptions can influence policymaking. While most chapters are up to date as of 2024, the situation in the Arctic is likely to remain subject to rapid changes. International Arctic governance has undergone fundamental changes since 2022, and it remains to be seen how it will develop in the years to come. As it is, this book provides a snapshot of sorts which can inform decision-makers both in the Arctic and beyond.

Medy Dervovic, Laura Ulatowski and Stefan Kirchner
Reykjavík/Rovaniemi, Paris, and Cork, January 2025

Figures and Tables

Figures

Tables

Abbreviations

A5	Arctic Five
ACA	Arctic Circle Assembly
AEC	Arctic Economic Council
AENA	Aeropuertos Españoles y Navegación Aérea
AES	Arctic Encounter Symposium
AEPS	Arctic Environmental Protection Strategy
AIV	Adviesraad Internationale Vraagstukken
AMAP	Arctic Monitoring & Assessment Programme
AMBI	Arctic Migratory Birds Initiative
AMSA	Arctic Marine Shipping Assessment
APECS	Association of Polar Early Career Scientists
ArCS	Arctic Challenge for Sustainability
ArCS II	Arctic Challenge for Sustainability II
ASEAN	Association of Southeast Asian Nations
ASM	Arctic Science Ministerial
ASSW	Arctic Science Summit Week
ASWF	Anti-Submarine Warfare Frigates
BBNJ	Biodiversity Beyond National Jurisdiction
BEAC	Barents Euro-Arctic Council
BELARE	Belgian Antarctic Expeditions
BELSPO	Belgian Science Policy Office
BNCAR	Belgian National Committee for Arctic and Antarctic Research
CAFF	Conservation of Arctic Flora and Fauna
CAO	Central Arctic Ocean
CAOFA	Agreement to Prevent Unregulated High Sea Fisheries in the Central Arctic Ocean
CCP	Chinese Communist Party
CFP	Common Fisheries Policy
CIAO	China-Iceland Aurora Observatory
CLCS	Commission on the Limits of the Continental Shelf
CNARC	China-Nordic Arctic Research Center
COEST	Council Working Party on Eastern Europe and Central Asia
COP	Conference of the Parties
CORES	Corporation of Strategic Reserves of Petroleum Products
CSIC	Spanish National Research Council
DAC	Dutch Arctic Circle

DG MARE	Directorate-General for Maritime Affairs and Fisheries
EEA	European Economic Area
EEZ	Exclusive Economic Zone
ELEPOZ	Hellenic Polar Zones Society
EU	European Union
FYP	Five-Year Plan
HaRP	Human Resource Development Platform for Japan–Russia Economic Cooperation and Personnel Exchange
HIECC	Hokkaido International Exchange and Cooperation Center
IASC	International Arctic Science Committee
IAWG	Inter-Agency Working Group
ILO	International Labour Organization
IMO	International Maritime Organization
INSROP	International Northern Sea Route Programme
INTER-ACT	International Network for Terrestrial Research and Monitoring in the Arctic
IPCC	Intergovernmental Panel on Climate Change
IPF	International Polar Foundation
ISAR	International Symposium on Arctic Research
ITLOS	International Tribunal for the Law of the Sea
JAMSTEC	Japan Agency for Marine-Earth Science and Technology
JANSROP	Japan Northern Sea Route Programme
J-ARC Net	Japan Arctic Research Network Center
JBIC	Japan Bank for International Cooperation
JCAR	Japan Consortium for Arctic Environmental Research
JEF	Joint Expeditionary Force
JOGMEC	Japan Organization for Metals and Energy Security
LIIA	Latvian Institute of International Affairs
LNG	Liquefied Natural Gas
MARPOL	International Convention for the Prevention of Pollution from Ships
METI	Ministry of Economy, Trade and Industry of Japan
MEXT	Ministry of Education, Culture, Sports, Science and Technology
MFA	Ministry of Foreign Affairs
MLIT	Ministry of Land, Infrastructure, Transport and Tourism
MoD	Ministry of Defence
MOFA	Ministry of Foreign Affairs
MOL	Mitsui O.S.K. Lines
MOSAiC	Multidisciplinary drifting Observatory for the Study of Arctic Climate
MP	Member of Parliament
NATO	North Atlantic Treaty Organization

NB8	Nordic-Baltic Eight
ND	Northern Dimension
NDEP	ND Environmental Partnership
NDPHS	ND Partnership in Public Health and Social Wellbeing
NDPTL	ND Partnership for Transport and Logistics
NDRC	National Development and Reform Commission
NEAFC	North-East Atlantic Fisheries Commission
NESPICO	Nederlandsche Spitsbergen Compagnie
NF	Northern Forum
NGO	Non-governmental Organization
NIPR	National Institute of Polar Research
NOAA	National Oceanic and Atmospheric Administration
NPFC	North Pacific Fisheries Commission
NSR	Northern Sea Route
OECD	Organisation for Economic Co-operation and Development
OSPAR	Convention for the Protection of the Marine Environment of the North-East Atlantic
PAME	Protection of the Arctic Marine Environment
PRC	People's Republic of China
PRIC	Polar Research Institute of China
ROK	Republic of Korea
ROTACS	Russian Optical Trans-Arctic Cable system
SIIS	Shanghai Institute for International Studies
SAO	Senior Arctic Official
SDWG	Sustainable Development Working Group
SOA	State Oceanic Administration
SOCIB	Balearic Islands Coastal Observation System
SOLAS	International Convention for the Safety of Life at Sea
STCW	International Convention on Standards of Training, Certification and Watchkeeping for Seafarers
TFEU	Treaty on the Functioning of the European Union
UArctic	University of the Arctic
UNCLOS	United Nations Convention on the Law of the Sea
UNDRIP	United Nations Declaration on the Rights of Indigenous Peoples
UNEP	United Nations Environment Programme
UNESCO	United Nations Educational, Scientific and Cultural Organization
UGS	Union of Greek Shipowners
USD	United States Dollars
VPN	Virtual Private Network
WWCAM	World Winter Cities Association for Mayors

Notes on Contributors

Julie Auffret-Cariou
holds a master's degree in International Relations and Political Science from Sciences Po Bordeaux. She was a visiting researcher at the Arctic Centre, University of Lapland (Rovaniemi, Finland) which gave her the opportunity to focus on the French Arctic Policy following its first Polar Strategy as well as the role of Indigenous representatives in Arctic politics. Her research interests include comparative politics, diplomacy, Arctic governance, Arctic policies, and the civil society.

Romain Chuffart
is the Nansen professor in Arctic Studies (2024–2025) at the University of Akureyri, Iceland. He holds a Ph.D. in law from Durham University in the United Kingdom. He is also the Managing Director of The Arctic Institute – Center for Circumpolar Security Studies, a think tank and nonprofit organization (Washington D.C., USA). His expertise includes public international law, human rights and the rights of Indigenous Peoples, international environmental law, Arctic law and policy, and ocean governance.

Konstantinos Deligiannis-Virvos
is a Ph.D. research fellow with the Norwegian Centre for the Law of the Sea (NCLOS) at the Law Faculty of UiT – The Arctic University of Norway. His doctorate thesis is titled "The Implementation of an Ecosystem Approach in Shipping". He comes from Greece and has studied law in the Democritus University of Thrace. He also holds two master's degrees, one in Public International Law from the National and Kapodistrian University of Athens, and one in the Law of the Sea from UiT – The Arctic University of Norway. He is a member of the Athens Bar Association and has practiced law in Greece. His research interests include public international law, the law of the sea, environmental law, shipping, and Arctic law and governance.

Medy Dervovic
is a Ph.D. candidate at Reykjavík University, Department of Law, Iceland, where he focuses on the normative impact of climate change on the law of the sea in the Arctic. He holds an LL.M. degree in Polar Law from the University of Akureyri, Iceland. He is also a Visiting Researcher at the Arctic Centre, University of Lapland (Rovaniemi, Finland), a researcher at the Stefansson Arctic Institute (Akureyri, Iceland), and a researcher at the Centre

for Law on Climate Change and Sustainability (Reykjavík, Iceland). Medy is the Editor-in-Chief of *A Compilation of International and Regional Instruments and Case-Law on Minorities and Indigenous Peoples' Rights* (Brill | Nijhoff, 2025–) His fields of research include the law of the sea, Arctic law and governance, Polar law, public international law, treaty law, environmental law, and human rights.

Gints Jegermanis
is a visiting lecturer at the University of Latvia and Riga Graduate School of Law. He served as ambassador of Latvia to Estonia (1998–2001), Denmark (2009–13) and Sweden (2013–17), as permanent representative to the UN in New York, and as counselor in Moscow (1995–98). He was a fellow at the Latvian Institute of International Affairs (2022–23), commentator (1990–93) and deputy editor-in-chief (1991–93) at the daily newspaper 'Diena', and a junior researcher at the Institute of Language and Literature, Academy of Sciences of Latvia (1987–90). His fields of expertise include international politics, geopolitics, Nordic countries and diplomacy.

Stefan Kirchner
is a government advisor based in Germany who works on energy security, environmental protection and disaster risk reduction, and an Adjunct Professor at University College Cork in Cork, Ireland. Formerly a Research Professor and Research Group Leader at the University of Lapland in Rovaniemi, Finland, he has taught international law at universities in Finland, Germany, Greenland, Italy, Lithuania and Ukraine. He is the author or co-author of more than 500 academic publications and has (co-)chaired the American Society of International Law (ASIL) Rights of Indigenous Peoples Interest Group, Law of the Sea Interest Group, Space Law Interest Group and Disaster Law Interest Group. He is a member of multiple editorial and advisory boards, including the editorial advisory committee of International Legal Materials, the advisory board of ASIL's International Courts and Tribunals Interest Group and the New Zealand-based International Disaster, Emergency and Law Network. His contribution only reflects his private opinion.

Marina Lomaeva
is a specially appointed assistant professor at Hokkaido University's Nitobe College Graduate Curriculum. She received her Ph.D. from Hokkaido University in December 2024. Her research interests include global and regional environmental governance, marine wildlife (particularly, marine mammal)

conservation, and the roles of subnational and non-state actors in multilevel governance, particularly in the North Pacific (Japan, Russia, the US, and Canada). She also explores Japan's Arctic policy, the emergence of the Pacific Arctic/Arcasia region, and Hokkaido's 'northern region' and Sapporo's 'winter city' concepts, focusing on the contributions of subnational entities to these processes.

Karen van Loon
is a research fellow at Clingendael's Security and Defence Programme, where she specializes in Arctic geopolitics and broader security and defence issues. Before joining Clingendael, she was a researcher in the European Affairs Programme at EGMONT – Royal Institute for International Relations. She has also held roles as an Educational Assistant at the Political Science Department of KU Leuven Kulak and as a Lecturer in the Master of Teaching Programme at the University of Antwerp. Her research interests include Arctic geopolitics, the future of NATO, and arms control.

Eline Lüschen
holds an M.A. in International Security from the University of Groningen, the Netherlands. She is a visiting researcher at the Arctic Centre, University of Lapland (Rovaniemi, Finland). Her field of research includes Arctic governance and security. Eline also works as an information specialist at the Inspectorate of Justice and Security in the Netherlands.

Fujio Ohnishi
is a specially appointed associate professor at the Arctic Research Center, and co-affiliated at the Department of Slavic-Eurasian Studies, Division of Humanities, Hokkaido University. He also acts as a vice chair of the Japan Consortium for Arctic Environmental Research. Having an academic background in International Relations and interdisciplinary regional studies, his current research interest focuses on order, geopolitics and security in the Arctic. His latest publications include: "Cold winds in the north: Three perspectives on the impact of Russia's war in Ukraine on security and international relations in the Arctic" (co-authored with P.S. Hilde and M. Petersson), *Polar Science*, Volume 41 (2024), 10105.

Rashmi Ramesh
is a doctoral candidate at the School of Conflict and Security Studies, National Institute of Advanced Studies, India, where she focuses on the geopolitics and governance in the Arctic. She holds a Master's degree in

Geopolitics and International Relations from Manipal Academy of Higher Education, Manipal, India. Previously, Rashmi was a visiting researcher at the Arctic Centre, University of Lapland (Rovaniemi, Finland), and served as the Arctic PASSION Ambassador 2023–24. Her fields of research include Arctic geopolitics and governance, Asia's interests in the Arctic, conflict and climate change, and India's foreign policy.

Juha Saunavaara
is an associate professor at the Hokkaido University Arctic Research Center. He has published in peer-reviewed journals and edited volumes covering a range of fields, including Arctic and Asian studies, history, geography, international relations, and tourism. His current research focuses on telecommunication and transport infrastructure in the Arctic, regional development, non-state actors' international cooperation and sustainable tourism.

Akiho Shibata
is a professor of international law and the Director of the Polar Cooperation Research Centre (PCRC), Kobe University in Japan. His research interests cover international law relating to both the Arctic and the Antarctic with publications such as *Emerging Legal Orders in the Arctic: The Role of Non-Arctic Actors* (co-edited, Routledge, 2019) and 'Ice sheet conservation and international discord: governing (potential) glacial geoengineering in Antarctica', *International Affairs*, Vol. 101, No. 1 (2025) (with Patrick Flamm).

Hiroki Takakura
is a social anthropologist and professor at the Center for Northeast Asian Studies, Tohoku University, Japan. His research interests cover human-animal relations, climate change, disaster resilience, ethnicity and the arctic human history including the ethnohistory of the Siberia and Northeast Asia. He is the author of *Anthropology and Disaster in Japan: Cultural Contributions to Recovery after the 2011 Earthquake and Tsunami* (Routledge, 2023), *Global Warming and Human – Nature Dimension in Northern Eurasia* (co-edited, Springer, 2017), *Arctic Pastoralist Sakha: Ethnography of Evolution and Microadaptation in Siberia* (Trans Pacific Press, 2015). Currently he engages with the project on the Siberian indigenous immigrants related to the Russo-Ukrainian war.

Ana Belén López Tárraga
is a journalist specialized in issues related to territorial development and cross-border cooperation. She is currently completing her Ph.D. studies in

social sciences, within the topic of territorial studies, in the Department of Geography at the University of Salamanca, where she is also a part-time lecturer. The European Arctic policy and its impact on the region at European, national and local scales has been the focus of her Ph.D. research. She enjoyed a fellowship as a visiting researcher at the Arctic Centre (University of Lapland) in Fall 2022. She combines her academic work with his job as a journalist in the European Grouping of Territorial Cooperation Duero-Douro, focused on cross-border cooperation between Spain and Portugal.

Pavel Tkach
is a researcher at the Arctic Centre of the University of Lapland (Finland) and the Managing Director of the Arctic Youth Network (Canada). His expertise is concentrated in the areas of law and governance. He is currently overseeing five international projects that focus on climate governance, youth engagement and education in the Arctic, as well as tourism development. His academic interests encompass the international relations of non-Arctic States and the legal frameworks that regulate climate interventions and intellectual property rights.

Apostolos Tsiouvalas
is a researcher at the Norwegian Centre for the Law of the Sea, UiT The Arctic University of Norway, Tromsø, Norway, and Senior Fellow at The Arctic Institute – Center for Circumpolar Security Studies, Washington D.C. He holds a Ph.D. in Law from UiT and an LL.M. degree in Polar Law from the University of Akureyri, Iceland and an M.Phil. in Indigenous studies from UiT. He has previously worked at the K.G. Jebsen Center for the Law of the Sea and the Sami Law Research Group of UiT, the Stefánsson Arctic Institute and the PAME Working Group of the Arctic Council. His current fields of research include the international law of the sea, legal geography, legal pluralism, critical legal theory, new materialism(s), and indigenous law/rights in the Arctic.

Laura Ulatowski
is a project officer at EIT Manufacturing. She holds a Master's degree in Urban and Economic Geography and has worked as Research Assistant at the Arctic Centre of the University of Lapland. Her professional expertise lies in regional development, regional innovation strategies, and tourism,

with a strong focus on fostering sustainable growth and innovation at the intersection of local and global challenges.

Marco Volpe
is a Ph.D. candidate at the Faculty of Social Science at the University of Lapland. He is a visiting researcher in the Arctic International Relations Team at the Arctic Centre in Rovaniemi and a Research Assistant for the Master's degree Course in Arctic Studies at the University of Milan. His research focuses on China's polar engagement from a Science Diplomacy angle and comprehends analysis of Chinese language-based literature. Recently he has become part of the Science Diplomacy Research Priority Team at the ICARP IV. He holds a Master's degree in Eastern Languages and Cultures from the University of Rome La Sapienza, a MRes in East Asian Studies from the University of Leeds and a Master's in Sustainable Development, Geopolitics of Resources and Arctic Studies from the Italian Society for International Organization.

CHAPTER 1

Asia's Foray into the Arctic: Perceptions and Identity Building

Julie Auffret-Cariou and Rashmi Ramesh

1 Introduction

Amidst the discussions on the role of non-Arctic States and their Arctic policies, Asia seemingly stands apart. The role of Asian States is much debated since China, India, Japan, Singapore, and South Korea were inducted as observers to the Arctic Council in 2013. Though those five States are not the only Asian States that have expressed an interest in the Arctic, this chapter focuses exclusively on the five Asian States that are Arctic Council observers as they have had a more active and diverse participation in the region. To delve more into this, this chapter is divided into four sections. To begin with, the debates surrounding the Asian States including, the perception, misperceptions, and skepticism, will be addressed followed by an emphasis on the shift from 2013 and the Kiruna Ministerial Meeting. In a third section, this chapter will give an overview of the major contours of Arctic policies of each of the five States, their approach to the Arctic, and the identities that they have constructed for themselves to justify their presence. The fourth and final section will ponder on the state of cooperation among the Asian observers and whether it is possible to speak about an Asian voice in the Arctic. It will also question the benefits of a stronger cooperation between the Asian observers themselves and with other actors in the Arctic, in terms of diplomacy and the impact of the Russia-Ukraine conflict on the Arctic.

2 Asian States' Entry into the Arctic

As the Arctic's prominence at the international level grew, non-Arctic States, inter-parliamentary organizations, and non-governmental organizations (NGOs) showed keen interest in becoming observers at the Arctic Council.

The Arctic Council Rules of Procedure states that observers must recognize, *inter alia*, Arctic States' sovereignty, sovereign rights, and jurisdiction

 | DOI:10.1163/9789004734685_002

in the Arctic, respect the values and interests of the Arctic indigenous people, and demonstrate Arctic interests and expertise relevant to the work of the Council. They do not have any voting rights, though they are welcome to attend the Council meetings, submit statements, and propose relevant projects through Permanent Participants or an Arctic State. Further, the observers' financial contributions are not to exceed that of Arctic States, unless decided by the Senior Arctic Officials (Arctic Council, 1998/2013).

Andrew Chater (2016a) traces the evolution of observers in the Arctic Council and charts this across three time periods. The first period (1991–1996) witnessed the efforts to create the Arctic Council, to replace the Arctic Environmental Protection Strategy (AEPS). The AEPS had eight observers, three of which were Indigenous peoples' organizations, three European States and two international institutions. The Arctic Council too welcomed observers, but the key difference is that the indigenous people's organizations successfully lobbied for an enhanced role. They were included as Permanent Participants who enjoy greater participatory rights than observers, but less than Member States. In the first period, the question of who would be included as observers naturally emerged. Denmark, Iceland, and Norway were against allowing environmental groups opposed to whaling to become observers in the Council. There was a general concern that disruptive environmental groups like Greenpeace might affect the working of the Council. This led to the decision to include more moderate environmental groups like the World Wildlife Fund (Chater, 2016a, p. 175).

The second period (1996–2004) witnessed debates about the influence of observers and their contributions to the work of the Arctic Council. They provided updates on the research conducted in their respective stations, technical suggestions, and suggestions on the Council's projects that may or may not have been considered by the States. Though they continued as the 'weak thread' in the Council, their increasing interests in the Arctic were evident. The observers grew in number, with 15 more joining, and the number of them who attended the meetings between 1998 and 2004 doubled (Chater, 2016a, pp. 176–177).

In the third period (2005–present), the global interest in the Arctic affairs burgeoned. This is in coherence with studies that emphasized the impact of climate change on the Arctic and, in turn, on the other parts of the globe. Non-Arctic States and NGOs saw a global concern, leading to the internationalization or globalization of the Arctic, not only in terms of trade, but also in political and socio-economic terms. The Arctic Climate Impact Assessment was published in 2004, a major report that highlighted climate change impacts on the Arctic and its related impact outside the region (Arctic Climate Impact Assessment, 2004). Since then, the observers began sponsoring projects more frequently and also demanded an enhanced role in the Council. During the 2008 Arctic Council meeting in Norway, the Netherlands stated that the "observers wish to cooperate not only on science but also decision-making" (Arctic Council, 2008). Around the same time, India, China, South Korea, Italy, Japan, and Singapore began to attend Council meetings and subsequently applied for observer status (Chater, 2016a, p. 178).

Additionally, in 2013, the Arctic Circle Assembly (ACA), an Iceland-based platform was established. Set up as a non-governmental networking platform to discuss Arctic issues, it grew into one of the foremost hosts for gathering representatives, stakeholders, and academic scholars from across the world, interested in the Arctic. In the eyes of the non-Arctic States – both observers and non-observers – the Arctic Circle provides stage to express freely and influence Arctic affairs. In the same year, on 15 May 2013, the Kiruna Ministerial Meeting welcomed six new States as observer States within the Arctic Council. Of them, five were Asian States, i.e., China, Japan, India, Singapore, and South Korea. Their candidacy had received much international attention, especially questioning what it meant for the governance of the region (Brigham, 2014). This new Asian interest reflected the growing implication of the Arctic within the global economy and politics.

However, Asian States have been increasingly active in the region from as early as the 1990s. In 1991, Japan established, in a joint effort with Norway, the Ny-Ålesund Research Station and the Chinese icebreaker *Xuelong* entered service in 1993 and was the only Chinese icebreaker until 2019. India, Singapore, and South Korea manifested their interests a bit later with South Korea establishing its own research station in Ny-Ålesund, Svalbard in 2002. India launched its Arctic Program, its first Arctic Ocean expedition in 2007, while Singapore was the first Asian State to build an icebreaker vessel in 2008 with its oil rig and shipbuilding company Keppel. This culminated in their welcoming to the Arctic Council in 2013 (Stokke, 2013). The chapter therefore argues that the period from 2013 till present, must be considered as the fourth phase, one where there were major shifts and a march towards a global Arctic in substantial terms.

3 A Marked Shift

The Kiruna Ministerial Meeting marked a turning point by including non-European/American States as observers in the Arctic Council for the first time. The global understanding of the Arctic with the conscience that "what happens in the Arctic does not stay in the Arctic" is a key component of Arctic politics (NATO Parliamentary Assembly, 2017). The global commitment to fight climate change was put forward as a primary justification of Asian States' presence in Arctic governance despite their lack of territorial claim (Dodds & Woon, 2020). At the same time, the evolving state of the region is unlocking new economic opportunities from natural resources to maritime routes and specialized technology. In this regard, Asian States are trying not to be excluded from discussions on Arctic matters.

Asian States have been increasingly active in the region through the Arctic Council, being part of the different working groups and discussions. The Arctic Council is seen as the core intergovernmental forum in the region. However, they understand that the Arctic governance framework is a combination of multiple arrangements, from sub-national to pan-regional levels (Young, 2005). Governance in the Arctic is the result of national legislations, bilateral, regional, and international arrangements. Asian States have adapted to this dynamic and took action beyond the limits of the Arctic Council. They have formed numerous bilateral cooperations with each other but mostly with already-active actors of the region, especially Arctic States. They also participate in Arctic Circle assemblies and forums.

Moreover, in the Arctic, science diplomacy has become an important part of Asian States' involvement, with China being in the top five of non-Arctic States in terms of research projects undertaken (Aksnes et al., 2016). Science diplomacy is a way for Asian States to have their voice heard in Arctic politics (Lanteigne, 2017).

In comparison to Italy's observer status, a lot of noise surrounded the admission of the Asian States, especially suspicion towards the aspiration of China (Babin & Lasserre, 2017). Arctic States expressed concern that such a move could have undermined their sovereignty as well as their voice within the Arctic Council and more broadly over the governance of the region. Moreover, Indigenous peoples worried that their position would be threatened as well in front of the strengthening of a statist approach (Stokke, 2013).

Overall, two main views emerged: one that sees the need to include the Asian actors in a global Arctic (Solli et al., 2013), and the other one which perceives Asia as an elephant in the room arriving with economic and military prowess, trying to change the terms of engagement in the Arctic (Babin & Lasserre, 2017). In this backdrop, expressions like 'scramble for the Arctic', 'the Arctic race', 'heating up of the Arctic because of Asia's entry' induced sensationalization, underlining the fear that the region would be lost to economic state interest (Koivurova, 2011; Pareek, 2021; Elzinga, 2016; Quaile, 2012). Moreover, the skepticism associated with this is directed more towards China, but in a way generalized about 'Asia'. Barring China, the other four Asian observers have excellent ties with the West.

The welcoming of those Asian States was conditioned to some criteria such as the recognition of sovereign rights and jurisdiction of Arctic States (Arctic Council, 1998/2013). Moreover, it should be remembered that they joined the Arctic Council as observer states meaning that their primary role is to observe the work of the Council. They do not have a voting right in the Arctic Council which was restated by the *Vision for the Arctic*: "[d]ecisions at all levels in the Arctic Council are the exclusive right and responsibility of the eight signatories to the Ottawa Declaration" (Arctic Council, 2013, p. 4). Nonetheless, they can participate in meetings, contribute through Working Groups, financing projects through another Arctic State or Permanent Participant, and taking an active part in subsidiary bodies.

While their entry was questioned, there were views that not doing so would probably lead to these States forming their own platform to discuss Arctic issues without necessarily involving the Members and Permanent Participants of the Arctic Council.

Asian States' will to be part of the region's governance is a symbol of the globalization of the Arctic and that it is no longer the sole preoccupation of the regional States. The challenges the region is facing, in terms of climate change or technology, cannot be dealt exclusively by the Arctic States but requires cooperation at a broader level. At the same time, the evolution of the region is promising new economic possibilities that other States do not want to miss out on. Nonetheless, if common ground appears in the Asian States' approach to the region, each of those States has its own objectives and policy concerning the region. Talking about Asian States in the Arctic as a whole might not be the best way to understand the sometimes-divergent interests of a very complex region. Thus, an understanding of the individual policies can provide insights that may be absent in generalizations.

4 Arctic Policies of the Asian Observers

Given the suspicion surrounding the Asian States' presence, providing justification and identity building became an imminent requirement. They had to "demonstrate their relevance" for coming North, and releasing policies was a step in that direction (Lanteigne, 2017). This section briefly discusses the overview of the Arctic policies and actions of the five Asian observers.

4.1 *China*

China has gathered limelight in the discussions on Asia in the Arctic. As a revisionist power, it has global ambitions, and economic and military clout required to pursue those ambitions. China's activities in the Arctic are often seen through the lens of suspicion, and the evident political differences with the West are one of the fueling factors. Beijing released the Arctic Policy in 2018, stating that its main goal is to "understand, protect, develop and participate in the governance of the Arctic, so as to safeguard the common interests of all countries and the international community in the Arctic, and promote sustainable development" (State Council of People's Republic of China, 2018, section III).

Capacity building, scientific research, response to climate change, environmental protection, resource utilization, development of shipping routes, and socio-economic development of the Arctic find a mention in the white paper (The State Council Information Office of the People's Republic of China, 2018). More importantly, China calls itself a "Near-Arctic State" (State Council of People's Republic of China, 2018, section II), an attempt at giving its Arctic activities an identity and a geographic rationale (Pursiainen, et al., 2021). With this denomination, China underlines its closeness to the Arctic especially in terms of the changes that, while occurring in the Arctic will have a definitive impact on its territories (State Council of People's Republic of China, 2018). The phrase has, though having a similar meaning as other countries' self-denominations such as the United Kingdom's "Arctic's nearest neighbor" (Foreign and Commonwealth Office, 2013, Foreword; Foreign, Commonwealth & Development Office, 2023, Foreword), garnered its share of criticism (Francis, 2020). In reaction to the idea of a "Near-Arctic State", the then US Secretary of State Mike Pompeo made a speech in 2019 at the Arctic Council stating: "there are only Arctic States and Non-Arctic States. No third category exists and claiming otherwise entitles China to exactly nothing" (Pompeo, 2019).

China has advocated for a more global Arctic (Manicom & Lackenbauer, 2013). It has often called on the Arctic States to strike a balance between regional and international interests in the North. With respect to its diplomatic approach, Beijing is mostly towards forging bilateral relations with the eight States, and has been successful so far (Pursiainen, et al., 2021). The Arctic States, though wary of its actions, see it as an indispensable partner that has invested in multiple sectors ranging across telecommunications, connectivity, science, fishing, tourism, shipping, and mining (Stepien et al., 2020).

4.2 *India*

While the focus is primarily on China due to its sheer prowess and ambitions, India's role in the Arctic is less discussed. There are speculations and questions about its activities in a geographical location that is far from its territory, yet the discussion is more about the curiosity generated by its observer status, rather than the alarming alertness among the Arctic States. This can be for two reasons. First, India is not a very active observer unlike its East Asian counterparts and does not have grand infrastructural projects and investments yet in the North. Second, there is generally a positive outlook towards India's foreign policy and it is perceived as a benign power holding the ability to maintain good relations with all the States and commitment towards international law, peace, and security. The perception is evident given how China's Arctic policy and India's Arctic policy were received by the Arctic region. Less skepticism has also meant less discussion. The three East Asian observers take most of the limelight, and India's Arctic policy is not much talked about (Lackenbauer, 2017).

Contrary to popular belief, India's role in the Arctic began in 1920, as a signatory to the Svalbard Treaty (1920). However, the engagement could not be sustained post-independence, as the government had a daunting task of rebuilding a nation-state, addressing socio-economic issues, one of the biggest refugee crises in history, and a war with Pakistan. The breakthrough arrived in the 1980s when India began its activities in Antarctica. About three decades later, in 2008, India established its first research station in the Arctic, Himadri, in Ny-Ålesund, Svalbard (National Centre for Polar and Ocean Research, n.d.).

The Arctic is of concern for India mainly because of the impact on monsoons. A study conducted by a group of Indian and Norwegian scientists concluded that the changes in the Arctic negatively affect the monsoon patterns in the subcontinent and result in extreme rainfall events in the later part of the monsoon, i.e., in September and October. Since nearly half the population engages in agriculture and related activities for livelihood in India, these events can have a substantial impact on food and water security of the State. Alongside, rising sea level, economic opportunities, and the common concerns with the Himalayas/Third Pole are the pull factors for India's presence in the Arctic (Government of India, 2022).

India released its draft policy in 2021, and the updated final version in early 2022 (Government of India, 2022). Titled as *India's Arctic Policy: Building a Partnership for Sustainable Development,* it lies on the principles of sustainable development and science diplomacy. It rests on six pillars:

science and research, climate and environment, economic and human development, transportation and connectivity, governance and international cooperation, and national capacity building.

India has energy and economic interests in the Russian Arctic. In 2018, India received its first natural gas shipment from the Arctic as part of Gas Authority of India Ltd.'s 20-year deal with Gazprom. However, in 2024, New Delhi announced that it will not buy LNG from Russia's Arctic 2 LNG project, which is sanctioned due to the Russia-Ukraine conflict (Reuters, 2024). But India-Russia cooperation in the Arctic is not ruled out yet. Both countries have set up a working group on the Northern Sea Route, where they continue to discuss the possibilities of training Indian sailors for polar navigation and development of joint projects for shipbuilding (Peri, 2024).

India also has been actively involved with Norway for scientific research in the Arctic. Heightened India-Nordic relations have also enabled the inclusion of the Arctic as an area of cooperation. India-Nordic Dialogues often discuss harnessing natural resources, green technology, sustainable development and scientific research (Ministry of External Affairs, 2022).

As a major identity push, the policy also mentions "harmoni[zing] polar research with the third pole – the Himalayas" as one of India's Arctic missions (Government of India, 2022, p. 2). The idea of belonging to one of the polar regions of the world and the vast scientific experience in the Antarctic further provides impetus to its activities in the Arctic.

The policy is not only an answer to the questions on India's role in the Arctic, but also a marked change in the manner in which Indian foreign policy has evolved over the years. This is the first policy document India has published specifically for a region and is also the first foreign policy document that was released in the form of a draft, for public opinion.

4.3 *Japan*

The drivers of Japan's Arctic policy are inter alia scientific engagement, climate change, and resources. To achieve those interests, the policy underlines three pillars to pursue: 1) research and development, notably to contribute to policy decision-making; 2) international cooperation including the formulation of responses to global issues and international rules; and 3) sustainable use, to be better present in the Arctic economy. Japan traces its activities in the Arctic to as early as the 1950s when it held its first Arctic observation projects, which enabled it to be the first non-Arctic State to become a member of the International Arctic Science Committee (IASC) (The Headquarters for Ocean Policy, 2015). It became an observer at the Arctic Council in 2013. Japan's Arctic research primarily focuses on climate change and sustainable development. As one of the strongest East Asian economies and a manufacturing hub that depends on the Middle East for hydrocarbons, it is looking for the resources that a melting Arctic can offer.

Additionally, Japan's geographic proximity to the Northern Sea Route (NSR) is seen as a future opportunity in terms of access to the European market (Almazova-Ilyina et al., 2020, p. 5; Chater, 2016b). Indeed, the NSR would reduce the distance and time needed to sail between the two areas. This is seen as a great opportunity for the reduction of shipping costs and emissions, while encouraging innovation. Despite new research highlighting a lesser gain than expected in terms of, among other things, time saving and equipment costs due to variable weather and sea-ice conditions, the NSR remains an important part of the economic benefits expected by Japan through the Arctic.

4.4 *Republic of Korea (ROK)*

The Republic of Korea's interests in the Arctic began in the 1990s, through scientific research (Holroyd, 2020). After applying for the observer status of the Arctic Council in 2008 based on its achievements in the research field, it became an observer at the Arctic Council in 2013. The ROK has already established two Masterplans for Arctic Policy at the initiative of the Ministry of Oceans and Fisheries, which can be considered as Arctic policies: the '1st pan-governmental Masterplan for Arctic Policy' (2013–2017) adopted as a follow-up of the obtention of the observer status, followed, in 2018, by a second plan entitled 'Master Plan for Promotion of Arctic Activities' (2018–2022). In 2022, the 'First Master Plan for Promoting Polar Activities 2023–2027' (Ministry of Oceans and Fisheries, 2022) was published evidencing a turning point in the Korean strategy as it implemented a legal-based plan for the activities in the Arctic and Antarctic (Seo, 2023). Those documents outline the framework of the Korean policy, based on a vision, with the ROK as a leading country in polar activities. It also highlights the policy goals of the ROK in the Arctic, namely: 'economic partnership with Arctic States', 'strengthening international cooperation' and 'strengthening scientific efforts' (Seo, 2023).

Similar to Japan and China, the ROK considers the Northern Sea Route as an important passage that can support its trade (Satikov & Kim, 2024). For this purpose, the ROK has extensive cooperation with Russia for developing a multi-model transportation and logistics route connecting the NSR with internal waterways. Economy, resources, and fishing form one of the major pillars of the ROK's Arctic Policy. However, there is an emphasis on the implications of a changing Arctic through the building of environmentally friendly icebreaking container ships (Satikov & Kim, 2024) but also through the engagement in favor of the 2018 Agreement to Prevent Unregulated High Seas Fisheries in the Central Arctic Ocean Agreement (CAOFA) even holding the second Conference of the Parties (COP) in June 2023 on its territory. Thus, despite the importance of economic concerns, the Republic of Korea also sees its involvement in the Arctic as a way to boost its political power and national image (Kim & Stenport, 2021).

4.5 *Singapore*

As a country located close to the equator, Singapore may not immediately seem like the one having an interest in the Arctic. Additionally, there is little history of engagement in the polar regions. To date, Singapore is the only Asian observer State to not yet have published an Arctic statement, policy, or a strategy but has spoken about its interests through government statements, events, and Arctic Council meetings. In 2012, it appointed a special envoy for Arctic affairs (The Arctic Institute: Center for Circumpolar Security Studies, n.d.).

Singapore's Arctic interest is an extension of its interests in the maritime domain. As a maritime hub, it is concerned about the Northern Sea Route opening up for more navigation owing to climate change. For the East Asian economies, the NSR is a shorter route, a potential alternative to the longer transit through the Suez Canal and Malacca Strait in the future, at the expense of Singapore's economy. Some analysts challenge the extent of threat to Singapore's status of a port hub. The navigability of the NSR comes with challenges to the shipping and insurance sectors (Watter & Tonami, 2012).

Apart from the commercial interests, environmental concerns also weigh in. As a low-lying small island State, Singapore is vulnerable to the changes in the sea level that is accelerated by the melting of sea ice and Greenland's ice sheet (Solli et al., 2013). It seeks to contribute to the climate change agenda, actively participate in Arctic Council Working Groups and share best practices in areas such as oil spills prevention, biodiversity conservation, shipping, and sustainable energy development (Ministry of Foreign Affairs, 2021).

5 Is There an Asian Voice in the Arctic?

Asian actors have promoted similar approaches on the Arctic. Indeed, the States put forward their will to understand, through scientific research, to protect, through the fight against climate change, to develop, through economic and social development especially thanks to shipping routes, technologies, and so on, and to participate in the governance of the Arctic, through the call for more participatory rights (Keyu, 2020).

However, the Asian discourses can also be compared to the ones of the European Observers of the Arctic Council. China, India, Japan, South Korea, and Singapore do not have a specific Asian perception of the Arctic (Stokke, 2014). Indeed, the environment, social progress, and especially science and technology are the least contentious areas of cooperation in the Arctic. The legitimacy and participation in the region usually arise from those very same fields. Therefore, it is worth noting that the policies put forward by the European observers and the Asian observers are not at odds with each other but rather rest on the same ideas (Heininen, 2020). The dichotomy of the European and Asian observers has been regularly highlighted especially by the discussions on the accession of Italy and the five Asian observer States which have been received very differently. However, looking at the policies and discourse, the said dichotomy is not as evident as it appears. It shows the importance of the perceptions of the Arctic States on the Asian observers which frame how their applications were received.

The different Arctic policies from China, India, Japan, and South Korea, as well as the discourse of Singapore, have shown the existence of areas of possible cooperation between the different States as well as with the rest of the Arctic actors.

As of now, no comprehensive long-term Asian cooperation in the Arctic can be shown as an example, nonetheless Asian States have stated their interest in a deeper and more active collaboration with each other with already some successes. Indeed, different types of cooperation which remained with limited impact have been successfully implemented previously such as a cooperation on the political level through the Trilateral High-Level Meeting or the scientific level through the Asian Forum for Polar Sciences (Danner, 2020).

Moreover, the Asian cooperation on the Arctic appears to be limited to the northeast Asian States that are China, Japan, and South Korea while India and Singapore have remained more isolated. It may be noted that apart from two Arctic institutions, the Arctic Council and the Arctic Science Ministerial (ASM), as well as the Association of Southeast Asian Nations (ASEAN), no other regional cooperation institution has given membership to all five States (Heng & Freymann, 2023). Looking at the different Arctic multilateral institutions, out of the five Asian observers, Singapore does not participate in the International Arctic Science Committee (IASC), both Singapore and India do not participate in the CAOFA and only the Korean Arctic Research Consortium, "an Arctic think-tank organization of Republic of Korea" (Arctic Economic Council, 2023) is part of the Arctic Economic Council (AEC).

The biggest area of cooperation would be trilateral academic cooperation between China, Japan, and South Korea through the co-organizations of events, establishment of memoranda of understanding between institutions, as well as the North Pacific Arctic Research Community (Lomaeva & Saunavaara, 2022). However, the amount of attention given to those events is significantly smaller than many other Arctic conferences which are attracting researchers from Asian States to Arctic States. Indeed, if the region has gained, all the more so since 2013, more and more interest from the Arctic community, and if China, Japan, and South Korea's research effort has been important, regional cooperation focusing exclusively on the Arctic remains very limited.

Nonetheless, in 2004, an NGO was established as the Asian counterpart of the International Arctic Science Committee: the Asia Forum for Polar Sciences which encompasses research from both the Arctic and the Antarctic (Kim & Jeong, 2015). Singapore does not participate because its polar research community is not significant enough to justify its participation. The other Asian observers participate, as well as Malaysia's National Antarctic Research Centre, and Thailand's Polar Science Consortium while Vietnam, Indonesia, the Philippines, and Sri Lanka are observers. However, it should be noted that China is represented through the Polar Research Institute of China and not the Chinese Arctic and Antarctic Administration that is the representative at IASC showing a dichotomy between the technical role of this body in comparison to the more long-term planning role of IASC. The Asia Forum for Polar Sciences has been an interesting vector of multilateral information exchange and discussion among the Asian States on the Polar regions. However, the impact of the forum has not been as great as other polar communities despite representing almost half of the world's population. It shows that strictly Asian platforms still suffer from a lack of recognition on polar research.

Therefore, it seems that despite a general interest about the region, there is still a limited cooperation of the Asian observers, both within the Arctic institutions as well as within Asian platforms, on the topic of the Arctic. Despite the limited areas and fora of cooperation, the Trilateral High-Level Dialogue on the Arctic allowed for three of the Asian States – China, Japan, and South Korea – to meet annually from 2016 to 2019 in order to discuss their cooperation in the Arctic (Keyu, 2020). This dialogue originates from the Sixth Trilateral Summit held in November 2015 during which the three

States decided to hold official meetings starting from the following year. Therefore, the Ambassadors for Arctic Affairs from South Korea and Japan and the Special Representative for Arctic Affairs from China met four times in the following years, first in 2016 and then 2019 in South Korea, in 2017 in Japan, and in 2018 in China. Additionally, the presence of experts, researchers, and industry representatives allow a platform of discussion between the State, economic, and research levels as a way to better frame the cooperation.

However, the scope of cooperation even within the framework of the Trilateral High-Level Dialogue on the Arctic remains limited. Indeed, this dialogue allowed States to hold discussion mainly on scientific cooperation and were limited to non-sensitive issues. In terms of implementation however, the results are very limited. Indeed, the different joint statements following the dialogues held since 2016 have always underlined the scientific research area as the main point of the cooperation calling for an increase in this domain (Ministry of Foreign Affairs of the Republic of Korea, 2016; Ministry of Foreign Affairs of Japan, 2017; Ministry of Foreign Affairs of the People's Republic of China, 2018; Ministry of Foreign Affairs of the Republic of Korea, 2019). The joint statements call for more sharing of data and results, as well as the launch of collaborative surveys and coordinated research. Nonetheless, its outcomes have remained very modest as there is no concrete action that is promoted in any of the joint statements. Therefore, it appears that the cooperation remained only a will rather than an actual policy.

Nevertheless, the Arctic has been put forward as one of the main areas of cooperation between the three northeast Asian observer States and to do so, the Trilateral High-Level Dialogue on the Arctic was recognized as the main tool. Indeed, in 2018, a joint statement closing the Seventh Trilateral Summit organized in May 2018 declared that the nations "endorse the Joint Statement of the Second Trilateral High-Level Dialogue on the Arctic held in Tokyo in June 2017, and reconfirm the importance of the trilateral cooperation on the Arctic, especially in the area of scientific research" (Ministry of Foreign Affairs of Japan, 2018). In parallel, in 2019, the 'Arctic' appeared as one of the mentioned areas of cooperation that needs to be pursued through the trilateral cooperation vision for the next decade of China, ROK, and Japan (Ministry of Foreign Affairs of the People's Republic of China, 2019). The interest in the continuation of such a cooperation and its development to more and more areas of the Arctic shows that despite the lack of formal advancement, there is a recognition of the benefits of creating a certain Asian voice in the Arctic.

However, even this limited scope of dialogue came to an end after its 2019 edition. Indeed, the pandemic led to the suspension of this forum which has, to this date, not been reconducted (despite mentions from 2023 of the three States' willingness of reviving this dialogue as it will be mentioned in a following paragraph), highlighting the difficulties to work in cooperation for those States. It appears that among the Asian States the approach on the Arctic is country-centered rather than regional-centered (Ji, 2013). This is due to different factors which make it difficult for the five Asian States to act in the same direction. Indeed, even though the Arctic observers are usually separated between the European States and the Asian States, it would be wrong to consider any of these groups to have homogenized interests.

First of all, the five Asian States present in the Arctic also have complicated relations with one another based on political, economic, as well as historical tensions (Keyu, 2020). Indeed, the five States have different political positions. Historically, China and Japan, as well as South Korea and Japan have complicated relations. Moreover, the changing politics in the region as well as in the international stage lead to competitive relations between India and China for instance, or between South Korea and Japan which have been increasingly close to the US following the growing tensions between China and the US. Therefore, there is a lack of mutual trust between the different States as well as areas of disagreement which makes it difficult to start cooperation between those different States.

Moreover, there are competing economic factors, especially in terms of the shipping routes (Keyu, 2020). Indeed, China, South Korea, and Japan are all interested in the Northeast Sea Route that could drastically reduce the length of the maritime travels to Europe. On the other hand, India as well as Singapore would suffer from a reduction of the maritime traffic which could stream from the redirection of boats through this route. Even among the three States interested in the maritime route, there are competing views on the shipping route design, the coastal ports developments, as well as the cooperation with the States along the routes, for instance Russia (Keyu, 2020). Therefore, the competition in terms of economic developments, through the shipbuilding national companies, or in terms of the ports of interests for instance, leads to difficulties for common investments which are necessary in the Arctic context due the high costs of adapting to the drastic conditions.

The industrial competition is another diverging sector which leads to disagreement between the States (Moe & Stokke, 2019). Indeed, China, Japan, Singapore, and South Korea are major actors in shipbuilding coupled with the presence of important national ports along the Northern Sea Route and an ever-growing demand for energy leading to an interest in new supply chains, potentially in the Arctic. It leads to competing interest in Arctic economic development. In 2013, Daewoo Shipbuilding & Marine Engineering (now known as Hanwha Ocean), the Korean shipbuilder, won the tender of around $5 billion for building fifteen ice-breaking liquefied natural gas (LNG) carriers for the Yamal LNG project in the Russian Arctic, the first being delivered in 2016 (The Maritime Observer, 2016). The economic impact of the development of such sectors is already noticeable, but due to the increased accessibility of the Arctic with ice-melting and new technologies, the economic benefit perceived, despite usual high costs of market entry, could grow significantly, leading to a strong competition. Therefore, each of the States has the ambition to become the leader in the shipbuilding industry and to develop their ports into hubs, moreover, they cooperate actively with Russia in order to develop a certain energy cooperation (Leksyutina, 2021). According to data from 2021, Japan is importing 3.6% of its raw petrol and 8.7% of its natural gas from Russia from which half of the petrol is coming from Sakhalin-I and -II projects and almost all of its natural gas from Sakhalin-II (Japan External Trade Organization, 2021). In such a State with limited natural resources, the closeness to the Arctic and its possibilities should not be forgotten. Therefore, if all of them are interested in the development of the Arctic and its different economic perspective, they have ambitions that could clash with one another making it difficult to be able to cooperate on those topics.

Therefore, there are conflicting relations and interests between the different Asian States which makes it difficult to develop a cooperation. However, 2023 brought a new perspective on the future possibilities of the Asian States to enhance their cooperation on the Arctic.

Indeed, the Arctic Circle Japan Forum, held on 4–6 March 2023 in Tokyo, was focused on 'Asia in the future of the Arctic' dealing with themes such as science, geopolitics, economy, oceans, climate, and technology (Arctic Circle, n.d.1). This occasion was the first time for all five Asian Arctic Ambassadors/representants from the Arctic Council to meet despite already three similar fora having been organized (China Forum on the Polar Silk Road in 2019, Korea Forum on Asia meets the Arctic in 2018, and Singapore forum in 2015 on the global collaboration on Arctic affairs) (Arctic Circle, n.d.2).

Aside from this unprecedented attendance, China, Japan, and South Korea have all mentioned their willingness to relaunch the Trilateral High-Level Dialogue that has been dormant since the pandemic in 2019 (Arctic

Circle, 2023). This announcement was made during the roundtable of the Arctic Circle Japan Forum that gathered all five of the Asian Ambassadors to the Arctic called 'Contributions of Observer States to the Future of the Arctic Council' showing how they see themselves playing an important part in the future of the Arctic. If neither India nor Singapore have hinted at a possible participation in such a forum, this roundtable highlights the prospects of future cooperation. Nevertheless, the prospects of such cooperation will depend on the readiness of the three States to go beyond the simple promise of further cooperation to the establishment of real effort.

The possibility of an increased cooperation between the Asian States offers new perspectives for the Arctic region that is currently in a difficult position following the war in Ukraine which debunked the notion of 'Arctic exceptionalism' (Pedersen & Steinveg, 2024). Indeed, Russia has been increasingly isolated diplomatically, even in the Arctic international dialogue, by the rest of the members with notably the meetings during its chairmanship (2021–2023) being boycotted by the seven other Arctic States (U.S. Department of State, 2022) while economic sanctions might have long-term impacts in terms of investment in the Russian Arctic. Russia represents 53 percent of the Arctic Ocean coastline (Arctic Council, n.d.) and a current claim of around 70% percent of the Arctic Ocean at the United Nations Commission on the Limits of the Continental Shelf, though overlapping other submissions such as the Danish one by over 800.000 square kilometers (Hossain, 2021) as well as the three largest residential areas of the region Murmansk, Norilsk, and Vorkuta (Lavelle, 2024). Therefore, Russian participation in discussion in all areas of cooperation in the Arctic appears fundamental to an effective preservation and development of the region

Asian observers appear as a potential alternative to the current unease in the Arctic discussion situation. Indeed, an Asian cooperation forum could appear as a neutral zone for discussion between the West and Russia. It has been the case with the CAOFA's Conferences of the Parties (COP) being held in South Korea in 2022, 2023 and 2024, thus enabling the participation of Russia and European/American States after the pause of the Arctic Council for more than year, following the beginning of the Russia-Ukraine conflict. Similarly, this neutral zone is fundamental for research. This willingness from Russia to get closer to India and China can also be seen in the invitation to the fourth Arctic Science Ministerial from Russia. Indeed, the administrative circular mentioned that:

> the meeting will be attended by representatives of Russia, Norway, India, and China, as well as representatives of the Arctic Council ob-

> server states, the main working groups of the Arctic Council, organizations and public associations, and heads of organizations of small indigenous peoples of the North.
>
> MINISTRY OF SCIENCE AND HIGHER EDUCATION OF THE RUSSIAN FEDERATION, 2023

India and China are both singled out, despite the mention of the Arctic observers, showing the will from Russia to give a special role to those two States.

Therefore, it seems that India and China could advocate for a return of cooperation with Russia, or at least serve as a vector for it. The implementation of a real platform for cooperation with for instance a deepened Trilateral High-Level Dialogue which would welcome India and Singapore as well could also serve as a neutral ground for discussion. Therefore, the development of a regional Asian voice could allow the preservation of the singularity of the Arctic as a zone of cooperation, especially in terms of scientific research, despite the geopolitical situation reducing the collaboration possible between Russia and the European and North American actors.

Moreover, a regional voice would permit Asian observers to become more important by offering a new and important network of discussion (Danner, 2020). Indeed, unofficial networks are fundamental in the advancement of matters and projects in the Arctic for the Arctic Council's observer States whose participatory rights are limited. The creation of a platform in Asia regrouping the different interests, or at least the common grounds that could be found, could give a stronger input from the five Asian observers. Additionally, they usually participate more in Ministerial and Senior Arctic Officials Meetings rather than in the Working Groups which allow more direct participation from observer States. According to AMAROK, the Arctic Council's project tracking tool, 125 projects have been finished as of 2019. Out of those projects, Japan had contributed to six, China and South Korea to five, and India and Singapore to two (Knecht, 2020). Therefore, their voice is quite low in the Arctic Council, and they are unable to contribute as much as they are asking for.

Finally, implementing real cooperation between those five States which, as we have demonstrated, have difficulties to work together because of a lack of trust and conflicting geopolitical interests, could serve as a diplomatic opportunity to improve their relations with one another thanks to the creation of a state of complex multi-dependence (Byers, 2017). Creating a framework for Asian cooperation in Arctic affairs which can promote less sensitive themes, comparatively to other challenges the region is facing, such as science diplomacy and on the long term serve as a basis for further cooperation on more conflicting issues.

Previous success in Arctic diplomacy can highlight the possibilities for the region. Indeed, China, Japan, and South Korea were for instance all able to sign and ratify the Central Arctic Ocean Fisheries Agreement despite their conflicted positions on the same topics in their own region (Danner, 2020). Indeed, the will to propose some framework on the fishing in the Arctic appeared in 2008 at the initiative of President Bush and was followed by the adoption of the 2015 Declaration concerning the Prevention of Unregulated High Seas Fishing in the Central Arctic Ocean by the United States, Canada, Denmark, Norway, and Russia (Oslo Declaration, 2015). In 2016, China, Japan, and South Korea were invited, along with Iceland and the EU, by the five Arctic coastal States to contribute to the negotiations on fisheries which were held in Washington D.C. (Balton, 2018). Despite important problems of overfishing in the Bering Sea including China, Japan, and South Korea, especially in the 1980s and 1990s, States were able to reach a common agreement for preventing unregulated high seas fisheries in the Arctic. Nonetheless, its redaction required six rounds of scientific and diplomatic negotiations before being signed on October 2018 (Morishita, 2019). It shows that the Arctic is still a sphere where the different States can work together, independently from the geopolitical rivalry that they are facing. Therefore, it appears that diplomatic relations within the Arctic, even without a formal platform, can lead to the evolution of perceptions of the Asian observers States on each other which could smoothen the tensions that are increasing in the region following the new geopolitical confrontation between the US and China.

It appears that talking about an Asian perspective or voice on the Arctic is homogenizing a region with very different interests and relations despite official similar discourse of science diplomacy and climate change tackling (which in the end are quite similar to the European observers' discourse). Nevertheless, if formal cooperation has failed for now between the five States, and even the more active Chinese, Japanese, and South Korean States, a deeper cooperation could lead to a change both in terms of the perceptions of those States by the rest of the Arctic States and by themselves. Indeed, more cooperation and a policy of bridge between the Western Arctic States and Russia could give a new strength and role to the Asian region in Arctic affairs. Similarly, developing a cooperation within the Arctic frame would allow discussion as well as formal and informal rules to be established between the five States which in turn permit better cooperation in a variety of other sectors.

6 Concluding Remarks

With the Asian States now developing at a fast pace, possessing the economic, demographic, and diplomatic strength, they aim to participate in the creation of international norms as equal actors to ensure that their interests are accounted for in the negotiations and their legitimacy in the larger global order is recognized. The Arctic is one such region that provides them an opportunity to assert their identity, ensures that they are part of an evolving process and are able to influence its discussion to a certain extent. The Asian perspective of the Arctic is tilting towards having an inclusive Arctic where their inputs on climate change and science are welcome. Science diplomacy is a steppingstone for the Asian States, on which they are expanding to look for economic opportunities and participate in governance issues.

While cooperating, they are treading the path carefully, keeping an approach that repeatedly recognizes the sovereignty of the eight Arctic States, working on Arctic strategies through bilateral and trilateral cooperation. Among each other, the cooperation remains limited as each of the five Asian observers is more centered on a national approach rather than a regional one. Nevertheless, developing more closely this regional cooperation could not only renew the role of the Asian observers by giving them a stronger voice but also potentially offer an alternative to the not fully functioning Arctic Council, which is still adapting to the new state of Arctic collaboration that began in the aftermath of Russia's illegal invasion of Ukraine in 2022. Lastly, cooperation within the scope of the Arctic could contribute to building a stronger Asian identity in the long-term, which would benefit the relations within the region in other fields, especially when the tensions are growing in the Indo-Pacific region.

Bibliography

Agreement to Prevent Unregulated High Seas Fisheries in the Central Arctic Ocean (adopted 3 October 2018, entered into force 25 June 2021). [2018 CAOFA] https://www.mofa.go.jp/files/000449233.pdf

Aksnes, D., Osipov, I., Moskaleva, O., & Kullerud, L. (2016). *Arctic research publication trends: A pilot study.* UArctic. https://www.uarctic.org/media/1596721/arctic-research-publication-trends-august-2016.pdf

Almazova-Ilyina, A.B., Vinogradov, A.D., Krasnozhenova, E., & Eidemiller, K. (2020). National interests of Japan and its emerging Arctic policy. *IOP Conference Series:*

Earth and Environmental Science, 539(1). https://doi.org/10.1088/1755-1315/539/1/012048
Arctic Circle (n.d.1). *Arctic circle Japan forum.* Arctic Circle. Retrieved 1 December 2024, from: https://www.arcticcircle.org/forums/arctic-circle-japan-forum
Arctic Circle (n.d.2). *Forums.* Arctic Circle. Retrieved 1 December 2024, from: https://www.arcticcircle.org/forums
Arctic Circle (2023, March 27). *Contributions of observer states to the future of the Arctic Council* [Video]. YouTube. https://www.youtube.com/watch?v=kTo24ax1COY
Arctic Climate Impact Assessment (2004). Impacts of a warming Arctic: Arctic climate impact assessment (ACIA) overview report. Cambridge University Press. https://www.amap.no/documents/doc/impacts-of-a-warming-arctic-2004/786
Arctic Council (n.d.). *The Russian Federation.* Arctic Council. Retrieved 16 November 2024, from: https://arctic-council.org/about/states/russian-federation/#:~:text=Russia%20stretches%20over%2053%20percent%20of%20the%20Arctic%20Ocean%20coastline
Arctic Council (2008). Meeting of senior Arctic officials. Final report. 19–20 November 2008. Kautokeino, Norway. http://hdl.handle.net/11374/862
Arctic Council (1998/2013). *Arctic Council rules of procedure.* http://hdl.handle.net/11374/940
Arctic Council (2013). *Vision for the Arctic.* http://hdl.handle.net/11374/287
Arctic Economic Council (2023). Memorandum of understanding between Arctic Economic Council and Korean Arctic Research Consortium (11 May 2023). https://arcticeconomiccouncil.com/wp-content/uploads/2023/05/230511-mou-aec-koarc-signed.pdf
Babin, J., & Lasserre, F. (2017). Asian states at the Arctic Council: Perceptions in western states. *Polar Geography, 42*(3), 145–159. https://doi.org/10.1080/1088937x.2019.1578290
Balton, D. (2018). The Arctic fisheries agreement: Looking to 2030 and beyond. In R.W. Corell, J.D. Kim, Y.H. Kim, A. Moe, D.L. VanderZwaag, & O.R. Young (Eds.), The Arctic in World Affairs: A North Pacific Dialogue on Arctic 2030 and Beyond – Pathways to the Future (2018 North Pacific Conference Proceedings, pp. 83–91). Korea Maritime Institute & The East-West Center
Brigham, L.W. (2014). The changing Arctic: New realities and players at the top of the world. *Asia Policy, 18*(1), 5–13. https://doi.org/10.1353/asp.2014.0029
Byers, M. (2017). Crises and international cooperation: An Arctic case study. *International relations, 31*(4), 375–402. https://doi.org/10.1177/0047117817735680
Chater, A. (2016a). Explaining non-Arctic states in the Arctic Council. *Strategic Analysis, 40*(3), 173–184. https://doi.org/10.1080/09700161.2016.1165467

Chater, A. (2016b, December 6). *What is Japan's Arctic interest?* The Polar Connection. https://polarconnection.org/japan-arctic-interest/

Chatterjee, S., Ravichandran, M., Murukesh, N., Raj, R.P., & Johannessen, O.M. (2021). A possible relation between Arctic sea ice and late season Indian Summer Monsoon Rainfall extremes. *npj Climate and Atmospheric Science*, *4*(36). https://doi.org/10.1038/s41612-021-00191-w

Danner, L.K. (2020). The promise of Arctic diplomacy: East Asian cooperation in the Arctic Council and beyond. *Journal of East Asia Security*, *1*(1), 1–8.

Declaration concerning the Prevention of Unregulated High Seas Fishing in the Central Arctic Ocean (adopted 16 July 2015). https://www.regjeringen.no/globalassets/departementene/ud/vedlegg/folkerett/declaration-on-arctic-fisheries-16-july-2015.pdf

Quaile, I. (2012, April 26). Race for the Arctic. *Deutsche Welle*. https://www.dw.com/en/chinas-arctic-ambitions-spark-concerns/a-15911711

Dodds, K., & Woon, C.Y. (2020). Introduction: The Arctic Council, Asian states and the global Arctic. In C.Y. Woon & K. Doods (Eds.), *'Observing' the Arctic: Asia in the Arctic Council and beyond* (pp. 1–27). Edward Elgar Publishing.

Elzinga, A. (2016). [Review of the book *The scramble for the Poles: the geopolitics of the Antarctic and Arctic* by K. Dodds & M. Nuttall]. *Antarctic Science*, *28*(3), 233–238. https://doi.org/10.1017/S0954102016000110

Foreign and Commonwealth Office (2013). Adapting to change: UK policy towards the Arctic. https://assets.publishing.service.gov.uk/media/5a757c1ded915d731495a53a/Adapting_To_Change_UK_policy_towards_the_Arctic.pdf

Foreign, Commonwealth & Development Office (2023). Looking North: The UK and the Arctic. The United Kingdom's Arctic policy framework. https://assets.publishing.service.gov.uk/media/63e38ed3e90e0762637e30d0/looking-north-the-uk-and-the-arctic-the-uks-arctic-policy-framework.pdf

Francis, E. (2020). *Arctic governance and China's claim of near Arctic state*. Middlebury Institute of International Studies. https://nps.edu/documents/114698888/121792798/Francis_Arctic_Governance_China_30_Dec_2020.pdf/4acb9f99-38d3-b96b-bdb1-aa98804e54d8?t=1609373841253

Government of India (2022). India's Arctic policy: Building a partnership for sustainable development. https://www.moes.gov.in/sites/default/files/2022-03/compressed-SINGLE-PAGE-ENGLISH.pdf

Headquarters for Ocean Policy (2015). Japan's Arctic policy. https://www8.cao.go.jp/ocean/english/arctic/pdf/japans_ap_e.pdf

Heininen, L. (2020). An Arctic boom of policies & strategies: 32 and counting. *Arctic yearbook*, 2020, 407–423. https://arcticyearbook.com/arctic-yearbook/2020/2020-briefing-notes/367-an-arctic-boom-of-policies-strategies-56-and-counting

Heng, C., & Freymann, E. (2023, July 7). *Outsiders wanting in: Asian states and Arctic governance*. Harvard Kennedy School's Belfer Center Policy Brief. https://www.belfercenter.org/publication/outsiders-wanting-asian-states-and-arctic-governance

Hossain, K. (2021, May 24). *Russia's proposed extended continental shelf in the Arctic Ocean: Science setting the stage for law* (Volume 25, Issue 8). American Society of International Law Insights. https://www.asil.org/insights/volume/25/issue/8

Japan External Trade Organization (2021). *Japanese Trade and Investment Statistics*. Japan External Trade Organization. Retrieved 16 November 2024, from https://www.jetro.go.jp/en/reports/statistics.html

Ji, Y.-J. (2013). Navigating the Arctic: Players from Asia. *Air Power Journal, 8*(3), 111–128. https://capsindia.org/wp-content/uploads/2022/09/Ji-Yeon-Jung.pdf

Keyu, G. (2020). A shifting northeast Asian security landscape and China-ROK-Japan Arctic cooperation. *The Journal of East Asian Affairs, 33*(2), 59–81

Kim, E., & Stenport, A. (2021). South Korea's Arctic policy: Political motivations for the 21st century global engagements. *The Polar Journal, 11*(1), 11–29. https://doi.org/10.1080/2154896X.2021.1917088

Kim, Y., & Jeong, J. (2015). The development of the Asian forum for polar sciences (AFoPS). *Polar Science, 9*(4), 338–344. https://doi.org/10.1016/j.polar.2015.08.004

Knecht, S. (2020). The Arctic Council, Asian observers, and the role of 'shadow networks' in the science–policy interface. In C.Y. Woon & K. Doods (Eds.), *'Observing' the Arctic: Asia in the Arctic Council and beyond* (pp. 29–53). Edward Elgar Publishing. https://doi.org/10.4337/9781839108211.00008

Koivurova, T. (2011). Scramble for resources or orderly development – What is happening in the Arctic? In L. Salmela (Ed.), *Nordic cooperation and the Far North* (Department of Strategic and Defence Studies, Series 2: Research Reports No. 46, pp. 1–14). Maanpuolustuskorkeakoulu – National Defence University.

Lackenbauer, P.W. (2017). India and the Arctic: Revisionist aspirations, Arctic realities. *Jindal Global Law Review, 8*(1), 23–54. https://doi.org/10.1007/s41020-017-0040-4

Lanteigne, M. (2017). Walking the walk: Science diplomacy and identity-building in Asia-Arctic relations. *Jindal Global Law Review, 8*(1), 87–101. https://doi.org/10.1007/s41020-017-0043-1

Lavelle, K.C. (2024). Regime, climate, and region in transition: Russian participation in the Arctic Council. In A. Obydenkova (Ed.), *Sustainable development, regional governance, and international organizations: Implications for post-communism* (pp. 53–65). Routledge.

Leksyutina, Y. (2021). Russia's cooperation with Asian observers to the Arctic Council. *The Polar Journal, 11*(1), 136–159. https://doi.org/10.1080/2154896X.2021.1892833

Lomaeva, M., & Saunavaara, J. (2022). Japan facing the Arctic and North: Interplay between the national and regional interests. In A. Likhacheva (Ed.), *Arctic fever: Political, economic & environmental aspects* (pp. 393–428). Springer. https://doi.org/10.1007/978-981-16-9616-9_15

Manicom, J., & Lackenbauer, W. (2013, April). *East Asian states, the Arctic Council and international relations in the Arctic* (Policy Brief No. 26). Centre for International Governance Innovation. https://www.cigionline.org/static/documents/no26.pdf

Ministry of External Affairs (2022, May 4). *2nd India-Nordic Summit.* Ministry of External Affairs, Government of India. https://www.mea.gov.in/press-releases.htm?dtl/35277/2nd_IndiaNordic_Summit#:~:text=India's%20partnership%20with%20the%20Nordic,countries%20to%20invest%20in%20India

Ministry of Foreign Affairs (2021, May 21). *Singapore's participation in the Arctic Council Ministerial Meeting, 20 May 2021* [Press release]. https://www.mfa.gov.sg/Newsroom/Press-Statements-Transcripts-and-Photos/2021/05/20210521-SG-Arctic-Council-Ministerial-Meeting#:~:text=Senior%20Minister%20of%20State%20(SMS,Meeting%20on%2020%20May%202021

Ministry of Foreign Affairs of Japan (2017). Joint statement: The second trilateral high-level dialogue on the Arctic (8 June 2017). https://www.mofa.go.jp/files/000263104.pdf

Ministry of Foreign Affairs of Japan (2018). Joint declaration of the seventh trilateral summit meeting of China-ROK-Japan (9 May 2018).https://www.mofa.go.jp/a_o/rp/page4e_000817.html

Ministry of Foreign Affairs of the People's Republic of China (2018). Joint statement: The third trilateral high-level dialogue on the Arctic (8 June 2018). https://www.mfa.gov.cn/eng/zy/gb/202405/t20240531_11367362.html

Ministry of Foreign Affairs of the People's Republic of China (2019). Trilateral cooperation vision for the next decade (24 December 2019). https://www.mfa.gov.cn/mfa_eng/zy/jj/2019zt/dbczrhldrhy/202406/t20240606_11379337.html

Ministry of Foreign Affairs of the Republic of Korea (2016). Joint press release of the first trilateral high-level dialogue on the Arctic among the Republic of Korea, Japan, and the People's Republic of China (28 April 2016). https://www.mofa.go.kr/eng/brd/m_5676/view.do?seq=316483

Ministry of Foreign Affairs of the Republic of Korea (2019). The fourth trilateral high-level dialogue on the Arctic, Busan, June 25–26, 2019 (27 June 2019). https://www.mofa.go.kr/eng/brd/m_5676/view.do?seq=320574

Ministry of Oceans and Fisheries (2022). 제1차 극지활동 진흥 기본계획 (2023~2027) [The first basic plan for promoting polar activities (2023–2027)]. https://www.mof.go.kr/synap/view.do?fn=MOF_ARTICLE_48185_2022121218503f0968e120&fd=202412

Ministry of Science and Higher Education of the Russian Federation (2023). *Administrative circular. The fourth Arctic Science Ministerial (ASM4): Delegation of authority from ASM4 (Russia) to ASM5 (Norway), April 14–15, 2023 г.* (30 January 2023). Retrieved 27 December 2024, from: https://arcticportal.org/images/news/2023/docs/ASM4_-_Administrative_circular.pdf

Moe, A., & Stokke, O.S. (2019). Asian countries and Arctic shipping. *Arctic Review on Law and Politics, 10*, 24–52. https://doi.org/10.23865/arctic.v10.1374

Morishita, J. (2019). The Arctic five-plus-five process on central Arctic Ocean fisheries negotiations. In Shibata, A., Zou, L., Sellheim, N., & Scopelliti, M. (Eds.). *Emerging legal orders in the Arctic: The role of non-Arctic actors* (pp. 109–131). Routledge

National Centre for Polar and Ocean Research (n.d.). *India in Antarctica.* National Centre for Polar and Ocean Research. Retrieved 15 October 2023, from https://ncpor.res.in/antarcticas/display/166-india-in-antarctica

NATO Parliamentary Assembly (2017, May 17). *"What happens in the Arctic, does not stay in the Arctic" – Climate change in the Arctic will have global consequences and cannot be ignored.* NATO Parliamentary Assembly. https://www.nato-pa.int/news/what-happens-arctic-does-not-stay-arctic-climate-change-arctic-will-have-global-consequences

Pareek, N. (2021). Asian observers in the Arctic framework: Hits and misses. *Global Affairs, 7*(3), 395–403. https://doi.org/10.1080/23340460.2021.1945478

Pedersen, T., & Steinveg, B. (2024). Russia's clashing ambitions: Arctic status quo and world-order revision. *Politics and Governance, 12*, 7311. https://doi.org/10.17645/pag.7311

Peri. D. (2024, October 14). *India-Russia discuss training of Indian sailors for polar navigation.* The Indu. https://www.thehindu.com/news/national/india-russia-discuss-training-of-indian-sailors-for-polar-navigation/article68752741.ece

Pompeo, M.R. (2019, May 6). *Looking North: Sharpening America's Arctic focus.* United States Department of State. https://2017-2021-translations.state.gov/2019/05/06/looking-north-sharpening-americas-arctic-focus/

Pursiainen, C., Alden, C., & Bertelsen, R. (2021). The Arctic and Africa in China's foreign policy: How different are they and what does this tell us? *Arctic Review on Law and Politics, 12*(1), 31–55. https://doi.org/10.23865/arctic.v12.2440

Reuters (2024, September 24). *India will not buy from Russia's sanctioned Arctic LNG 2 project, oil secretary says.* Reuters. https://www.reuters.com/world/india/india-will-not-buy-russias-sanctioned-arctic-lng-2-project-oil-secretary-says-2024-09-27/

Satikov, R.V., & Kim, V.M. (2024). Policy of the Republic of Korea in the polar regions in 2023–2033. *Arctic and North, 54*, 91–95. https://doi.org/10.37482/issn2221-2698.2024.54.110

Seo, H. (2023). South Korea and the Arctic. In K. Hossain & M. Roncero (Eds.), *Arctic law in 1000 words.* (Juridica Lapponica No. 50, pp. 157–160). University of Lapland. https://lauda.ulapland.fi/bitstream/handle/10024/65637/Seo_Hyunkyo.pdf?sequence=1&isAllowed=y

Solli, P.E., Rowe, E.W., & Lindgren, W.Y. (2013). Coming into the cold: Asia's Arctic interests. *Polar Geography, 36*(4), 253–270. https://doi.org/10.1080/1088937X.2013.825345

State Council of People's Republic of China (2018, January 26). China's Arctic policy. Retrieved 15 October 2023, from: https://english.www.gov.cn/archive/white_paper/2018/01/26/content_281476026660336.htm

Stepien, A., Kauppila, L., Kopra, S., Käpylä., J., Lanteigne., Mikkola, H., & Nojonen, M. (2020). China's economic presence in the Arctic: Realities, expectations and concerns. In T. Koivurova & S. Kopra (Eds.), *Chinese policy and presence in the Arctic* (Studies in Polar Law, Volume 3, pp. 90–136). Brill. https://doi.org/10.1163/9789004408425_007

Stokke, O.S. (2013). The promise of involvement: Asia in the Arctic. *Strategic Analysis, 37*(4), 474–479. https://doi.org/10.1080/09700161.2013.802520

Stokke, O.S. (2014). Asian stakes and Arctic governance. *Strategic Analysis, 38*(6), 770–783. https://doi.org/10.1080/09700161.2014.952946

Sun, Y. (2018, August 27). *The intricacy of China's Arctic policy* (Policy Paper). Stimson Centre. https://www.stimson.org/2018/intricacy-chinas-arctic-policy/

The Arctic Institute: Center for Circumpolar Security Studies (n.d.). *Singapore.* Retrieved 1 September 2024, from https://www.thearcticinstitute.org/country-backgrounders/singapore/

The Maritime Observer (2016, January 18). *DSME launches world';s first icebreaking LNG carrier.* The Maritime Observer. https://maritime-executive.com/article/dsme-launches-worlds-first-icebreaking-lng-carrier

Treaty concerning the Archipelago of Spitsbergen (adopted 9 February 1920, entered into force 14 August 1925) 2 LNTS 7. [1920 Svalbard Treaty]

U.S. Department of State (2022, March 3). Joint statement on Arctic Council cooperation following Russia's invasion of Ukraine. Retrieved 16 November 2024, from https://2021-2025.state.gov/joint-statement-on-arctic-council-cooperation-following-russias-invasion-of-ukraine/

Watters, S., & Tonami, A. (2012). Singapore: An emerging Arctic actor. Arctic Yearbook, [*2012*], 105–114. https://arcticyearbook.com/images/yearbook/2012/Scholarly_Papers/5.Tonami_and_Watters_Singapore.pdf

Young, O.R. (2005). Governing the Arctic: From cold war theater to mosaic of cooperation. *Global Governance: A Review of Multilateralism and International Organization, 11*(1), 9–15. https://doi.org/10.1163/19426720-01101002

CHAPTER 2

Belgium's Polar Leadership to Build Arctic Expertise: A Policy in the Making

Romain Chuffart and Karen van Loon

1 Introduction

Despite being a small European country geographically far from the polar regions, Belgium's involvement in the Arctic primarily stems from its interest in scientific research, environmental and geo-economic interests, and international cooperation in the region. As with other non-Arctic States, geographical proximity is not the only element to understanding a country's engagement in regional governance (see Chuffart et al., 2020; see also Depledge, 2017). In the case of Arctic governance, willingness to engage in relationship building is often regarded as primordial to be considered a legitimate actor (Chuffart et al., 2021; Chuffart & Raspotnik, 2019). However, until the early 2020s, the Arctic did not seem to factor significantly into Belgium's foreign policy. This chapter traces the evolution and history of Belgium's ongoing political development as it relates to engaging in Arctic governance. Besides current drafting and negotiations that are part of the development of an Arctic policy document, what becomes evident is that there are a considerable number of actors within the different government levels that have been involved in some shape or form in the broader picture of Arctic governance.

2 Belgium as a Polar Nation

To fully appreciate why the Arctic region was not traditionally featured in Belgium's foreign policy agenda, it is essential to delve into the country's history as a polar nation as primarily conducted through Antarctic exploration and scientific research within the Antarctic Treaty System (Molenaar, 2021). Antarctic exploration history underscores Belgium's long-standing interest and involvement in polar research, despite its geographic distance from the poles.

 | DOI:10.1163/9789004734685_003

Belgium's first foray into polar exploration is notably marked by its pioneering achievement in organizing the first expedition to overwinter in Antarctica. This expedition, led by Baron Adrien de Gerlache, a naval officer hailing from Hasselt, embarked on a historic journey aboard the RV *Belgica* from 1897 to 1899. This voyage is celebrated as a cornerstone of the Heroic Age of Antarctic Exploration. It stands out not only for its scientific accomplishments but also for including an unpaid Norwegian first mate, Roald Amundsen, who was just 25 years old at the time. Amundsen would later gain fame as one of the most illustrious polar explorers, highlighting the expedition's role in nurturing future generations of explorers. Lesser known are the three major expeditions that de Gerlache undertook in the Arctic Ocean between 1905 and 1909 at the service of the French Duke of Orleans, to Novaya Zemlya, Iceland, and Greenland (Barr, 2009).

The *Belgica* expedition's legacy is a testament to Belgium's early commitment to understanding and exploring the polar regions, a commitment that extended well beyond this singular voyage into the 20th century. This enduring interest underscores Belgium's broader engagement with polar research and exploration. Moreover, Belgium's involvement in Antarctic affairs did not wane with the passage of time. The country played a pivotal role in the governance and legal framework of Antarctica (Antarctic Treaty, 1959). As one of the twelve original signatories of the Antarctic Treaty, Belgium helped lay the foundation for the modern regime governing the southern continent (Molenaar, 2021). This treaty, a landmark agreement that came into force in 1961, set the stage for collaborative international research and ensured that Antarctica would remain a zone free of territorial disputes and military activities.

This backdrop of Belgium's Antarctic exploration and legal engagement illustrates a nuanced picture of the country's polar interests. It demonstrates that Belgium has been, historically, deeply invested in the polar regions through scientific, exploratory, and legal channels. While the Arctic may not have been the primary focus of Belgium's foreign policy in the past, the country's profound legacy in Antarctica suggests a broader interest in polar affairs. This legacy not only enriches Belgium's national narrative but also positions it as a country with valuable expertise and a vested interest in both polar regions' future.

Under the Antarctic Treaty System, science serves as a foundational element of Antarctic governance and collaboration, reflecting the commitment of various States to advancing scientific knowledge.

In the context of this scientific dedication, Belgium has made significant contributions to Antarctic research, mirroring its historical and ongoing interest in polar exploration and study. For instance, the establishment of the Roi Baudouin Base during the International Geophysical Year of 1958–1959 marked Belgium's initial foray into Antarctic scientific endeavours. Positioned on a floating ice shelf in Dronning Maud Land, this base symbolized Belgium's early dedication to polar research, although it was decommissioned in 1967. Subsequently, recognizing the critical importance of marine research, the Belgian government initiated the construction of a new research vessel in the late 1970s. Launched in 1984, the *RV A692 Belgica*, named in homage to its historic predecessor, underscored Belgium's ongoing commitment to oceanographic exploration.

Advancing into the 2000s, the Belgian Science Policy Office (BELSPO), in collaboration with the International Polar Foundation led by Alain Hubert, embarked on numerous scientific expeditions through the Belgian Antarctic Expeditions (BELARE) program (International Polar Foundation, 2007) A significant milestone was achieved in 2009 with the inauguration of the Princess Elisabeth research station on Dronning Maud's Land (International Polar Foundation, n.d.). The station is Antarctica's only zero-emission station as it operates entirely on renewable energy. It welcomes international scientists annually to facilitate a broad spectrum of research activities which serve to emphasize Belgium's role in promoting global scientific cooperation in the Antarctic

After nearly four decades dedicated to oceanographic research, the *RV A692 Belgica* was retired, and the Belgian government, through BELSPO, acquired a successor, which maintained the name of its predecessor *RV Belgica*. Set to continue Belgium's tradition of marine scientific research, this new vessel, operational since 2021, represents a modern commitment to advancing scientific knowledge. In a notable act of international cooperation and support for environmental research, Belgium signed an agreement with Ukraine in September 2021 to transfer the *RV Belgica* as part of the European Union for Improving Environmental Monitoring in the Black Sea project (*Odessa Journal*, 2022) This transfer not only exemplifies Belgium's willingness to extend its legacy of scientific exploration but also its commitment to enhancing scientific and environmental monitoring efforts globally. In October 2021, the vessel, stationed in Odessa started operating under the name *RV Borys Aleksandrov* to contribute to research activities in the Black Sea (*Odessa Journal, 2022*). Although the vessel showcased international scientific collaboration and environmental stewardship, it did not last long as the *RV Borys Aleksandrov* was damaged during a Russian attack on the port of Odesa on 23 July 2022 (Yakimyuk, 2023).

During the Arctic Science Summit Week (ASSW) in March 2022 in Tromsø, the International Arctic Science Committee (IASC) approved the Belgian application for IASC membership and welcomed Belgium as its 24th member country. Belgium is currently a member of the Council, IASC's policy and decision-making body. IASC membership provides Belgium with an opportunity to consolidate its scientific cooperation on Arctic research by continuing to participate in the various IASC working groups and initiatives that strengthen capacity building. It is also a testament of the quality of the ongoing research in over a dozen research groups at nine Belgian universities.

3 The Evolution of the Belgian Arctic Policy

3.1 *Arctic Political Developments at the Federal Parliament*

Given Belgium's extensive expertise in Antarctic research, one might question why the country has not taken a more proactive stance in Arctic governance. The absence of a comprehensive Belgian Arctic policy document further underscores Belgium's cautious approach towards articulating its interests in the region. Such a policy would not only signal Belgium's strategic intentions but also contribute to its recognition as a credible actor in Arctic affairs – a non-Arctic State that nonetheless possesses a profound understanding of the region's dynamics. Recent political developments within Belgium, however, have begun to attract the attention of Arctic specialists (van Loon, 2024). These internal shifts may indicate a growing awareness of the importance of Arctic issues, potentially paving the way for Belgium to adopt a more defined role in Arctic governance. As the global strategic importance of the Arctic continues to rise, Belgium has argued that its involvement in other regional governance regimes (e.g., the Antarctic) positions it as a potentially influential player both nationally and through the European Union's Arctic policy, should Belgium choose to engage more directly with Arctic governance mechanisms and regional actors (Chamber of Representatives, 2021a).

To understand current policy developments, it is vital to retrace the historical steps through which Belgium went through to reach its current position. The formal timeline can be traced back to the early 2010s. In 2011, the Belgian Federal Parliament's lower house, the Chamber of Representatives, passed a resolution focused on the "protection of the Arctic" (Chamber of

Representatives, 2011). This legislative measure was a foundational step in defining Belgium's participation in Arctic matters at a parliamentary level, establishing a strategic emphasis on environmental stewardship within the Arctic domain. The significance of this resolution lies in its endeavour to align Belgium's Arctic policy more effectively with the concurrent Arctic strategy of the European Union, thus integrating Belgium's efforts into a wider regional policy landscape. It specified seven distinct directives to guide the federal government's foreign policy agenda and provide a thorough framework for Belgium's strategic engagement with the Arctic. The first directive asked, among other, to:

> promote at the European and international levels the strengthening of international governance of the Arctic by aiming for the adoption of an international protocol for the protection of the Arctic Ocean, based on the United Nations Convention on the Law of the Sea (UNCLOS), drawing inspiration from the principles of the Antarctic Treaty, and taking into account the fact that the Arctic is inhabited and that it is therefore appropriate to respect the rights and needs of the populations and nations of the Arctic region; this protocol will confirm the value of the area as a "common heritage of mankind," put an end to the appropriation of international waters, and adopt all necessary measures to protect indigenous cultures, biodiversity, and natural resources.
>
> CHAMBER OF REPRESENTATIVES, 2011, p. 4, transl.

As will be explained in more details below, the ambivalence between narrating the Arctic as an empty region at the forefront of climate change and as a cultural and social space will characterize much of the Federal Parliament's efforts to engage with the region.

Since 2013, a bipartisan group of Belgian Senators, spearheaded by Senator Bert Anciaux, a former minister in the Flemish government, has been persistently introducing draft resolutions aimed at the "Protection and Conservation of the Arctic Region" (Senate, 2013; Senate, 2019). This draft resolution broadly outlines the multifaceted nature of Arctic affairs, touching upon environmental challenges, the potential for economic activities, governance issues, and the possibility of conflicts in the region. While the resolution acknowledges the presence and rights of Indigenous peoples and Arctic inhabitants, its primary focus is on the geopolitical implications of changes within the Arctic. Among its recommendations, it urges the Belgian Federal Government to assert a more significant role in formulating a cohesive European Union (EU) Arctic policy, to support the EU's continued efforts to obtain observer status on the Arctic Council, and to engage in Arctic-related discussions within various multilateral frameworks, including the International Maritime Organisation (IMO) and the North Atlantic Treaty Organization (NATO). Notably, the latest version of this draft resolution from 2019 advocates for Belgium, within the EU context, to push for an international moratorium on mineral resource exploitation in the Arctic – a proposal that echoes previous EU initiatives and stances on Arctic affairs (Senate, 2019).

The involvement of the EU in Arctic matters has influenced the positioning of the Belgian government regarding Arctic issues. For example, in September 2020, then Minister of Foreign Affairs Philippe Goffin reiterated Belgium's support for the integrated EU Arctic policy of 2016 and the conclusions drawn by the Council of the European Union in 2019 during a session of the Chamber of Representatives' Commission for External Relations (Chamber of Representatives, 2020c). These developments underscore a growing EU interest in the Arctic, raising questions about Belgium's potential to expand its engagement in the region. However, in 2020, the Belgian Ministry of Foreign Affairs (MFA) was still very much focused on the Antarctic and not on the Arctic (Chamber of Representatives, 2020b, p. 29). Despite its niche status among Brussels' foreign affairs civil servants and politicians at the time, Arctic discussions are gradually becoming more frequent in parliamentary meetings and debates. For example, in October 2021, then-EU Special Envoy for Arctic Matters Michael Mann was invited to participate in a meeting of the Parliament's foreign affairs committee to discuss Arctic developments, indicating an increasing awareness and potential for Belgium to engage more deeply in Arctic governance.

The year 2021 marked a pivotal moment in Belgium's approach to Arctic engagement. A cross-party group of Members of Parliament (MP) introduced a draft resolution urging the Belgian government to closely monitor the security challenges arising from developments in the Arctic (Chamber of Representatives, 2021a). This resolution is divided into two sections: the first addressing geopolitical and security concerns, and the second offering insights into Belgian policymakers' perceptions of the Arctic. It emphasized strategic and geo-economic implications of a warming Arctic. Specifically, it points to the investment in the Zeebrugge Liquefied Natural Gas (LNG) terminal, in Belgium's largest harbour of Antwerp-Bruges, making it one of the principal EU transshipment hubs for Russian LNG. The prospect of new Arctic shipping routes, emerging as a result of rapidly diminishing summer ice, could significantly affect the Port of Antwerp-Bruges' commercial activities (Chamber of Representatives, 2021a).

In addition, even following Russia's full-scale illegal invasion of Ukraine, Belgium is still among the top three EU importers of LNG from Novatek's Yamal LNG facility with Zeebrugge serving as a major re-export hub for Russian gas in 2024 (Humpert, 2024). Since 2018, the provider Fluxys has operated under a 20-year contract with Novatek for the transshipment of up to 8 million tons of LNG annually (Fluxys, 2020). Although Russian gas and LNG are not subject to EU sanctions, a reform of EU gas market rules was set in motion in late 2023 to allow EU countries to choose whether to stop deliveries of Russian pipeline gas and LNG by giving them a legal option to prevent Russian firms from booking capacity on their gas infrastructure (Humpert, 2024). Given the importance of LNG transshipment for Belgium, Belgium's Energy Minister Tinne Van der Straeten commented that it was not clear whether Belgium would use such a legal mechanism (Abnett, 2024). On 22 November 2024, Fluxys announced that that it would adapt its operational rules to ensure full compliance with the 14th EU sanctions package against Russia (Council of the European Union, 2024), which will apply to existing contracts starting March 26, 2025 (Fluxys, 2024).

The draft resolution concludes by an analysis of geographical closeness and proximity as not entirely relevant to specific regional engagement by stating that "although Belgium is located approximately 4,300 km from the North Pole, the country has a strategic interest in monitoring regional developments." (Chamber of Representatives, 2021a, p. 12). As discussed in the introduction, this is a common strategy adopted by non-Arctic States to position themselves as legitimate actors in the Arctic governance. Far from saying that geography does not matter, what it does is show the interconnectivity of global and regional affairs and climates.

Following an expert hearing in November 2021, the draft resolution underwent some minor revisions, and small amendments were introduced to reflect Belgium's stance on geostrategic tensions and great power rivalry in the Arctic, its economic interests in the region and the opportunities that the Arctic has to offer to Belgian businesses, and the need to stay committed to scientific cooperation in the region. Throughout the document, the focus on issues related to climate change intensified (Chamber of Representatives, 2021d). In December 2021, a final draft text was adopted by the Parliament's External Relations Commission (Chamber of Representatives, 2021e). The final text of the resolution was adopted almost unanimously on 22 December 2021 in a plenary session of the Chamber of Representatives (Chamber of Representatives, 2021f) with only the French-speaking Workers' Party of Belgium voting against the motion.

3.2 *A Growing Interest among Parliamentarians*

This growing interest in the Arctic within Belgian political circles reflects the broader international recognition of the Arctic's significance in geopolitical, environmental, and economic terms. One theme across the political documents and discussions around Belgium's Arctic efforts is that as it contemplates a more assertive role in Arctic affairs, the evolution of its policy stance and actions could contribute meaningfully to the collective efforts addressing social and environmental challenges mainly through scientific research and innovation (van Loon, 2024). This is even more noticeable in the amended version of the 2021 Parliamentary draft resolution where several Members of Parliament (MPs) redrafted the preamble to include references to relevant international environmental law treaties, as well as references to ocean governance and the rights of Indigenous peoples, through the ILO Convention No. 169, and that Arctic climatic changes will lead to global impact, "including on climate conflicts and migrations, along with all the related social and security consequences." (Chamber of Representatives, 2021c, p. 11). The revised preamble's language ended up in the final adopted text of the 2021 resolution (Chamber of Representatives, 2021f). Therefore, whether through advocacy for sustainable governance, environmental protection, or engagement in multilateral Arctic frameworks, Belgium's potential contributions could enhance its profile as a concerned and constructive non-Arctic State invested in the future of this increasingly pivotal region on the global stage.

As of March 2024, the policy has still not been formally adopted. This has prompted some Belgian MPs to regularly ask the MFA and other Federal Public Services to update Belgium's Federal Parliament on the policy drafting-process. These requests for updates and engagement on Arctic issues highlight that Belgium's parliamentary interests in the Arctic revolve around four distinct topics: upholding the international rule-based legal order, military security, economic development, and climate change. For example, in a written question to the Ministry of Defence (MoD) submitted on 25 May 2021, MP Jasper Pillen highlighted the strategic importance of the Arctic region from both economic and military perspectives, prompting a discussion on Belgium's preparedness for operations in the increasingly accessible Arctic Ocean (Chamber of Representatives, 2021b). The question specifically addressed the readiness of the Belgian naval component for Arctic mobilization, the capabilities of future multi-purpose frigates in Arctic conditions, and the training of other military units for operations in polar regions. The Ministry of Defence's response underscored a proactive approach to Arctic engagement, detailing annual training for naval officers in Antarctic navigation to adapt to icy waters, the operational readiness of future Anti-Submarine Warfare Frigates (ASWF) in Arctic, albeit non-ice-covered, waters, and the comprehensive Arctic and cold environment training regimen of the Special Operations Regiment, including participation in exercises such as Joint Arctic Training and Cold Response in Norway. This exchange reveals how Belgium's interest in the Arctic is increasingly being channelled through a military and security lens, reflecting a broader trend among nations to prepare for the geopolitical and environmental challenges posed by the Arctic region's changing landscape.

In 2022, another written question to the MoD, stressed the importance of developing bilateral relations with Arctic States. Pillen asked about Belgium's potential involvement in Air Policing missions over the Arctic region, specifically in response to Iceland's expressed interest outlined in Iceland's Policy on Matters Concerning the Arctic Region (Parliament's Resolution 25/151) of October 2021. Pillen's query, submitted on 25 January 2022, with a response sought to ascertain whether Belgium would consider deploying Air Policing efforts in the Arctic if requested by Iceland or another NATO ally (Chamber of Representatives, 2022a, pp. 327–328). The Ministry's response, published on 10 March 2022, pointed out Belgium's active contribution to NATO's collective air surveillance task since 2004, highlighting its particular focus on Baltic airspace security. Notably, the response detailed Belgium's involvement through a Belgian fighter pilot assigned to the Portuguese Air Force as part of an exchange program, participating in the Air Policing mission for Icelandic airspace until 30 March 2022. At the ministerial level, this engagement underscores Belgium's commitment to NATO's collective defence responsibilities and its readiness to support allied airspace security, including potential future missions in the strategically significant Arctic region. In the context of the development of Belgium Arctic interests, this exchange reflects the nuanced security considerations in contributing to collective measures within the NATO framework, emphasizing the importance of interoperability and bilateral and multilateral collaboration among allies in addressing the evolving security dynamics of the Arctic.

In August 2022, Jasper Pillen requested an update on the progress of the draft policy for Belgium's strategic engagement in the Arctic, emphasizing the region's escalating geostrategic significance and the imperative of climate change considerations (Chamber of Representatives, 2022b, p. 314). The specific updates Pillen sought revolved around 1) whether the MFA was working with external partners such as think tanks or universities to inform the policy-drafting process; 2) what were the different state organs involved in the drafting process and whether there was a coordinated process; and 3) whether bilateral meetings with other States, which had already released or were in the process of drafting their own Arctic policies or strategic frameworks, were being held (Chamber of Representatives, 2022b, p. 314). In its response on 28 September 2022, the MFA outlined Belgium's active steps toward formulating its Arctic policy, including collaboration with the Egmont Institute, an independent non-profit think tank focused on international relations based in Brussels, to engage stakeholders through seminars and discussions, thereby enriching the policy draft with diverse insights (Chamber of Representatives, 2022b, pp. 315–316). The initiation of the network 'Group of Friends of the Arctic' and the provision of substantial funding to the Egmont Institute were highlighted as pivotal efforts to solidify Belgium's stance on Arctic issues. Additionally, Belgium's involvement in the 2022 Arctic Circle Assembly (ACA) and its admission to IASC were presented as significant strides towards Belgium's integration into international Arctic discourse, showcasing the country's dedicated and forward-thinking approach to its Arctic engagement in light of changing global dynamics.

Representative Pillen tabled a similar question in April 2023. This time, his concerns were mainly about the allocation of financial resources to the policy-drafting process, including Egmont Institute's staff assignments, budget allocations, and external collaborations related to the strategy's development (Chamber of Representatives, 2023a, p. 317). The Ministry's response, dated 26 May 2023, reaffirmed the heightened importance of the Arctic for Belgium across various dimensions – scientific cooperation, economic opportunities, geostrategic challenges, and climate change. It detailed the allocation of a grant to the Egmont Institute in 2022 for foundational work on the strategy, highlighting the recruitment of a researcher hired and supported administratively by Egmont's staff, including the EU's former Ambassador for the Arctic, to compile the necessary groundwork (Chamber of Representatives, 2023a, pp. 318–319). The Ministry outlined a plan for extensive intra-Belgian consultations post-draft submission, spanning scientific, economic, environmental, political, and security aspects to shape the strategy's final draft. Moreover, the Ministry acknowledged collaborations beyond the Egmont Institute, involving consultations with a broad spectrum of stakeholders, including several federal Ministries (e.g., Ministry of Foreign Affairs, Climate, Defence, and Health), BELSPO, climate change researchers, representatives from regional governments in Belgium, and their export and foreign investment agencies, and European institutions, to ensure a comprehensive and inclusive strategy formulation process (Chamber of Representatives, 2023a, pp. 318–319). Once again, despite the concerns around the drafting of the policy as such, this dialogue between Pillen and the Ministry encapsulates a proactive and collaborative approach to developing a nuanced and strategic Belgian stance on Arctic affairs, demonstrating a commitment to engage as many Belgian Arctic stakeholders as possible in the process.

Finally, on 24 October 2023, Representative Goedele Liekens submitted a question to seek updates from the Ministry of Foreign Affairs, European Affairs and Foreign Trade and the Federal Cultural Institutions regarding the development of Belgium's Arctic policy (Chamber of Representatives, 2023c, pp. 358–359). The aim was to assess the progress made since the Chamber's 2021 resolution, which called for a strategy attentive to the climate crisis and security challenges in the Arctic. Specific questions addressed the involvement of the MFA with the Egmont Institute that was funded to support the development a policy document, any updates regarding the status of intra-Belgian consultations, the advancement towards finalizing the Belgian strategic plan for the Arctic, and the anticipated timeline for its submission to parliamentary debate. The Minister of Foreign Affairs' response articulated a keen awareness of the Arctic's growing significance for Belgium, emphasizing climate change, scientific and economic cooperation opportunities, and the geostrategic challenges of the region. Highlighting Belgium's proactive engagement, the MFA's response noted Belgium's participation in the 2023 ACA in Reykjavík, where Belgium, represented by its ambassador to Norway and Iceland and a team from Egmont Institute, contributed to discussions on the Arctic's value for Belgium and its relevance to energy security. She further notified that the MFA received a strategy project from the Egmont Institute over the summer 2023, which was followed by internal consultations with relevant governmental services.

After the 2023 ACA, a collaborative effort was outlined involving the MFA, the Environment Ministry, the MoD, and BELSPO, based on the Egmont Institute's project, to develop a comprehensive policy plan for Belgium regarding the Arctic. According to the MFA, this plan will also incorporate feedback from regional and community levels, underscoring a holistic approach to Belgium's Arctic strategy (Chamber of Representatives, 2023c, p. 359). The ministry assured that this preparatory work is moving forward and will be presented to the Parliament in due course, with continued support from the Egmont Institute to enrich Belgium's involvement in Arctic policy discussions and initiatives.

3.3 *Increased Engagement at the Ministry of Foreign Affairs*

Since 2022, the Arctic is explicitly featured in Belgium's foreign policy. Hadja Lahbib, Minister of Foreign Affairs, European Affairs and Foreign

Trade and Federal Cultural Institutions, briefly referred to the region for the first time in her annual General Policy Note on External Relations, European Affairs, and Foreign Trade, in the chapter on foreign trade linking the Arctic to the blue economy, noting that:

> I will also pay particular attention to the "blue economy" theme, but also to the Arctic region, which is set to gain in importance, both in terms of climate change and geostrategic and economic challenges, as stipulated in the resolution to draw up a Belgian strategy for this region, adopted on 22/12/2021 in Parliament.
>
> CHAMBER OF REPRESENTATIVES, 2022c, p. 24, transl.

In 2023, the Arctic took a more prominent role in Minister Lahbib's General Policy Note. In the introduction, she referred to the Arctic in the context of the future of Europe, mentioning that: economic security and open strategic autonomy are concepts that need to be fleshed out, and which affect our markets and our investment policy. This is one of the reasons why it is important to develop an Arctic Strategy (Chamber of Representatives, 2023d, p. 5, transl.). Moreover, she dedicated a paragraph to the Arctic in the chapter on security:

> The Arctic is of great strategic, economic and security importance to our country. A secure, stable, sustainable, prosperous, and peaceful Arctic region, characterized by peaceful multilateral cooperation, is an advantage for Belgium, and our country is striving to achieve it. We will continue to work towards this within the EU framework and at the international level, focusing on strengthening and respecting the international rule of law and its values, and paying particular and continuous attention to the rights and concerns of Indigenous Peoples, in line with Belgium's human rights policy. A Belgian strategy is currently being prepared, which will be characterized by its integrated approach and should enable us to secure our interests in the Arctic. Aspiring to become an Arctic Council observer for our country is an integral part of this.
>
> CHAMBER OF REPRESENTATIVES, 2023d, p. 41, transl.

It is worth noting that this language mirrors the EU discourse, referring to the Arctic as a secure, stable, sustainable, prosperous, and peaceful region (European Commission, 2021). The paragraph also stresses the importance that Belgium attaches to upholding the international rules-based order and respecting human rights, particularly those of the Indigenous Peoples in the region. The policy note shows that the rule of law plays a key role in the development of Belgium's Arctic policy. It also mentions, for the first time in official statements, Belgium's aspirations to become an Observer in the Arctic Council.

In October 2023, Zakia Khattabi, Minister of Climate, the Environment, Sustainable Development, and Green Deal, was scheduled to share Belgium's vision on the Arctic and the climate during the Arctic Circle Assembly. This would have been the first appearance of a Belgian government official on an international Arctic forum. However, severe weather conditions prevented her from participating. At the same conference, Jan Bayart, Belgian Ambassador to Norway and Iceland, participated in the panel 'The like-minded, the willing, the capable…the Belgians' (Arctic Circle, 2023) and in an international panel on offshore energy showcasing how Belgium already has strong ties with Arctic partners and is active in the region.

These developments show that, in parallel to the process of the development of Belgium's Arctic policy framework, the Belgian Ministry of Foreign Affairs is attaching greater importance to the Arctic in its foreign policy and is working towards solidifying its role as an Arctic stakeholder by creating greater visibility on the national and international stage.

3.4 *The Arctic and Belgium's Defence and Security*

Already in 2016, the Belgian Defence's Strategic Vision (2016–2030) touched upon the growing strategic importance of the Arctic region, with an observation that most experts anticipate that the northern periphery will maintain its security stability. In December 2021, Belgium released its first National Security Strategy, in which the Arctic is mentioned in the chapter on conventional and hybrid state threats: "[i]n addition, the race is on to control untapped regions such as the Arctic, the deep seabed and outer space, which risk becoming new hotbeds of conflict. Belgium must also defend its interests in these areas of high-tech expertise." (Prime Minister of Belgium, 2021, p. 18, transl.). The region is also featured in the section dedicated to economic security:

> The maritime sector is of growing economic importance. Belgium must continue to make its contribution in the various multilateral organizations to protect the international navigation system, including freedom of navigation. As northern shipping routes become increasingly accessible, both observer status on the Arctic Council and an analysis of the opportunities and threats emanating from the Arctic re-

> gion are recommended. Certain economic interests also call for political action in the field of energy transition. Belgian companies are among the world's leading players in coastal wind energy and hydrogen production. A maritime strategy drawn up in concert with economic players can enable Belgium to play an active role in protecting its economic interests.
>
> PRIME MINISTER OF BELGIUM, 2021, p. 32, transl.

While on the one hand, Belgium puts the Arctic in the same category of remote places such as the deep sea and outer space, Belgian Defence describes it at the same time as a zone that is severely impacted by climate change where regions connect and that is part of a multilateral governance system.

Since Russia's illegal annexation of Crimea in 2014 (United Nations General Assembly, 2014), military interests in the Arctic have increased, translating into a greater military presence in the region and more frequent military exercises, in which Belgium participates on a bilateral basis or in the framework of its NATO membership. By partaking in these major multinational exercises, such as Nordic Response 2024 and Arctic Challenge Exercise 2023, Belgian Defence is working on its readiness to operate in the Arctic in support of the needs of its allies (NATO, 2022; Belgian Defence 2023). These exercises also provide Belgium with the opportunity to increase its interoperability and share its expertise.

Belgium is the only North Sea country that is not a member of regional defence partnerships that are open to non-Arctic States such as the Joint Expeditionary Force (JEF) and the Northern Group (Karen van Loon, 2024). This might be a relevant track for Belgium to pursue in the future. It will be interesting to see if and how Russia's full-scale invasion in Ukraine and Finland and Sweden's accession to NATO will impact Belgium's Arctic Policy.

4 Participation in Arctic Governance

4.1 *Formal Regional Governance*

While the release of an Arctic policy would mark the beginning of a coordinated foreign-policy agenda on Arctic affairs, it should not always be considered the end-all and be-all of Arctic engagement. As Chuffart and others remark in the case of the EU, both a multilateral player and a bilateral actor, non-Arctic actors can also be instrumental in Arctic governance in being active within international legal regimes and political forums that are directly and indirectly relevant to the Arctic (Chuffart et al., 2021). Such mapping exercises help get a sense of the broad constellations of relevant governance venues where non-Arctic States are willing to spend political and financial resources.

Through the development of the European Union's Arctic policy documents, Belgium appears to be a natural stakeholder in European Arctic affairs, particularly given its long-standing international role as an advocate for the rule of law as a State Party to relevant international agreements. In ocean governance, for instance, this commitment is evident in Belgium's accession to the United Nations Convention on the Law of the Sea (UNCLOS) in 1998. More recently, Belgium actively participated in the negotiations of the Implementing Agreement under the UNCLOS on the Conservation and Sustainable Use of Marine Biological Diversity of Areas beyond National Jurisdiction (BBNJ, 19 June 2023). Belgium became a signatory to the BBNJ agreement on 20 September 2023 but has yet to ratify it (High Seas Alliance, 2024). In addition, it has submitted its candidacy to host the BBNJ Secretariat (Kingdom of Belgium, Federal Public Services, 2023).

Also, Belgium demonstrated its formal support for Indigenous rights by voting in favour of the United Nations Declaration on the Rights of Indigenous Peoples in 2007 (United Nations General Assembly, 2007).

Despite these engagements, Belgium has not pursued observer status within the Arctic Council, unlike several of its European counterparts. This suggests that while Belgium possesses the scientific knowledge and legal acumen relevant to Arctic issues, it has yet to leverage these assets fully in the context of Arctic governance. This transferability could prove invaluable, especially with an acute awareness of the Arctic's unique social, environmental, cultural, and legal complexities.

4.2 *Informal Arctic Governance*

Political processes and decision-making regarding the Arctic region often marginalize non-Arctic States, limiting their ability to participate in more formal settings like the Arctic Council (Steinveg, 2023, p. 84). As outlined above, participation in Arctic-relevant conferences is also regarded as governance spaces where non-Arctic States can have an impact more easily (see Depledge & Dodds, 2017). As Steinveg demonstrates, conferences such as Arctic Frontiers (Norway), Arctic Circle Assembly (Iceland), or Arctic Encounter (Alaska) often obscure the distinction between governance and dialogue, as they serve not as intergovernmental bodies or governmental forums but as alternative spaces for discussion (see Steinveg, 2021, 2022). In short, they broaden the scope and structure of Arctic governance and allow for more actors to be regarded as both legitimate and relevant in regional governance (Steinveg, 2022, p. 248). While they can serve as what Steinveg terms "instruments of statecraft" (Steinveg, 2022, p. 248) to build a coherent Arctic identity to non-Arctic States (Steinveg, 2023, p. 45), they also allow for "communication and outreach" around Arctic involvement (Steinveg, 2021, pp. 49–50). As she points out, "in addition to the legitimizing function, there is an element of publicity to conference participation, which provides the opportunity for non-Arctic States to advance their interests in the region" (Steinveg, 2023, p. 85). This double purpose of Arctic conferences has also been felt domestically in Belgium. For instance, Egmont Institute co-organized panels and held closed-door bilateral side meetings at Arctic Circle Assembly in 2022 and 2023 to showcase the breadth of Belgium's polar expertise with key individuals such as the EU's current and former Special Envoy for Arctic Affairs, Belgium's Ambassador to Norway and Iceland, and relevant Belgian experts.

The International Polar Foundation (IPF), the organization mandated to act as an Antarctic Operator of Belgium's Princess Elisabeth Antarctica Research Station, has also organized the Arctic Futures Symposium in Brussels. The conference has often attracted more high-level politicians and diplomats from Arctic States with partners and contributors such as regional diplomatic representations to the European Union, Nordic Embassies, the Arctic Economic Council, the Arctic Mayors' Forum, and EU-funded research projects (Arctic Futures, 2023).

Proving Steinveg's analysis, the role of conferences as alternative governance spaces did not go unnoticed at the Belgian Parliament. In May 2023, Representative Pillen asked the Belgian MFA to clarify the impact of Belgium's participation in the eighth edition of the Arctic Encounter Symposium (AES) from 29–31 March 2023 in Anchorage, Alaska where Belgium was represented by an attaché from its embassy in the United States. According to the MFA, AES offers an opportunity for Belgium to stay up to date about developments in the region, meet actors operating or having specific interests there, remain visible and active in international forums on the Arctic, and gather relevant knowledge to inform internal deliberation on the development of a Belgian strategy for the Arctic region (Chamber of Representatives, 2023b, pp. 354–356). According to the AES 2023 program, the Belgian representation attended informally as no official representatives were included in the final available version (Arctic Encounter Symposium, 2023). In its response, the MFA remarked that the Belgian Embassy in Washington subsequently shared its observations with the MFA and the Egmont Institute. The MFA also asserted that the Embassy would continue to closely monitor the evolution of the United States' Arctic policy, especially through contacts made during AES, and will inform stakeholders in Belgium through the MFA (Chamber of Representatives, 2023b, p. 356). During AES 2024, Belgium will be officially represented by Jean-Arthur Régibeau, Ambassador of Belgium to the United States (Arctic Encounter Symposium, n.d.). This continued participation, yet at a higher level, shows that, like its gradual increase in official participation during the Arctic Circle Assembly, Belgium sees the value of international Arctic conferences and uses them as an opportunity to network and put the country firmer on the radar as an Arctic stakeholder.

5 Building on Belgium's Scientific Interests

As discussed above in Section 2, Belgium's primary interest in the polar regions has historically been scientific research. A cursory examination of the contributors to the Multidisciplinary drifting Observatory for the Study of Arctic Climate (MOSAiC) project, the first year-round expedition into the central Arctic exploring the Arctic climate system, reveals the active involvement of several Belgian scientists, or those based in Belgium, in Arctic-focused research projects (MOSAiC, n.d.). With a total budget of €140 million, MOSAiC was designed by an international consortium of leading polar research institutions and led by Germany's Alfred Wegener Institute, Helmholtz Centre for Polar and Marine Research. This participation underscores the significant contributions of individual researchers to Arctic studies. However, the integration of Arctic considerations into Belgium's foreign policy and scientific diplomacy efforts should not depend solely on the initiative of individual scientists. Rather, it necessitates a systematic approach. Advancing international scientific collaboration through science diplomacy, enhancing investments in Arctic research across both the natural and social sciences, and fostering increased dialogue with residents of the Arctic region are crucial steps. These actions would enable a more cohesive and coordinated engagement of Belgium's research community and policymakers in Arctic affairs.

As a result, research has been at the forefront of Belgium's engagement in the polar region. In the evolving landscape of polar research, Belgium has reaffirmed its commitment to advancing scientific knowledge in the Arctic region, as highlighted by the inquiries and subsequent responses regarding the RV *Belgica*. Belgium sees the vessel as a pivotal asset in Belgian and European marine research for the coming decades. However, the RV *Belgica*'s capabilities are currently underutilized due to budgetary constraints that have precluded its return to the Arctic in 2024 (Institute of Natural Sciences, 2024). As Representative Verhaert remarks, the strategic importance of Arctic science, integral to Belgium's broader Arctic strategy as mentioned in the Minister of Foreign Affairs' policy note, underscores the necessity of ensuring the vessel's operational deployment to the polar region (Chamber of Representatives, 2024a, pp. 423–424).

According to Thomas Dermine, Secretary of State for Recovery and Strategic Investments, responsible for Scientific Policy (Minister of Economy and Labour), Belgium is actively preparing for a scientific expedition with the new RV Belgica in 2025 (Chamber of Representatives, 2024a, p. 424). The investment in Arctic science is further manifested through BELSPO's specific research initiatives. For instance, a specific call for research projects on the new *RV Belgica* was launched in 2021. Two of the six selected research projects focus on the study of the Arctic region (Greenland and Iceland). And several projects are coordinated by Belgian universities as principal investigators. Two of these projects with the University of Ghent, Royal Belgian Institute of Natural Sciences, and the Royal Netherlands Institute for Sea Research, which explores climate change impacts on carbon cycling and food webs in Arctic fjords (BELSPO, 2021a) and with the Royal Belgian Institute of Natural Sciences, the Antwerp University, and the *Université Libre de Bruxelles*, which researches natural analogues and system-scale modelling of marine enhanced silicate weathering (BELSPO, 2021b) received BELSPO funding of €997,645 and €999,530 respectively.

Additionally, a specific call was launched in 2022 to conduct scientific polar research in the polar regions. Under that call, six Arctic-specific projects were selected, mainly focusing on ecological polar research with Gent University, Liège University, and Louvain Catholic University in collaboration with international partners (Chamber of Representatives, 2024a, p. 424). At the research level, these efforts collectively demonstrate Belgium's strategic engagement with Arctic research, aiming to enhance understanding of the region's complex environmental and geopolitical challenges, and reinforce its presence in international polar science dialogues. BELSPO also financially supports Belgian Arctic scientists who have become IASC members via the Belgian National Committee for Arctic and Antarctic Research (BNCAR) of the Royal Academy. The Belgian government has already asserted that these new research programs of BELSPO starting in 2024 support research in line with the federal strategic priorities proposed by the relevant departments which in turn will be in line with the Belgian Arctic strategy (Chamber of Representatives, 2024a, p. 424).

6 Conclusion

Navigating Belgium's engagement in Arctic governance necessitates a cautious and informed approach, especially in light of its historically documented colonial legacy (Chamber of Representatives, 2020a; 2024b). It is imperative for Belgium to consciously avoid perpetuating colonial narratives that view the Arctic as an 'empty region' only requiring protection and conservation. This entails a nuanced understanding of the Arctic's significance juxtaposed against Belgium's historical backdrop, advocating for an approach to Arctic affairs that is rooted in respect, collaboration, and mutual benefit rather than exploitation.

The global environmental crises, accentuated by climate change underscores the necessity for robust environmental governance. Belgium's contributions to global ecological systems underscore the interconnected nature of local actions and global environmental outcomes. This interconnectedness necessitates a cohesive approach within Belgium's intricate federal and federated governance structures to environmental policy and international cooperation, posing a significant challenge yet essential for Belgium's credibility as a global environmental actor.

Belgium's profound expertise in Antarctic science and diplomacy presents an untapped potential for increased Arctic engagement. This foundation could be leveraged to explore participation avenues in Arctic governance, including pursuing Observer status at the Arctic Council or engaging through alternative platforms. However, the pathway to meaningful involvement in Arctic governance is fraught with complexities, as illustrated by the European Union's ongoing *ad hoc* Observer status and the rejection of Estonia's recent application which highlights the stringent criteria for Observer State aspirants.

The experiences of non-Arctic States and non-state actors in Arctic governance offer valuable lessons. These examples illuminate the importance of crafting long-term strategies aimed at fostering closer ties with the Arctic, Arctic States, and local and Indigenous communities. For Belgium, this may involve enhancing Arctic-focused initiatives within its borders, thus nurturing a portfolio of Arctic interests through persistent engagement and commitment reaffirmation.

As demonstrated by other non-Arctic States' involvement in Arctic governance, the construction of an Arctic identity indicates that participation in Arctic governance is a continuous, strategic process requiring deliberate decision-making regarding the nature of relationships Belgium seeks to establish (Chuffart et al., 2020, p. 342). These relationships could range from bilateral cooperations with specific Arctic States and non-state partners to active engagement in multilateral forums, with a focus on upholding the rule of law and advancing climate action.

Belgium is thus faced with the critical task of selecting and prioritizing Arctic relationships to cultivate. This decision process should align with Belgium's unique strengths, including its scientific expertise and dedication to environmental stewardship, while also carefully considering the ethical dimensions of its colonial history. By adopting a path that respects the intricacies of Arctic governance and amplifies the voices of Indigenous and local communities, Belgium can make a substantive contribution to the Arctic region's sustainable and equitable development.

As Belgium evaluates its prospective role within Arctic affairs, it must balance its ambitions with the obligations inherent in becoming a responsible and ethical Arctic participant. This balance requires thoughtful reflection on Belgium's internal capabilities, historical context, and the dynamic landscape of Arctic governance. Likely, Belgium will adopt its Arctic policy framework in the near future. All signs point toward a comprehensive and strategic approach in line with the European Union's own Arctic policy.

Bibliography

Abnett, K. (2024, January 22). Unclear if Belgium will use EU option to block Russian gas imports -minister. *Reuters*. https://www.reuters.com/markets/commodities/unclear-if-belgium-will-use-eu-option-block-russian-gas-imports-minister-2024-01-22/

Antarctic Treaty (adopted 1 December 1959, entered into force 4 August 1961) 402 UNTS 71.

Arctic Circle (2023). *2023 Program*. https://prismic-io.s3.amazonaws.com/arctic-circle-www/4195b0f3-c55a-4c27-a8ba-afa0cddee751_2023+Arctic+Circle+Assembly+Program.pdf

Arctic Encounter Symposium (2024). *Arctic encounter Anchorage – April 10–12, 2024*. https://www.arcticencounter.com/arctic-encounter-anchorage-2024

Arctic Encounter Symposium (2023). *Arctic encounter 2023, March 29–31: Agenda*. https://drive.google.com/file/d/1JIkG4wkCCmWnxmFYqWZkbLQrvITEhT5r/view

Arctic Futures (2022). *Arctic futures symposium 2022: Summary report*. https://www.arcticfutures.org/uploads/archives_files/ARCTIC-FUTURES-SYMPOSIUM-2022-SUMMARY-REPORT.pdf

Arctic Futures (n.d.). *Partners*. Arctic Futures Symposium. Retrieved 28 November 2023, from https://www.arcticfutures.org/partners

Barr, W. (2009). The Arctic voyages of Louis-Philippe-Robert, Duc d'Orléans. *Polar Record, 46*(1), 21–43. https://doi.org/10.1017/S0032247409008377

Belgian Defence (2023, December 2023). Opérations 2024 : Un engagement sans faille [Operations 2024: an unwavering commitment]. https://beldefnews.mil.be/operations-2024-un-engagement-sans-faille/?lang=fr

BELSPO (2021a). *Climate chANGe impacts on carbon cycling and fOod wEbs in Arctic fjords* (*CANOE*). https://www.belspo.be/belspo///fedra/proj.asp?l=de&COD=RV%2F21%2FCANOE

BELSPO (2021b). *DEHEAT - Natural analogues and system-scale modeling of marine enhanced silicate weathering.* https://www.belspo.be/belspo////NewRV/projects/DEHEAT_en.pdf

Chamber of Representatives (2011). *Proposition de résolution pour la protection de l'arctique* [Proposal for a resolution for the protection of the Arctic] (*Doc 53 1000/001 (2010/2011)*). https://www.lachambre.be/FLWB/PDF/53/1000/53K1000001.pdf

Chamber of Representatives (2020a). *Commission spéciale chargée d'examiner l'état indépendant du Congo (1885–1908) et le passé colonial de la Belgique au Congo (1908–1960), au Rwanda et au Burundi (1919–1962), ses conséquences et les suites qu'il convient d'y réserver* [Special commission to examine the independent state of Congo (1885–1908) and Belgium's colonial past in Congo (1908–1960), Rwanda, and Burundi (1919–1962), its cconsequences, and the appropriate measures to be taken] (*DOC 55 1462/001*). https://www.lachambre.be/FLWB/PDF/55/1462/55K1462001.pdf

Chamber of Representatives (2020b). *Exposé d'orientation politique, Affaires étrangères: Affaires européennes, commerce extérieur et nstitutions culturelles fédérales* [Policy orientation statement: Foreign affairs, European affairs, foreign trade, and federal cultural institutions] (*DOC 55 1610/019*). https://www.dekamer.be/FLWB/PDF/55/1610/55K1610019.pdf

Chamber of Representatives (2020c). *Compte rendu intégral avec compte rendu analytique traduit des interventions, commission des relations extérieures* [Complete report with an analytical summary translated of interventions, Foreign Relations Commission] (Doc CRIV 55 COM 256) https://www.lachambre.be/doc/ccri/pdf/55/ic256.pdf

Chamber of Representatives (2021a). *Proposition de Résolution demandant d'accorder une attention accrue aux défis sécuritaires liés aux évolutions dans la région arctique (déposée par M. Jasper Pillen et Mmes Marianne Verhaert, Kattrin Jadin et Goedele Liekens)* [Proposal for a resolution calling for increased attention to security challenges related to developments in the Arctic region (submitted by Mr. Jasper Pillen and Mses. Marianne Verhaert, Kattrin Jadin, and Goedele Liekens)] (*DOC 55 2027/001*). https://www.lachambre.be/doc/flwb/pdf/55/2027/55k2027001.pdf

Chamber of Representatives (2021b). *Questions et réponses écrites* [Written questions and answers] (*Doc QRVA 55056*). https://www.lachambre.be/QRVA/pdf/55/55K0056.pdf

Chamber of Representatives (2021c). *Proposition de résolution demandant d'accorder une attention accrue aux défis sécuritaires liés aux évolutions dans la région arctique. Amendements* [Proposal for a resolution calling for increased attention to security challenges related to developments in the Arctic region. Amendments] (*DOC 55 2027/002*). https://www.lachambre.be/doc/flwb/pdf/55/2027/55k2027002.pdf#search=%22arctique%20%2055k%20%3Cin%3E%20keywords%22

Chamber of Representatives (2021d). *Proposition de résolution demandant d'accorder une attention accrue aux défis sécuritaires liés aux évolutions dans la région arctique. Amendements* [Proposal for a resolution calling for increased attention to security challenges related to developments in the Arctic region. Amendments] (*DOC 55 2027/003*). https://www.lachambre.be/FLWB/PDF/55/2027/55K2027003.pdf

Chamber of Representatives (2021e). *Proposition de Résolution demandant d'accorder une attention accrue aux défis sécuritaires liés aux évolutions dans la région arctique, texte adopté par la commission des relations extérieurs, proposition de résolution visant l'élaboration d'une stratégie belge pour la région arctique attentive à la crise climatique et aux défis en matière de sécurité dans cette région. Nouvel intitulé* [Proposal for a resolution calling for increased attention to security challenges related to developments in the Arctic region, text adopted by the committee on foreign relations, proposal for a resolution aiming at developing a Belgian strategy for the Arctic region, focused on the climate crisis and security challenges in the region. New Title] (*DOC 55 2027/006*). https://www.lachambre.be/FLWB/PDF/55/2027/55K2027006.pdf

Chamber of Representatives (2021f). *Résolution visant l'élaboration d'une stratégie belge pour la région arctique attentive à la crise climatique et aux défis en matière de sécurité dans cette région* [Proposal for a resolution aiming at developing a Belgian trategy for the Arctic region, focused on the climate crisis and security challenges in the region] (*DOC 55 2027/007*). https://www.dekamer.be/doc/flwb/pdf/55/2027/55k2027007.pdf

Chamber of Representatives (2022a). *Questions et réponses écrites* [Written questions and answers] (*Doc QRVA 55079*). https://www.lachambre.be/QRVA/pdf/55/55K0079.pdf

Chamber of Representatives (2022b). *Questions et réponses écrites* [Written questions and answers] (*DOC QRVA 55092*). https://www.lachambre.be/QRVA/pdf/55/55K0092.pdf

Chamber of Representatives (2023a). *Questions et réponses écrites* [Written questions and answers] (*DOC QRVA 55112*). https://www.lachambre.be/QRVA/pdf/55/55K0112.pdf

Chamber of Representatives (2023b). *Questions et réponses écrites* [Written questions and answers] (*DOC QRVA 55113*). https://www.lachambre.be/QRVA/pdf/55/55K0113.pdf

Chamber of Representatives (2023c). *Questions et réponses écrites* [Written questions and answers] (*DOC QRVA 55124*). https://www.lachambre.be/QRVA/pdf/55/55K0124.pdf

Chamber of Representatives (2024a). *Questions et réponses écrites* [Written questions and answers] (*DOC QRVA 55127*). https://www.lachambre.be/QRVA/pdf/55/55K0127.pdf

Chamber of Representatives (2024b). *Commission spéciale chargée d'examiner l'état indépendant du Congo et le passé colonial de la Belgique au Congo, au Rwanda et au Burundi, ses conséquences et les suites qu'il convient d'y réserver. Constats des experts* [Special commission to examine the independent state of Congo and Belgium's colonial past in Congo, Rwanda, and Burundi, its consequences, and the appropriate measures to be taken. Findings of the experts] (*DOC 55 1462/006*). https://www.lachambre.be/doc/flwb/pdf/55/1462/55k1462006.pdf#search=%221462%20%2055k%20%3Cin%3E%20keywords%22

Chuffart, R., Hataya, S., Inagaki, O., & Arthur, L. (2020). Assessing Japan's Arctic engagement during the ArCS project (2015–2020). *The Yearbook of Polar Law Online*, *12*(1), 328–348. https://doi.org/10.1163/22116427_012010020

Chuffart, R., & Raspotnik, A. (2019). The EU and its Arctic spirit: Solving Arctic climate change from home? *European View*, *18*(2), 156–162. https://doi.org/10.1177/1781685819883l4

Chuffart, R., Raspotnik, A., & Stępień, A. (2021). Our common Arctic? A more sustainable EU–Arctic nexus in light of the European green deal. *The Polar Journal*, *11*(2), 284–302. https://doi.org/10.1080/2154896X.2021.1978757

Council of the European Union (2024). Council Decision (Cfsp) 2024/1738 of 24 June 2024 amending Decision 2014/145/CFSP concerning restrictive measures in respect of actions undermining or threatening the territorial integrity, sovereignty and independence of Ukraine. https://eur-lex.europa.eu/legal-content/EN/TXT/PDF/?uri=OJ:L_202401738

Depledge, D. (2017). *Britain and the Arctic*. Springer. https://doi.org/10.1007/978-3-319-69293-7

Depledge, D., & Dodds, K. (2017). Bazaar governance: Situating the Arctic circle. In K. Keil & S. Knecht (Eds.), *Governing Arctic Change: Global Perspectives*, (pp. 141–160). Springer. https://doi.org/10.1057/978-1-137-50884-3_8

European Commission (2021). Joint Communication to the European Parliament, the Council, the European Economic and Social Committee and the Committee of the Regions: Stronger EU Engagement for a Peaceful, Sustainable and Prosperous Arctic. Join/2021/27 Final. https://eur-lex.europa.eu/legal-content/EN/TXT/?uri=JOIN:2021:27:FIN

Fluxys (2020, January 7). *Zeebrugge LNG terminal: Transshipments under Yamal long-term contract started.* Fluxys. https://www.fluxys.com/en/press-releases/fluxys-belgium/2020/20200107_press_long_term_contract_started

Fluxys (2024, November 22). *Fluxys LNG ready to implement the 14th EU sanctions package.* Fluxys. https://www.fluxys.com/en/press-releases/fluxys-belgium/2024/241122_press_fluxys-lng-ready-to-implement-14th-sanctions-package

High Seas Alliance (2024). *Signature and Ratification Progress Table* https://highseasalliance.org/treaty-ratification/table-of-countries/

Humpert, M. (2024, March 6). *EU countries divided on how to phase out Russian Arctic LNG.* High North News. https://www.highnorthnews.com/en/eu-countries-divided-how-phase-out-russian-arctic-lng

Institute of Natural Sciences (2024). *RV Belgica campaign timeline for 2024.* Institute of Natural Sciences. https://odnature.naturalsciences.be/belgica/en/timeline/2024

International Polar Foundation (n.d.). *Building the Station.* http://www.antarcticstation.org/station/construction

International Polar Foundation (2007, June 11). *BELARE: Belgian Antarctic Expeditions.* http://www.antarcticstation.org/multimedia/picture_gallery/belare_belgian_antarctic_expeditions/

van Loon, K. (2024, January 9). *Looking towards the north: Belgium's role in the* Arctic. Egmont Institute. https://www.egmontinstitute.be/looking-towards-the-north-belgiums-role-in-the-arctic/

Kingdom of Belgium, Federal Public Services (2023). *Brussels. The diplomatic hub for the ocean. Bid for the BBNJ secretariat.* https://www.bbnjbrussels.be/brussels-the-diplomatic-hub-for-the-ocean.pdf

Molenaar, E.J. (2021). Participation in the Antarctic treaty. *The Polar Journal, 11*(2), 360–380. https://doi.org/10.1080/2154896X.2021.1972257

MOSAiC (n.d.). *An entire year trapped in the ice.* Retrieved 1 December 2024, from https://mosaic-expedition.org/expedition/

NATO (2022, April 6). *NATO ships complete exercise Cold Response.* NATO. https://mc.nato.int/media-centre/news/2022/nato-ships-complete-exercise-cold-response-

Odessa Journal (2022, October 28). Ukraine to restore research vessel damaged by Russian missile attack. *Odessa Journal.* https://odessa-journal.com/public/ukraine-to-restore-research-vessel-damaged-by-russian-missile-attack

Prime Minister of Belgium. (2021). *Stratégie de Sécurité Nationale* [National Security Strategy]. https://premier.be/sites/default/files/2025-02/Strategie_de_securite_nationale.pdf

Senate (2013). *Proposition de résolution pour la protection et la conservation de la région arctique (Document parlementaire 5-2198/1)* [Proposal for a resolution on the protection and conservation of the Arctic region]. https://www.senate.be/www/?MIval=publications/viewPub.html&COLL=S&LEG=5&NR=2198&VOLGNR=1&LANG=fr

Senate (2019). *Session extraordinaire de 2019 : Proposition de résolution pour la protection et la conservation de la région arctique (7–25/1)* [Extraordinary session of 2019: Proposal for a resolution on the protection and conservation of the Arctic region]. https://www.senate.be/www/webdriver?MItabObj=pdf&MIcolObj=pdf&MInamObj=pdfid&MItypeObj=application/pdf&MIvalObj=117440535

Steinveg, B. (2021). The role of conferences within Arctic governance. *Polar Geography, 44*(1), 37–54. https://doi.org/10.1080/1088937X.2020.1798540

Steinveg, B. (2022). Arctic conferences as arenas for power games and collaboration in international relations. *The Polar Journal, 12*(2), 240–260. https://doi.org/10.1080/2154896X.2022.2137086

Steinveg, B. (2023). *Arctic governance through conferencing: Actors, agendas and arenas*. Springer. https://doi.org/10.1007/978-3-031-23332-6

United Nations General Assembly (2007). *United Nations Declaration on the Rights of Indigenous Peoples*, 2 October 2007, A/RES/61/295.

United Nations General Assembly (2014). *Territorial integrity of Ukraine*, 27 March 2014, A/RES/68/262.

Yakymiuk, I. (2023, May 6). Під час російської атаки на одеський порт пошкодили науково-дослідне судно – директор антарктичного центру [During the Russian attack on the Odesa port, a research vessel was damaged – the director of the Antarctic Center]. *Суспільне Одеса* [Suspilne Odesa]. https://suspilne.media/odesa/467867-pid-cas-rosijskoi-ataki-na-odeskij-port-poskodili-naukovo-doslidne-sudno-direktor-antarkticnogo-centru/

CHAPTER 3

China's Arctic Policy: How Scientific Research Interplays with Arctic Governance

Marco Volpe

1 Introduction

The opening-up reform launched by Deng Xiaoping in the early 1980s and the Jiang Zemin's Go Out Policy, formally announced in March 2000, projected China into the global market. China's improved economic power drove its leadership's attention to new areas. In the last two decades, the African continent has been the focus of China's outbound policy.

The exploitation of the Arctic's rich untapped resource basins, the emergence of new potential shipping routes, and the prospect of easier access to fishery resources in the high seas are all phenomena linked to climate change. These developments make the region highly attractive to many non-Arctic States, including China, despite the uncertainties surrounding high seas fisheries. The years 2013 and 2018 respectively represent two key moments for China's engagement in the Arctic region: China's admission as an observer to the Arctic Council and the official release of China's Arctic strategy.

The rapid economic growth fueled by the opening of China's market to global trade has led the West to view China as a threat to the existing international order. China's threat theory assumes that China's rise, rather than having peaceful meanings, actively aims to overturn the status quo principally led by the US to establish China as the main global power (Liu, K. 2022). In the Arctic context, where China does not fulfil the territorial definition of being one of the eight regional States, speculations about potential risks related to the party-state's growing regional presence have been widespread. To alleviate China's threat perceptions among the regional actors, the Chinese leadership has paid particular attention to status-building and legitimation of its regional role in the Arctic. In a context of well-defined territorial boundaries and decades-old disputes solved through multilateral and bilateral agreements, China tries to improve its role in regional governance by abiding by international law, respecting sovereignty, and strengthening economic relationships.

 | DOI:10.1163/9789004734685_004

Against this backdrop, Arctic scientific research goes beyond a soft power tool. Enhancing the understanding of global climate changes and their impact on regions far from the Arctic region emphasizes the perception of the Arctic as a global space that requires global governance mechanisms, legitimizing China's increasing activities. Over the past decade, for example, China has invested in Arctic research and resource exploitation and increasingly partaken in official and unofficial forums discussing Arctic governance. What is more, the Chinese government has increased funding in Arctic research which could also improve credibility and strengthen international cooperation opportunities.

China's Arctic policy was officially released in 2018. It mentions scientific research 17 times and China's Arctic scientific engagement appears throughout the whole document. The document mentions how China will:

> constantly increasing investment in scientific research, building modernized research platforms, and improving the capacity in, and level of, research on the Arctic. It is making a greater effort to advance research in the fields of natural science, climate change and ecological environment, accelerate the development of basic subjects such as physics, chemistry, life science and earth science, strengthen social science research including Arctic politics, economy, law, society, history, culture and management of Arctic activities, and promote innovation in both natural and social sciences.
>
> STATE COUNCIL, 2018, section IV (1)

This passage highlights how China will invest in developing scientific research work on technological development to strengthen and improve its research capabilities and enlarge the scope of research not only to natural science but also to social sciences that look at political, environmental, governance, and socio-cultural aspects of the region.

In this chapter, the author looks at how Arctic research represents a key point of China's strategy in light of the deep interconnectedness between scientific knowledge production and participation in Arctic governance. In order to do that, in the following section, the author takes into account the existing relations between science and international relations highlighted by Weiss (2005) and applies them to China's case in the Arctic. Namely: how science affects the substance of international relations by creating new regimes addressing global challenges through the example of China's participation in the negotiation of the 2018 Agreement to Prevent Unregulated High Seas Fisheries in the Central Arctic Ocean (CAOFA), and how the relationship between science and international relations changes the architecture of the international system by analyzing the role of the China-Nordic Arctic Research Center (CNARC) as a non-state-led and international platform which gathers research institutes from China and Nordic countries. In the third section, the author provides an updated overview of China's scientific research infrastructures, expeditions, and activities in the Arctic and analyzes national and subnational strategies which mention the Arctic to better grasp the interplay between China's improving attention to scientific research and national interests.

2 Science in International Relations

A relatively extensive literature has investigated the role of science in international relations and the influence it has in international affairs. Skolnikoff (1993) has conducted one of the most relevant works. The author finds the role of science in international affairs as incremental, focusing the discourse on the massive change the production of nuclear weapons and intercontinental ballistic missiles had on the traditional military force. Weiss (2005) goes beyond and explores the mutual influence of science, technology and international relations providing a framework that helps in understanding typical patterns of such an interaction. He classifies four different interactions: how science and technology 1) change operational processes; 2) affect the substance of international relations; 3) change the architecture of the international system; and 4) affect the information, ideas, and perceptions on which the international system is based.

In understanding how science affects the substance of international relations, climate change and endangered species are just some of the issues that have facilitated the adoption of new treaties and agreements, creating a blend of domestic and international concerns, driving cooperation and policy-making across borders. Weiss (2005) defines science and technology as "intermestic" issues in which domestic and international considerations penetrate. Looking at the cross-border effect of climate change and the necessity to protect local biodiversity in the Arctic, the adoption of the CAOFA provides an excellent example of how science and technology intervene in international regime shaping (Dervovic & Heinrich, 2023). The Agreement was signed in 2018 and entered into force in 2021. For the first time in the recent decades, the Arctic five (A5) (Canada, Russia, Denmark, the USA, and Norway) were joined by other four non-Arctic States (China, South Korea, Iceland, and Japan) and the European Union in producing a legally binding agreement on Arctic specific issues. The only precedent example is the Svalbard Treaty signed in 1920 which granted Norway sovereignty over the Svalbard archipelago while allowing other signatory countries, including non-Arctic States, equal rights to engage in commercial activities, such as fishing and mining, within the territory.

Looking at how science and technology are changing the architecture of international systems refers to the process of affecting the balance of power which does not necessarily consider the action perpetrated by state actors, but it values the role of networks, international organizations, and other non-state actors. The absence of a comprehensive international binding treaty and the multilevel governance system in the Arctic create room for non-state-led platforms, which, thanks to different knowledge production assets, intervene in decision-making progress at different levels and through many different ways. Here the author looks at one of the most representative and long-lasting platforms which see a consistent engagement of Chinese actors: CNARC. Established in Shanghai in 2013, the international consortium of Chinese and Nordic research centres celebrated its tenth anniversary in 2023.

2.1 *Science and Technology Affecting the Substance of International Relations: China and the CAOFA*

The CAOFA Agreement aims to prevent overfishing in the largest high seas area in the Arctic, the Central Arctic Ocean (CAO). As the first modern Arctic-related international agreement not exclusively negotiated among Arctic countries, it sees the involvement of non-Arctic States and posits the precautionary approach as a key principle in regulating areas beyond national jurisdiction. In the first phase of the negotiations, the Arctic five were collaborating on what would become the Declaration Concerning the Prevention of Unregulated High Seas Fishing in the Central Arctic Ocean (Oslo Declaration, 2015). The Icelandic disagreement with the five-state format of the negotiations paved the way for the A5 plus 5 format which included China, South Korea, Japan, the EU, and Iceland in the second phase of negotiations that culminated in the formal signing of the Agreement to Prevent Unregulated High Seas Fisheries in the Central Arctic Ocean, on 3 October 2018 (Vylegzhanin et al, 2020). The integration of the precautionary principle in the CAOFA reflects the shared interests that Arctic and non-Arctic States have in ensuring environmental security, including the protection of marine biodiversity (Vylegzhanin et al, 2020, p. 15).

The scientific meetings discussing fish stocks in the Central Arctic Ocean started in Anchorage in 2011, where scientific experts from the five Arctic coastal States only were involved (National Oceanic and Atmospheric Administration (NOAA), 2011). The focal point of the discussion was the sustainability of existing subsistence harvests and commercial fisheries in coastal areas and sub-arctic seas, and how they may be affected by climate change. The participants agreed on the necessity to schedule further meetings to develop a well-coordinated research plan and inclusion of scientists from countries outside the Arctic coastal States to improve the collective ability to address priorities identified, such as:

> develop and improve monitoring of physical and biological marine environment; improve understanding of vital rates [...]; improve understanding of life stage and habitat linkages of key fish and invertebrate species [...]; develop predictions of potential changes in fish production [...]; study ecosystem processes [...] and refine models and perform scenario modeling of ecosystem responses to climatic change [...].
>
> NOAA, 2011

The second meeting was held in Tromsø in 2013. Fisheries experts from the five Arctic coastal States and experts from international research organizations took part in the discussion (NOAA, 2013). Representatives from China started participating in the third scientific conference that was held in Seattle in 2015. Besides China, representatives from other non-Arctic countries such as Japan, South Korea, and Iceland joined the scientific meetings. Presentations by non-Arctic coastal States consisted of describing their nation's research and monitoring activities in the Arctic (NOAA, 2015). In the meeting, it was highlighted that:

> other States may have an interest in this topic and looked forward to a broader process involving additional States beginning before the end of 2014. The purpose would be to develop a set of interim measures, compatible with the Ministerial Declaration, that would include commitments by additional States. The outcome could be a binding international agreement.
>
> NOAA, 2015, p. 14

At this advanced stage of discussion, the involvement of distant-water fishing fleets in CAOFA negotiations consistently grew. A parallel exercise prior and during the negotiations was started. What is called the 'Asia Dialogues' includes four different meetings: the 'Roundtable on Central

Arctic Ocean (CAO) Fishery issues' held in Shanghai in 2015; one meeting in Incheon, Korea in 2016; one working session on 'An International Marine Science Coordinating Organization of the Central Arctic Ocean' and a one-day workshop on 'Implementation for the Agreement to Prevent Unregulated High Seas Fisheries in the Central Arctic Ocean: Conditions for success' in Korea in 2018 (Harrison et al., 2020). The first Roundtable organized at Tongji University in Shanghai gathered over 40 experts. The aim was to assess how the precautionary approach can be applied in the Central Arctic Ocean before any commercial fishing activities take place. From the Chinese side, there were experts from many different academic institutions which included Tongji University, Ocean University of China, Shanghai Ocean University, Shanghai Jiao Tong University, and Dalian Maritime University (Ocean Conservancy, 2017). The issues discussed were international scientific cooperation on CAO/Arctic Ocean issues, China's significant research capacity and the necessity to create stronger links with the international scientific community, and China's strong interest in being involved in the CAO management process. The participants at the Roundtable observed that the involvement of key non-Arctic States with significant fishing capacity in the high seas would be a key to success in developing and implementing precautionary measures in the CAO. Zhou and Chen (2015) reported the position of Prof. Huang Shuolin, Vice-President of Shanghai Ocean University, who pointed out that only 8% of the Arctic international waters is under the jurisdiction of the North East Atlantic Fisheries Commission (NEAFC) so far and the remaining 92% lacks restraint of regional regulations. Prof. Huang also stated that at present, all the other related international conventions or regional regulations on Arctic Ocean international waters have no sufficient legal effect. Even though mutual or multilateral agreements have been negotiated and implemented, they have effects only on their Parties, and cannot develop a uniform regulation on fishery management and utilization in the Arctic international waters (Zhou & Chen, 2015).

The second Roundtable held in Korea was organized in three different sessions. The first session discussed the national and international approaches to Arctic issues; the second session focused on the level of the current understanding of the Arctic Ocean system and the emerging importance of chemical and biological links between continental shelves and deep-ocean basins; the third section looked at the future and the discussion highlighted the importance of involving non-Arctic States in both scientific activities and eventual management regimes. The participation of non-Arctic States as "'equal partners'" in the International Maritime Organization's Polar Code was often recalled as an example which could be replicated in the context of the Central Arctic Ocean Agreement (Ocean Conservancy, 2017). Participants in the roundtable agreed on the precautionary approach as an absolute necessity, and there was consensus that effective management of Arctic marine resources requires both scientific understanding and the involvement of stakeholders and communities, including Indigenous peoples (Harrison et al., 2020). The Working Session at Hokkaido University in December 2016 brought together a small group of experts from Korea, Japan, China, and the US to discuss the options of creating a new international science coordinating organization for the CAO. The working session was useful to discuss the purpose, mandate, principles underlying the scientific organization, implementation and governance issues, and conditions for success. The working session also focused on the creation of a platform to determine the scientific priorities and monitoring requirements under the Agreement, to integrate CAO research with existing scientific efforts, and to provide appropriate analysis for decision-making by the Parties to the Agreement (Harrison et al, 2020). The fourth 'Asia Dialogue' was the one-day workshop on the implementation of the Agreement. Among the speakers who discussed its implementation during the Arctic Circle, Prof. Guo Peiqing from the Ocean University of China raised the issue of the Agreement's enforcement. He specifically inquired about the implications of commercial activities during the interim period (before ratification) and the mechanisms for monitoring and applying sanctions once the Agreement is in force, particularly concerning States that fall under an 'umbrella' signatory like the EU members.

As outlined here, the gradual involvement of China's and other non-Arctic States' representatives started in 2015. China's "under-the-radar" presence is extremely meaningful as it was the first time for China to sit and negotiate an agreement for the Arctic region (Liu, 2021). The enlargement to Asian parties is connected to the distant-water fishing capacity. For China, this is particularly relevant as the increasing demand for fish (Lin, 2012) has led to an expansion and improvement of the Chinese distant-water fishing fleet (Pan & Huntington, 2016). More information is needed to foresee sustainable fisheries in the CAO and China might contribute to improving knowledge of marine living resources in the Central Arctic Ocean. As Min (2016) noted, the CAOFA is at the intersection of geopolitics, policy, diplomacy, and science. The precautionary approach, as the leading principle of the Agreement, helps avoiding the 'first-exploit, manage-second' disaster scenario showing how the necessity of acquiring more scientific knowledge has harmonized the perspectives of Arctic and non-Arctic States in implementing the Agreement. It can be the opportunity to understand how to manage Arctic resources sustainably and protect the ecosystem and the rights of the people who depend on fishery resources. Chinese special envoy to the Arctic Gao Feng summarizes the role of China and the importance and innovative structure of the Agreement as follows:

> China also actively participated in the negotiation on the Agreement to prevent unregulated high seas fisheries in the Central Arctic Ocean. The conclusion of the Agreement is an important progress of the Arctic rule-making and governance, as well as a good case of multilateral governance of the Arctic participated by the Asian countries including China, Japan and Korea. It has profoundly influenced regulating high seas fisheries in the Arctic Ocean and on protected living resources in the Arctic.
>
> ARCTIC CIRCLE, 2019, 6:14–7:05

2.2 *Science and Technology Changing the Architecture of the International System: The Example of* CNARC

A pilot study conducted in 2016 under the UArctic Science & Research Analytics Task Force has found that scientific production related to the Arctic has increased from less than 5.000 papers per year to almost 11.000 in the period 1996–2015 (Aksnes et al., 2016). Another study conducted under the UArctic Thematic Network on Arctic Research Analytics and Bibliometrics found that the Arctic publications have risen from 9.500 in 2016 to 11.500 in 2021 (Aksnes et al., 2023). While both studies found that in terms of publication output the US emerged as the largest contributor, China showed a relative growth of 260% in the period between 2006–2015 (Andreeva and Hønneland, 2023). In the period between 2015–2022, China has the highest relative growth (132%) of all states. As shown, China consistently increased its production of scientific knowledge that pertains to Arctic research. Research institutions operating in the United States led the country to consistently be the partner number one regarding China's Arctic publications. Until 2018, Canada was the second most cooperative country. Additionally, the United Kingdom, Norway, and Germany have extensively cooperated with China, while Sweden, Denmark, Finland, France, Japan, Iceland, and South Korea have steadily increased scientific cooperation with China (Chen, 2023).

The outbreak of the war in Ukraine has led to the suspension of scientific cooperation between Russia and the Arctic 7, significantly compromising the collaborative approach within the realm of scientific collaborations.

Nevertheless, scientific research continues to be a cornerstone of China's Arctic policy, which in recent years has increasingly focused on the Central Arctic Ocean and the Gakkel Ridge area. Russia has included the Gakkel Ridge area in its submission to the Commission on the Limits of the Continental Shelf (CLCS) for the extension of its continental shelf. However, this area was not included in the CLCS's recommendation (Todorov, 2023). Despite the improvement in Sino-Russian relations, particularly in the energy sector, Russia's concerns about China's interests and activities in the Gakkel Ridge highlight the limitations of their cooperation. Notably, the Gakkel Ridge was the focus of China's 13th Arctic expedition, conducted in July 2023 (Kubny, 2023).

The growth of China's scientific output related to the Central Arctic Ocean has not yet resulted in extensive collaboration with international researchers. According to Scopus, 45% of articles by Chinese scientists on the Central Arctic Ocean are published in outlets operated or sponsored by Chinese research institutes. Furthermore, approximately 65% of articles authored by Chinese researchers on this topic between 2010 and May 2024 were solely written by Chinese scientists (Landriault, 2024). Nonetheless, China's scientific community is firmly embedded within the framework of the international scientific community. Research programs in the Arctic are developed by many different regional and international actors that work on Arctic cooperation in research, such as the International Arctic Scientific Committee (IASC), the Arctic Council, the University of the Arctic (UArctic), the International Arctic Social Sciences Association, and the Barents Euro-Arctic Council. Since 1996, China has been a member of IASC which was established in 1990 by the eight Arctic States to facilitate cooperation in the Arctic research community. Yang Huigen, a research professor at the Polar Research Institute of China (PRIC), served as one of the Vice-President of the IASC. As an observer of the Arctic Council, China attends Arctic Council meetings and takes part in the work of the Arctic Council working groups. The initial suspension of the Arctic Council's working groups, decided by the Arctic 7 immediately after Russia's invasion of Ukraine, was partially lifted in February 2024, under Norway's Chairshsip of the Council. The increasing tensions within the Council have placed China in a difficult position, as its role in the Arctic Council is closely tied to its ambitions to enhance its influence in Arctic governance.

Although China initially expressed concerns about the legitimacy of continuing the Arctic Council's work without Russia (Jonassen, 2022), its potential exclusion from the Council – or from any new forum formed without Russia – could undermine efforts related to fisheries and other economic interests. This scenario might prompt China to emphasize the global significance of the Arctic and advocate for opening its governance to the broader international community (Dyck, 2024).

Chinese scientists are engaged in many of these institutions where they participate or develop joint research projects. CNARC is one of these institutions. Like many other Arctic international platforms, CNARC is a non-state-led entity which provides a space for discussing and promoting Arctic science. CNARC initially counted ten founding institutions, six Nordic and four Chinese, including research centres and universities, with the common purpose of providing a platform for academic cooperation and increasing awareness and undertaking of the Arctic region (Nielsson, 2023). According to Prof. Yang Jian from the Shanghai Institute for International Studies (SIIS), in the first five years CNARC has realized four main objectives: 1) the understanding of governance structures has extended beyond Arctic countries to include non-Arctic nations. 2) the Chinese government has adopted the concept of 'governance' to apply to its Arctic cooperation, 3) Chinese media and businesses have begun to take concrete actions to practice the concept of governance, and 4) China's positive role in Arctic governance is gradually being acknowledged (Yang, 2017). Prof. Yang also highlights the long-term mechanism for Arctic governance which focuses on "building a diversified, efficient, and open Arctic academic exchange network by means of academic conferences, economic roundtables, visiting scholars and academic exchange" (Yang, 2017, p. 293). Before the COVID-19 pandemic, CNARC held yearly symposia and roundtables. The COVID-19 pandemic forced CNARC to move meetings online and since 2018 no new members have joined. The summer seminar on 'Arctic Issues and China-Nordic Cooperation' hosted by the SIIS in August 2023 was the first in-person event after the pandemic. In this event, participants discussed the impact of great power politics on regional governance amid the Russia-Ukraine conflict, and new issues of economic and technological cooperation in the Arctic (Shanghai Institutes for International Studies, 2023). CNARC's 8th Symposium was held in December in 2023 in Guangzhou and the University of Iceland and China Institute for Marine Affairs (CIMA) of the Ministry of Natural Resources were accepted as members.

A close examination of CNARC symposia reveals that these events serve as significant opportunities for knowledge-sharing. They provide ample space for social science disciplines, facilitating debates on current and relevant Arctic legal, political, economic, and societal issues. For example, the 7th CNARC Symposium focused on the theme 'Arctic Fisheries, Polar Silk Road, and Sustainable Development Practices'. Approximately 120 participants from China, Finland, Denmark, Sweden, Norway, and Russia attended the event. The 7th Symposium report prepared by Han (2019) highlights the opinions of Arctic experts on many different topics. Prof. Lassi Heininen analyzed the Finnish Arctic Council Chairmanship that covered the period 2017–2019, valuing Finnish capacity to maintain low tensions and high stability thanks to constructive cooperation between the eight Arctic States. The balance of economic activities and environmental protection was the key to connecting priorities among the Arctic Eight. Prof. Þorsteinn Gunnarsson from the Icelandic Centre for Research (Rannís) discussed the vision, goals, roadmap, and cooperation mechanism of Sustaining Arctic Observing Networks, created to develop a set of recommendations on how to achieve long-term Arctic-wide observing activities. For example, the Polar Data Project focuses on promoting effective governance and establishing co-funding mechanisms to provide researchers and others with access to all Arctic observational data. Group discussions are key moments for academic debate. In the group discussion session on 'Polar Silk Road: Vision, Progress and Outlook', Prof. Arild Moe touched upon the prospects of liquefied natural gas in the Arctic and its significance for China and explored the role of the Arctic in the broader Chinese supply picture. Governance has been analyzed by Prof. Zhao Huiyu from Shanghai Jiao Tong University who believed that UNCLOS and the Arctic legal regime do not cover the entire governance and ecological protection needs of China's 'Arctic Belt and Road' strategy, suggesting that new cooperative policies and governance mechanisms in terms of Arctic environmental governance need to be established. In the group discussion session on 'China-Nordic Policy Synergies on Arctic Sustainable Development', Prof. Camilla T.N. Sørensen touched upon Arctic geopolitics. She stressed how Arctic politics and security have become increasingly intertwined with great power policy, highlighting how in a context of intensified U.S.-China great power rivalry can make it even more difficult for China as the only non-Arctic great power to ensure its access to and influence in the region. Prof. Zhang Pei from SIIS assessed how the 'Polar Silk Road' should be viewed as a natural extension and integral part of the 'One Belt and One Road' initiative. He mentioned how China should promote cooperation with the Nordics as a whole and, at the same time, study the national development strategies of individual Nordic countries.

As shown from this brief presentation and example from the 7th Symposium, CNARC offers room for fruitful discussions between Chinese and international scholars and experts. Often symposia's participants come from the academic, business, and political spheres. Cross-sectoral debate is extremely beneficial in the perspective of a holistic discussion on Arctic issues. CNARC's purpose of fostering academic cooperation which increases awareness, understanding, and knowledge of the Arctic and its global impacts, is even more important now as the security aspect of China-Nordic relations is entangled in a more tense and complex geopolitical scenario (Nielsson, 2023). Finland and Sweden joining NATO is rapidly changing the security landscape in the Arctic. China is steadily rising as a strategic priority in NATO's Arctic agenda. The Chair of the NATO Military Committee, Admiral Rob Bauer in 2022 stated that "a matter of increasing concern is the growing cooperation between Beijing and Moscow [...]. [...] in their joint statement in February 2022, [they] pledged to intensify practical cooperation in the Arctic" (Arctic Circle, 2022, 9:23–9:53). In 2023, he reiterated that "China's intentions for the region remain opaque" (Arctic Circle, 2023b, 4:44).

3 Arctic Scientific Research: A National Priority with Global Aftermaths

3.1 *The Official Perspective*

The publication of China's Arctic Policy in 2018 was a ground-breaking moment for China's engagement in the Arctic. China's release of its official policy a few years after Japan and Korea, fueled concerns and speculation among Arctic actors. In the official Arctic Policy, China self-defines a "near-Arctic State": "China is an important stakeholder in Arctic affairs. Geographically, China is a 'Near-Arctic State', one of the continental States that are closest to the Arctic Circle" (State Council, 2018, section II). In the subsequent statement, emphasis is placed on how environmental changes directly affect China's climate system: "The natural conditions of the Arctic and their changes have a direct impact on China's climate system and ecological environment, and, in turn, on its economic interests in agriculture, forestry, fishery, marine industry and other sectors." (State Council, 2018, section II).

From the 2010s, the Arctic started receiving much more attention in the Chinese national and subnational Five-Year Plans (FYP). In the 12th FYP (2011–2015), Arctic engagement is discussed in the framework of promoting the maritime economy and is focused on improving scientific research. The plan states: "Strengthen integrated marine surveying and mapping, and carry out polar and oceanic scientific investigation actively" (State Council, 2011, section XIV(II)). The goals of improving soft and hard power through high-quality scientific research and expansions of multilevel presence in the Arctic and Antarctic have been reached by the end of the 12th FYP (Brady, 2017, p. 17). In the 13th Five-Year Plan (2016–2020), renewed emphasis is placed on improving scientific research, developing blue economic corridors, building a new icebreaker and to foster China's "active role in formulating international rules in areas such as the internet, the deep sea, the polar regions, and aerospace" (State Council, 2016, section LII (III)). Among the maritime projects, the plan lists 'Polar exploration' which includes:

> 1) establish a new shore-based Arctic observation through cooperation; 2) establish a new Antarctic research station; 3) build new advanced icebreakers; 4) improve Antarctic aviation capabilities; 5) complete the basic framework for a land-sea-air observation platform in the polar regions; 6) research and develop exploration technology and equipment suitable to the polar environments; 7) establish a service platform for the provision and application of information regarding the polar environments and potential polar resources.
>
> STATE COUNCIL, 2016, section XLI(III)

In the 14th FYP (2021–2025) published by the State Council (2021 section XXXIII(III)), the Arctic finds its place in Chapter 33, dedicated to the expansion of the maritime economy where China plans to: engage actively in the development and implementation of international maritime governance mechanisms and regulations, fostering the establishment of a fair and equitable global maritime order and advancing the concept of a shared marine future; strengthen practical collaboration with coastal nations in areas such as marine environmental monitoring and protection, scientific research, and search and rescue; participate in pragmatic cooperation and build the "Polar Silk Road".

The development opportunities linked to the fast changes happening in the Arctic have also influenced subnational plans which offer a more localized and detailed policy planning. For geographical reasons, the Arctic region has received much more attention in the subnational plans from the Northeast provinces, which have historically suffered an economic development gap compared to the Southern provinces. Since the early 1980s, the opening-up policy brought Southern provinces immense economic benefits thanks to the better connectivity with global trade and the export-oriented economy. Before 1978, the Northeast Chinese provinces of Heilongjiang and Liaoning were among the richest provinces in the country in terms of GDP per capita. The policy environment, based on the creation of Special Economic Zones, the incentives for foreign direct investments, along with the easier access of coastal provinces to international trading networks, have facilitated impressive regional growth (Weiss, 2006). To remedy the economic development imbalance in summer 2003, Wen Jiabao (Chinese Premier from 2003 to 2013) paid a visit to Northeast provinces and said that "rejuvenating the traditional industrial bases in the Northeast and turn them into national or international bases for the manufacture of equipment and important raw materials was a historic task" (Dong, 2005, p. 1–2). 'Revitalization' is the common perspective when discussing the Northeast economies of Heilongjiang, Jilin, and Liaoning (Eiterjord, 2023b). Current Chinese leader Xi Jinping outlined how the Northeast provinces are now acquiring a strategic role for the development of new commercial channels: "Northeast China is an important gateway for the country's northward opening up, and its strategic position and role in strengthening regional cooperation in northeast Asia and the interplay between domestic and international flows are increasingly prominent" (Xinhua, 2023).

Eiterjord (2023a) points out how Northeast provinces' subnational five-year plans look at benefits that can be generated through the development of Arctic shipping routes. The Polar Silk Road emerges as a common key factor to boost regional development. For the Heilongjiang province it will "promote the transformation [of the province] from being 'peripheral' to becoming a 'Northeast Asian hub'" (Ministry of Transport, 2022). In 2017, the president of the Tumen River International Cooperation Society highlighted how the development of the River is the only strategic channel for China to enter the Sea of Japan, and this is also the coastal area closest to Arctic shipping routes (Li, 2018). For the Liaoning Province, the city of Dalian is at the core of the policy as it might represent the international shipping center in the country's Northeast. Based on the opportunities that the Polar Silk Road in terms of connectivity and regional cooperation between Arctic and near-Arctic regions might provide, the city's 14th five-year plan for the economic and social national development calls for integrating into the Polar Silk Road and "establishing [itself] as a homeport for Arctic shipping" (Dalian Municipal People's Government, 2021). Eiterjord (2023b) highlights that the development of the Polar Silk Road differs for the provinces of Heilongjiang and Jilin, where it is shaped by cross-border opportunities between China and Russia, whereas for Liaoning Province, it is driven by the strategic position of Dalian as a gateway city.

October 2022 was a key moment for China's national politics and policy-planning as the Chinese Communist Party (CCP) held the 20th Congress in Beijing. As usual, ahead of the Party Congress, the current leader Xi Jinping read the Congress Report that conventionally celebrates the achievements and introduces future policies for specific geographical regions. In the last Congress Report, science and technology (科技 / keji) were mentioned more often than in the last report released in 2017 (Mercator Institute for China Studies, 2022). Science is labelled as a "productive force", and a "primary driver of growth" (International Department, Central Committee of the CCP, 2023). From the Congress Report also emerges China's intention to better allocate innovation resources and better define the roles of national research institutes, advanced-level research universities, and leading high-tech enterprises. Science is tightly linked to growth, which in the last decades has been a key tool for the CCP's legitimization power. The attention to the research institutes shows how specific and high-level knowledge is required in order to have an adequate approach to specific issues of national and international interests. The Congress Report states that China: "will increase investment in science and technology through diverse channels [...]. [...] We will expand science and technology exchanges and cooperation with other countries, cultivate an internationalized environment for research, and create an open and globally-competitive innovation ecosystem" (International Department, Central Committee of the CPC, 2023). In the Arctic, China does not have sovereign rights and activities are modelled upon its rights to conduct scientific research in the high seas and its obligations imposed by the UNCLOS and the CAOFA. In this framework, developing science and technology means to increase capabilities to access the polar regions and produce relevant scientific knowledge which can affect its role within the Arctic governance. Cooperation with other countries is another key point not only because a significant portion of waters and terrestrial areas in the Arctic are under Arctic States' sovereignty, but also because only producing, sharing, and interpreting data collected from every part of the region can help understanding the changing climate and other environmental factors. Additionally, the pressing need for specialized expertise can enhance the role of scientists and experts in shaping a bottom-up process, which might see knowledge production in scientific networks, platforms, and consortiums of research institutes influencing policymakers.

China's Arctic policy provides an overview of all China's Arctic interests ranging from participation in Arctic governance, investing in sustainable development, respecting the status quo, endorsing international law, developing opportunities linked to shipping routes, exploiting natural resources, and conducting scientific research. From the official release in 2018, the self-definition as a 'near-Arctic State' was criticized by vast Western literature, that, by echoing China's narrative about its presence in the Arctic, risks mischaracterizing China as a peer or near-peer competitor in the region, while its presence remains far weaker than Beijing advises (Lackenbauer et al., 2022). However, the absence of the 'near-arctic State' definition in the FYPs could mean that the status concept was meant for the external public, to create a narrative outside of China to improve external recognition rather than to domestic audiences. Alternatively, it could suggest that the concept wasn't initially imposed through official channels but rather originated from academic discussions and was later adopted by the leadership.

The last three FYPs consider a timespan of 15 years of policy planning. Polar scientific research gradually takes shape and expands its reach to enhancement of infrastructures and improvement of research capabilities. The progress in technology development and research capabilities is clearly shown by the building of new infrastructures and the recently domestically-built icebreaker, which improved China's capability to conduct scientific research at the poles. Being a consistent scientific knowledge producer, China can enhance its role in regional governance (Eiterjord, 2023a). Strategic plans show that science and technology development are key priorities in the coming years. While in the 12th and 13th FYPs, the prioritization of science at national and international levels is framed under the improvement of China's position in maritime global governance, the 14th FYP shows a much clearer link between scientific and technological progress to realize Xi Jinping's concepts and plans. The realization of the 'community with a shared future' through the Polar Silk Road, envisioned as an additional 'blue economic passage' of the Belt and Road Initiative, was already framed in the *Vision for Maritime Cooperation on the Construction of the Belt and Road* jointly released by the National Development and Reform Commission (NDRC) and the State Oceanic Administration (SOA) in 2017 (State Council, 2017). Becoming more self-reliant in science and technology could lead China to enhance its ability to conduct scientific research in the Arctic, positioning itself as a leader in Arctic science and bolstering its credibility and influence in international discussions and decision-making processes related to Arctic governance. The interplay of CAOFA and the 2023 Biodiversity Beyond National Jurisdiction Agreement (BBNJ Agreement) in the Arctic might be highly relevant for China's fishery policy and, more broadly, for its place in the Arctic governance. While parties to both agreements face challenges related to the inclusion or exclusion of fisheries in the category of marine genetic resources and the debate over the privileged role of Arctic coastal States (Liu, 2022), their shared goal of enhancing scientific knowledge in areas beyond national jurisdiction – aimed at better understanding marine living resources and developing management systems – could help knowledge-producing actors to gain greater influence at the international level.

3.2 *China's Arctic Research Facilities and Arctic Expeditions*

As China emerges as a more prominent player on the global stage, its long-term policy planning in the polar regions and in funding allocated to science and technology development have enabled it to establish a robust structure which comprises the building of polar research stations, deployment of icebreakers, and development of comprehensive research programs that have grown significantly and constantly in the last years. For non-Arctic States, active engagement in Arctic scientific research contributes to expanding academic endeavors and engages with foreign-policy objectives and shows visibility (Andreeva & Hønneland, 2023). After China became an official observer State of the Arctic Council in 2013, its involvement in Arctic affairs has significantly grown. The status within the Arctic Council is tightly linked to scientific research as "observers should continue to make relevant contributions through their engagement in the Arctic Council primarily at the level of Working Groups" (Arctic Council, n.d.).

China's engagement in the Arctic is a component of the long-term planning of improving China's position within both polar regions and it has evolved through several distinct phases. In 1983, China joined the Antarctic Treaty. During the latter half of the 1980s, China constructed the Great Wall and Zhongshan Stations in Antarctica and established the Polar Research Institute of China (PRIC). From the late 1990s onward, China began conducting scientific research expeditions in polar regions. Starting in the early 2000s, the polar regions were incorporated into China's FYPs, leading to a substantial increase in its polar activities through research expeditions and deeper involvement in governance.

China established its first research station in the Arctic in 2004. The Yellow River Station is located in Ny-Ålesund, in the Svalbard archipelago. In 2018, China and Iceland jointly opened the China-Iceland Aurora Observatory (CIAO), located at Kárhóll, approximately 60 km east of Akureyri in Northern Iceland. Chinese organizations involved in the CIAO project include: PRIC, the National Space Science Centre and the Institute of Geology and Geophysics of the Chinese Academy of Sciences, the China Research Institute of Radio Wave Propagation, the National Centre for Space Weather, the Institute of Space Physics and Applied Technology of Peking University, the School of Electronic Information of Wuhan University, the School of Earth and Space Science of the University of Science and Technology of

China, and the School of Space Science and Physics of Shandong University (Brady, 2017). In 2012, China's Meteorological Administration built a ground receiving station for its satellites in Kiruna and later opened the China Remote Sensing Satellite North Polar Ground Station near Kiruna in 2016, which is the first-ever Chinese-owned satellite station anywhere in the world (Doshi et al., 2021). In 2019, China launched the *Ice Pathfinder* (*BNU-1*) developed by the Beijing Normal University. The *BNU-1* is the first satellite dedicated to remote-sensing observation and designed to conduct polar climate and environmental observations (Chen, 2023). The importance of polar satellites is linked to safe navigation in Arctic shipping as they can observe weather and ice conditions and also further promote research on climate science.

The COVID-19 pandemic and China's strict policies to contain and limit its diffusion have deeply influenced and constrained Chinese Arctic research outreach. In December 2022, Lipin already noticed that there were plans to resume research work in both Yellow River Station in Ny-Ålesund and in the China-Iceland Arctic Observatory (Lipin, 2022), which shows that China prioritized its well-established scientific projects and partnerships in Norway and Iceland (Volpe, 2023).

One of the prominent features of China's Arctic engagement is its consistency in Arctic research expeditions. China inaugurated Arctic scientific expeditions in 1999 with the first journey of the Chinese icebreaker *Xuelong* to the North Pole. On that occasion Chen Liqi, the chief scientist leading the team stated that:

> global climate changes are the result of the integrated effect of many factors. During the expedition, we employed various means, such as yachts and helicopters, to carry out multi-site simultaneous observation of the integrated effect of the ice, the atmosphere, and the sea.
>
> China.org.cn, n.d

More than 50 Chinese Polar researchers from various fields along with researchers from Japan, Russia, and South Korea joined the first Chinese Arctic expedition. According to Chen Lianzeng, deputy Director of National Bureau of Oceanography, the second Arctic expedition in 2003 marked a more advanced technology in Arctic expeditions (Xinhua, 2003). Qu Tanzhou, the administration's polar region expedition office director, said that the fourth Arctic expedition set a new record on both its duration and the number of people involved. Seven scientists from the United States, France, Finland, Estonia, and South Korea took part in the mission (Xinhua, 2010). The fifth expedition was conducted on the *Xuelong* and included the survey of the marine environment and sea–ice–air system, geologic record of rapid changes in the marine environment and the research on the carbon flux, nutrients and biogeochemical cycle in the Arctic (Arctic Portal, 2012).

When approaching the sixth expedition, Wang Yong, head of the division of science programs of the Chinese Arctic and Antarctic Administration, stated that Chinese scientists will collect information on climate change, consider future uses of the Northern Sea Route and explore the region's resources. Wang Yong made clear that besides understanding of effects that a warming Arctic might have on China's and global climate, the expedition will improve China's capacities for the utilization of the Northern Sea Route and to exploit Arctic natural resources (Wang, 2014). The seventh expedition was completed in 2016 and saw the participation of American and French scientists. Xia Limin, from the State Oceanic Administration and research team leader, stated that it will help to "promote peace, stability and sustainable development in the Arctic region" (Xinhua, 2016). The ninth expedition was dedicated to interdisciplinary studies and focused on issues such as marine radioactivity, microplastics, and ocean acidification (Xinhua, 2018). The tenth Arctic expedition was carried out on China's oceanographic research vessel *Xiang Yang Hong 01* for the first time. The eleventh research expedition in 2020 was conducted on board the domestic-built Chinese icebreaker *Xuelong 2*. The vessel is 122.5 meters long with an ice-breaking capacity of 2-3 knots average speed in 1.5 m of ice with 20 cm snow cover. It is classified as Polar Class 3 and is owned by the PRIC. The possibility of using *Xuelong 2* represented a breakthrough for China's polar scientific operations. *Xuelong* was designed as an ice-strengthened cargo ship, not completely fitting China's polar program and inhibiting the ability to conduct in-depth scientific investigations in the Arctic and in-depth seabed research in the Antarctic (Brady, 2017). During its ice trials in 2020, the project manager at Aker Arctic, a Finnish company specialized in icebreaker design services, remarked that:

> *Xue long 2* performed splendidly at the actual task she was designed and built for, which is an excellent validation for the vessel's operational capability [...] The new ship allows a new dimension of flexibility in terms of scheduling and areas of operation, as the icebreaking capability of *Xue long 2* is much higher than that of the old vessel. *Xue long 2* can reach considerably closer to the research stations earlier than previously. This was the design target, which was also achieved.
>
> AKER ARCTIC, 2020, pp. 9–10

The thirteenth Arctic expedition was completed in September 2023 and it included scientists from Thailand and Russia. It was organized by the Ministry of Natural Resources and it focused on long-term monitoring of key environmental elements: 49 comprehensive marine surveys were completed, 5 sets of submersible buoys were deployed, 142 groups of meteorological soundings were carried out, 6 short-term and 1 long-term ice stations were completed, and a total of 26 sets of quasi-disposable ice-based buoys have been deployed to conduct tests on various parameters, including sea surface meteorology, atmospheric composition, aerosols, marine debris, gravity, sea surface temperature and salinity, current profiles, sea ice extent, and ship stress. These tests have resulted in the collection of a significant amount of valuable data (Yu, 2023). Sharma (2023), from the Manohar Parrikar Institute for Defence Studies and Analyses, summarized the important outcome of this Chinese Arctic research expedition: the deployment of a series of domestically developed unmanned buoys to make observations and record data on various parameters and the collection of biological samples to replenish China's Nation GeneBank in Shenzhen show how China does not "ignore the ongoing transformation in the Arctic region and is seeking to understand the region's scientific and environmental dimensions".

4 Conclusion

China's 2018 Arctic policy launch generated renewed momentum for China's Arctic engagement. The self-definition as a 'near-Arctic State' received particular attention and animated the international debate about China's strategic interests in the area. Geopolitical implications, the renewed energy cooperation with Russia, and the interest in exploiting Arctic natural resources have fostered concerns among Arctic and non-Arctic States. However, the literature has deeply overlooked how China's improvement of its Arctic scientific research capabilities might directly influence its role in Arctic governance.

This chapter discussed two main examples of how science influences international relations in the case of China in the Arctic. The CAOFA demonstrates the impact of science on the lawmaking process, while CNARC illustrates how sharing scientific knowledge through non-state-led platforms can enhance understanding and cooperation. While China's participation in the CAOFA negotiations testifies an increased role in Arctic governance, it also provides an excellent opportunity to become a leading actor in scientific knowledge production. Governance in the Arctic is evolving, driven in part by CAOFA's advancements and "existing strategies for decision making may become increasingly inapplicable to new Arctic arrangements [...]. [...] new decision-making strategies such as sub-coalitions and systematic independent arbitration [...] should be explored" (Shahbazi, 2022, p. 32). The deep interconnectedness between science and governance in the Arctic highlights the importance of technological development and investments in scientific research to enhance China's influence in Arctic governance. The chapter also analyzed who the actors are. CNARC, as a non-state-led consortium which sees a consistent participation of Chinese research centres and universities and their counterparts from the Nordic countries, provides an international platform for a holistic debate on the Arctic and, along the years, has expanded the understanding of Arctic governance structure from the Arctic countries to non-Arctic countries (Yang, 2017). Sharing scientific knowledge, discussing business opportunities, the impact of climate change on Indigenous peoples, and Arctic resource exploitation, can improve reciprocal understanding, enlarge cooperative grounds and enhance bottom-up progress to influence decision-makers in a context of increasing polarization. In terms of geopolitical relevance, it could be a valuable space to better deconstruct the Sino-Russian cooperation in the Arctic, which, as the Chair of the NATO Military Committee Admiral Rob Bauer has reiterated at the Arctic Circle Assembly, is perceived as a growing menace for stability in the Arctic region.

China does not hide its interests in the region that range from natural resource exploitation, sustainable development, shipping routes, to scientific research, governance, and tourism. While at the national level, science and technology are discussed as key priorities under a broad perspective, subnational plans look at the possibility to develop Arctic shipping routes for Northeast regional development. Still, better capacities to predict weather conditions might be important for Arctic shipping routes. As it is shown, China is conducting Arctic scientific research expeditions on a yearly basis, with some recent impediments due to the COVID-19 pandemic. The recently domestic-built icebreaker *Xuelong 2* has been used for the last three Arctic expeditions. Moreover, China is in the process of constructing a new multifunctional ice-going vessel capable of navigating through thick one-year ice with a maximum thickness of 120 centimeters (Wenger, 2023). China is clearly investing in polar scientific research and its Arctic scientific engagement and improved research should not be solely seen as the possibility to better understand environmental and climate change-related issues. China's national planning and the growing attention and increased investment in science can make China a knowledge-producer, affecting its credibility and its attractiveness to actors which do not carry the same financial capability.

Bibliography

Aker Arctic (2020). *Xue Long 2 in successful ice trials* [Brochure]. https://akerarctic.fi/app/uploads/2020/03/xue_long2_in_successful_ice_trials-1.pdf

Andreeva, S., & Hønneland, G. (2023). *Arctic Research and its Actors. A pre-study of Research Strategies and Priorities.* (Report No. 6/2023). Fridtjof Nansen Institute. https://www.fni.no/getfile.php/1317848-1696327774/Filer/Publikasjoner/FNI%20Report%206%202023%281%29.pdf

Aksnes, D.C., Blöcker, C., Colliander, C., & Nilsson, L.M. (2023). Arctic research trends: Bibliometrics 2016–2022. *UArctic, Umeå University, and Canada Arctic.* https://umu.diva-portal.org/smash/get/diva2:1787024/FULLTEXT01.pdf

Aksnes, D.C., Osipov, I., Moskaleva, O., & Kullerud, L. (2016). Arctic research publication trends: A pilot study. *UArctic and the Far Eastern Federal University.* https://research.uarctic.org/media/1596721/arctic-research-publication-trends-august-2016.pdf

Arctic Circle (2018, November 9). *China's Arctic policy white paper: Gao Feng at the #ArcticCircleFaroeIslands Forum.* [Video]. YouTube. https://www.youtube.com/watch?v=4V6lkoyZEnY

Arctic Circle (2019, October 11). *China's special representative for Arctic affairs, Gao Feng – Full speech* [Video]. YouTube. https://www.youtube.com/watch?v=j-B2yLvlGM0

Arctic Circle (2020, December 13). *The status of "near Arctic state" and its impact* [Video]. YouTube. https://www.youtube.com/watch?v=Qqg9UiOrS_c

Arctic Circle. (2022, October 19). *Nato and the Arctic* [Video]. YouTube. https://www.youtube.com/watch?v=6n6GEuOo_dM

Arctic Circle (2023a, March 27). *Contributions of observer states to the future of the Arctic Council* [Video]. YouTube. https://www.youtube.com/watch?v=kTo24ax1COY

Arctic Circle (2023b, October 26). *The NATO perspective on the Arctic* [Video]. YouTube. https://www.youtube.com/watch?v=R5KmhabOXic

Arctic Council website (n.d.). Role of Arctic Council observers. *Arctic Council.* Retrieved July 11, 2024, from https://arctic-council.org/about/observers/#:~:text=Role%20of%20Arctic%20Council%20observers,observer%20status%20has%20been%20granted

Arctic Portal (2012). *The 5th Chinese national Arctic research expedition.* Arctic Portal. Retrieved June 10, 2024, from https://arcticportal.org/ap-library/yar-features/805-chinare5

BBNJ Agreement (2023). Agreement under the United Nations Convention on the Law of the Sea on the Conservation and Sustainable Use of Marine Biological Diversity of Areas beyond National Jurisdiction (adopted 19 June 2023). https://treaties.un.org/pages/ViewDetails.aspx?src=TREATY&mtdsg_no=XXI-10&chapter=21&clang=_en

Brady, A.-M. (2017). *China as a Polar Great Power.* Cambridge University Press. https://doi.org/10.1017/9781316832004

CGTN (2021, July 13). *China's Xuelong 2 sets sail for new Arctic expedition.* CGTN. Retrieved June 12, 2024, from https://news.cgtn.com/news/2021-07-13/China-s-Xuelong-2-sets-sail-for-new-Arctic-expedition-11RgRorlYIw/index.html

Chen, Y. (2023). China's Arctic policy and engagement: Review and prospects. *Asia Policy, 18*(1), 29–38. https://doi.org/10.1353/asp.2023.0005

China.org.cn. (n.d.). *China's first Arctic expedition.* China.org.cn. Retrieved July 17, 2024, from http://www.china.org.cn/english/features/40958.htm

Dalian Municipal People's Government (2021). 大连市国民经济和社会发展第十四个五年规划和2035年远景目标纲要 [*Outline of the 14th five-year plan for the economic and social development of Dalian and long-range objectives toward 2035*]. https://www.ndrc.gov.cn/fggz/fzzlgh/dffzgh/202106/P020210628415825765328.pdf

Dervovic, M. & Heinrich, K. (2023). Law-Science Nexus in International Law-Making: Perspectives from Arctic Fisheries Governance. *Nordic Journal of International Law, 92*(4), 599–622. https://doi.org/10.1163/15718107-bja10073

Ding, M., Tian, B., Zhang, T., Tang, J., Peng, H., Bian, L., & Sun, W. (2018). Shipborne observations of atmospheric black carbon aerosol from Shanghai to the Arctic Ocean during the 7th Chinese Arctic Research Expedition. *Atmospheric Research, 210*, 34–40. https://doi.org/10.1016/j.atmosres.2018.04.016

Dong, L. (2005). China's drive to revitalize the Northeast. *China Perspectives, 58.* https://doi.org/10.4000/chinaperspectives.462

Doshi, R., Dale-Huang, A., & Zhang, G. (2021). *Northern expedition, China's Arctic activities and ambitions.* (April 2021). Foreign Policy at Brookings. https://www.brookings.edu/wp-content/uploads/2021/04/FP_20210412_china_arctic.pdf

Dyck, C. (2024). On thin ice: The Arctic Council's uncertain future. *Marine Policy, 163*, 106060. https://doi.org/10.1016/j.marpol.2024.106060

Eiterjord, T. (2023a, November 30). *The Arctic in China's subnational 14th five-year plans.* The Arctic Institute. https://www.thearcticinstitute.org/arctic-chinas-subnational-14th-five-year-plans/

Eiterjord, T. (2023b, December 7). *Polar expertise in China's 14th five-year plan.* The Arctic Institute. https://www.thearcticinstitute.org/polar-expertise-chinas-14th-five-year-plan/

Han, L. (2019). CNARC symposium 2019 report – "Arctic fisheries, polar silk road, and sustainable development practices", 8 May 2019, Shanghai. CNARC. Retrieved June 17, 2024, from https://www.cnarc.info/symposia/7th-cnarc-symposium

Harrison, P., Shin, H.C., Huntington, H.P., Balton, D., Benton, D., Pan, M., Fujio, O., Guo, P., Grebmeier, J.M., Highleyman, S., Jakobsen, A., Meloche, M., Romanenko, O., & Zilanov, V.K. (2020). *How non-government actors helped the Arctic fisheries agreement.* (Polar Perspectives No. 2). Polar Institute and Wilson Center. https://www.wilsoncenter.org/sites/default/files/media/uploads/documents/Polar%20Perspective%202%20FINAL.pdf

International Department, Central Committee of the CPC (2023). Full text of the report to the 20th National Congress of the Communist Party of China. Retrieved 17 July 2024, from: https://www.idcpc.org.cn/english2023/tjzl/cpcjj/20thPartyCongrssReport

Jonassen, T. (2022, October 15). *China: "Will not acknowledge Arctic Council without Russia".* High North News. https://www.highnorthnews.com/en/china-will-not-acknowledge-arctic-council-without-russia

Kubny, H. (2023, July 24). *China on its 13th Arctic expedition.* Polar Journal. https://polarjournal.ch/en/2023/07/24/china-on-its-13th-arctic-expedition/

Lackenbauer, P.W., Lajeunesse, A., & Dean, R. (2022). Why China is not a peer competitor in the Arctic. *Journal of Indo-Pacific Affairs, 5*(5), 80–97.

Landriault, M. (2024, June 5). *Chinese scientists are increasingly shaping the future of the Arctic amid China's rising presence.* The Conservation. https://theconversation.com/chinese-scientists-are-increasingly-shaping-the-future-of-the-arctic-amid-chinas-rising-presence-230509

Li, T. (2018). 实施 "五大突破" 连接 "冰上丝绸之路" ——我国向北开放战略实施路径探析 [Implementing the "five major breakthroughs" to connect the "ice silk road" – An analysis of the implementation path of my country's northward opening strategy]. https://aoc.ouc.edu.cn/2022/0912/c9821a377052/pagem.htm

Lipin, M. (2022, December 5). China begins to revive Arctic scientific ground projects after setbacks. *Voice for America.* Retrieved July 17, 2024, from https://www.voanews.com/a/china-begins-to-revive-arctic-scientific-ground-projects-after-setbacks-/6860756.html

Liu, D. (2022). The interplay between the CAOF agreement and BBNJ agreement: A Chinese perspective. *Sustainability, 14*(21), 14575. https://doi.org/10.3390/su142114575

Liu, K. (2022). The *global times* and the China threat narrative: An empirical analysis. *Journal of Chinese Political Science, 27*, 1–18. https://doi.org/10.1007/s11366-021-09754-3

Liu, N. (2021, June 10). *China and the agreement to prevent unregulated high seas fisheries in the central Arctic Ocean*. The Diplomat. Retrieved 17 July 2024, from https://thediplomat.com/2021/06/china-and-the-agreement-to-prevent-unregulated-high-seas-fisheries-in-the-central-arctic-ocean/

Mercator Institute for China Studies (2022, October 20). Key takeaways from Xi's report to the party congress. *MERICS*. Retrieved 12 June 2024, from https://www.merics.org/en/merics-briefs/key-takeaways-xis-report-party-congress

Ministry of Foreign Affairs of People's Republic of China (2015, October 17). *Keynote speech by Vice Foreign Minister Zhang Ming at the China country session of the third Arctic Circle Assembly*. Embassy of the People's Republic of China in Iceland. Retrieved 3 July 2024, from http://is.china-embassy.gov.cn/eng/zbgx/kjjl/201510/t20151018_3164910.htm

Ministry of Transport (2022, April 15). 《黑龙江省"十四五"综合交通运输发展规划》介绍——访黑龙江省交通运输厅 党组成员、副厅长 周贵才 [Introduction to the 14th five-year plan for comprehensive transportation development in Heilongjiang Province——Interview with Zhou Guicai, member of the Party Leadership Group and Deputy Director of the Heilongjiang Provincial Department of Transportation. Retrieved 17 July 2024, from https://www.mot.gov.cn/zxft2022/fzhgh_hlj/

Nielsson, E, T. (2023). The China-Nordic Arctic research center: One decade in. *Arctic Yearbook*, [2023]. https://arcticyearbook.com/arctic-yearbook/2023/2023-commentaries/513-the-china-nordic-arctic-research-center-one-decade-in

National Oceanic and Atmospheric Administration (NOAA) (2011). *Report of a meeting of scientific experts on fish stocks in the Arctic Ocean*. NOAA Fisheries. https://apps-afsc.fisheries.noaa.gov/documents/Arctic_fish_stocks_third_meeting/508_Documents/508_First%20Meeting%20Sci%20Experts%20Arctic%20Fisheries%2030%20Aug%202011.pdf

NOAA (2013). *Report of 2nd scientific meeting on Arctic fish stocks, Tromsø 28-31 October*. NOAA Fisheries. https://apps-afsc.fisheries.noaa.gov/documents/Arctic_fish_stocks_third_meeting/508_Documents/508_Report%20of%202nd%20Scientific%20Meeting%20on%20Arctic%20Fish%20Stocks%2028%2031%20October%202013_unlocked.pdf

NOAA (2015). *Final report: Third meeting of scientific experts on fish stocks in the central Arctic Ocean*. NOAA Fisheries. https://apps-afsc.fisheries.noaa.gov/documents/Arctic_fish_stocks_third_meeting/508_Documents/Meeting-and-Breakout-Reports/508_3rd_Arctic_Fish_Final_Report_10_July_2015_final-unlocked.pdf

Ocean Conservancy (2017). *Preventing unregulated commercial fishing in the central Arctic Ocean (CAO): A compilation of reports from meetings of experts in Shanghai (China), Incheon (Korea) & Sapporo (Japan)*. Ocean Conservancy. https://oceanconservancy.org/wp-content/uploads/2018/09/Preventing-Unregulated-Commercial-Fishing-CAO.pdf

Oslo Declaration (2015). Declaration concerning the prevention of unregulated high seas fishing in the central Arctic Ocean (adopted 16 July 2015). https://www.regjeringen.no/globalassets/departementene/ud/vedlegg/folkerett/declaration-on-arctic-fisheries-16-july-2015.pdf

Pan, M. & Huntington, H.P. (2016). A precautionary approach to fisheries in the central Arctic Ocean: Policy, science, and China. *Marine Policy*, *63*, 153–157. https://doi.org/10.1016/j.marpol.2015.10.015

Shahbazi, A. (2023). *Sustaining tomorrow's central Arctic Ocean today: Using best practices to guide central Arctic Ocean fisheries agreement's implementation*. WWF. https://files.worldwildlife.org/wwfcmsprod/files/Publication/file/7zhj2wrz1i_CAOFA_Full_Report_pages_web_version.pdf

Shanghai Institutes for International Studies (SIIS) (2023, August 24). *Nordic scholars visit SIIS*. SIIS. Retrieved July 17, 2024, from https://www.siis.org.cn/Visits/15088.jhtml

Sharma, B. (2023, November 10). *China's 13th Arctic expedition*. Manohar Parrikar Institute for Defence Studies and Analyses. Retrieved August 29, 2024, from https://www.idsa.in/idsacomments/china-13th-arctic-expedition-bsharma-101123

Skolnikoff, E. (1993). *The elusive transformation: science, technology, and the evolution of international politics*. Princeton University Press.

State Council (2011). 中华人民共和国国民经济和社会发展第十三个五年规划纲要 [The 12th five-year plan for economic and social development of the People's Republic of China. https://www.ndrc.gov.cn/fggz/fzzlgh/gjfzgh/201109/P020191029595702423333.pdf

State Council (2016). *The 13th five-year plan for economic and social development of the People's Republic of China: 2016-2020*. (Compilation and Translation Bureau, Central Committee of the Communist Part of China, Trans.). https://en.ndrc.gov.cn/policies/202105/P020210527785800103339.pdf

State Council (2017). *Vision for maritime cooperation under the belt and road initiative*. Retrieved June 19, 2024, from https://english.www.gov.cn/archive/publications/2017/06/20/content_281475691873460.htm

State Council (2018). *China's Arctic policy*. Retrieved July 1, 2024, from https://english.www.gov.cn/archive/white_paper/2018/01/26/content_281476026660336.htm

State Council (2021). 中华人民共和国国民经济和社会发展第十四个五年规划和 2035 年远景目标纲要. [Outline of the People's Republic of China 14th five-year plan for national economic and social development and long-range objectives for 2035]. https://www.gov.cn/xinwen/2021-03/13/content_5592681.htm

Todorov, A. (2023, March 2). *Russia's Arctic shelf bid and the commission on the limits of the continental shelf, explained.* Harvard Kennedy School: Belfer Center for Science and International Affairs. https://www.belfercenter.org/publication/russias-arctic-shelf-bid-and-commission-limits-continental-shelf-explained#:~:text=On%20February%206%2C%202023%2C%20the,shelf%20close%20to%20an%20end

Volpe, M. (2023, April 18). *From the 20th Chinese communist party congress to the Arctic: The cooperation triptych.* The Arctic Institute. https://www.thearcticinstitute.org/20th-chinese-communist-party-congress-arctic-cooperation-triptych/

Vylegzhanin, A.N., Young, O.R., & Berkman, P.A. (2020). The central Arctic Ocean fisheries agreement as an element in the evolving Arctic Ocean governance complex. *Marine Policy, 118,* 104001. https://doi.org/10.1016/j.marpol.2020.104001

Wang, Q. (2014, July 3). *China embarks on sixth Arctic trek to explore the North Pole.* China Daily. Retrieved August 3, 2024, from https://www.chinadaily.com.cn/china/2014-07/03/content_17639357.htm

Wenger, M. (2023, June 29). *China starts construction of its third polar-going vessel.* Polar Journal. https://polarjournal.ch/en/2023/06/29/china-starts-construction-of-its-third-icebreaker/

Weiss, C. (2005). Science, technology and international relations. *Technology in Society, 27*(3), 295–313. https://doi.org/10.1016/j.techsoc.2005.04.004

Weiss, J. (2006). *Development in north east People's Republic of China.* (ADBI Research Policy Brief No. 19). Asian Development Bank Institute. https://www.adb.org/sites/default/files/publication/157262/adbi-rpb19.pdf

Xinhua (2003, September 27). *Second Arctic expedition returns.* China.org.cn. http://www.china.org.cn/english/MATERIAL/76154.htm

Xinhua (2008, July 9). *China's third Arctic expedition ready to sail.* China.org.cn. http://www.china.org.cn/china/sci_tech/2008-07/09/content_15977047.htm

Xinhua (2010, June 26). *China to begin fourth scientific expedition to North Pole.* China Daily. https://www.chinadaily.com.cn/china/2010-06/26/content_10024635.htm

Xinhua (2016, July 11). *China begins 7th Arctic expedition.* China Daily. https://usa.chinadaily.com.cn/china/2016-07/11/content_26045249.htm

Xinhua (2018, July 20). *Icebreaker sets sail on China's 9th Arctic research expedition.* Xinhuanet. http://www.xinhuanet.com/english/2018-07/20/c_137337962.htm

Xinhua (2019, October 1). *Xiangyanghong 01 returns to Qingdao after completing Arctic expedition.* China.org.cn. http://www.china.org.cn/china/2019-10/01/content_75264306.htm

Xinhua (2020, July 16). *China's polar icebreaker sets sail for Arctic*. The State Council Information Office. http://english.scio.gov.cn/m/chinaprojects/2020-07/16/content_76277760.htm

Xinhua (2023, September 10). *Xi stresses striving for full revitalization of northeast China*. Xinhuanet. https://english.news.cn/20230910/389cbdb1029d49a0991adfda8006607c/c.html

Yang, J. (2017), Four impacts of the China-Nordic Arctic research center, In R.W. Corell, J.D. Kim, Y.H. Kim, O.R. Young (Eds.), *The Arctic in world affairs: A North Pacific dialogue on building capacity for a sustainable Arctic in a changing global order (2017 North Pacific Arctic conference proceedings)* (pp. 291–299). Korean Maritime Institute and East-West Center.

Yu, T. (2023, September 27). *China's 13th Arctic Ocean scientific expedition team triumphantly made important progress in independent equipment research and development and other aspects*. Shanghai Observer. https://web-shobserver-com.translate.goog/staticsg/res/html/web/newsDetail.html?id=660824&sid=300&_x_tr_sl=zh-CN&_x_tr_tl=en&_x_tr_hl=en&_x_tr_pto=sc

Zhou, C., & Chen, J. (2015, January 21). *The centre Arctic Ocean: Building fisheries management mechanism as early as possible* (M. Pan, Trans.). China Ocean News. http://www.arcticandnorth.ru/Encyclopedia_Arctic/China%20Ocean%20News%20story.pdf

CHAPTER 4

From Ambition to Reality: Envisioning a Future Greek Arctic Strategy

Apostolos Tsiouvalas and Konstantinos Deligiannis-Virvos

1 Introduction

The Arctic region is on the verge of experiencing changes that will have significant socio-ecological and geopolitical impacts both within the region and beyond it. What were once local issues have now become global concerns. States, as well as non-State actors and corporate entities outside the Arctic, demonstrate an ever-increasing interest in getting involved in Arctic matters. Climate change is an issue affecting different regions around the globe, thus prominently linking different regional responses to it. Especially in the Arctic, anthropogenic climate change is, *inter alia*, directly causing the melting of sea ice in the Arctic Ocean and Greenland's ice sheet – affecting the marine ecosystems and people living in the area in a more rapid and fundamental way compared to other regions in the world (UNEP, 2022, p. 2). Furthermore, the effects of the warming of the Arctic and the related melting of the sea ice have repercussions for other regions too. According to the Intergovernmental Panel on Climate Change (IPCC) 2019 Special Report, the global average sea level will rise by between 0.6 and 1.1 meters by 2100, followed by global coastal erosion. Such changes are driven by changes in both the Arctic and Antarctica due to the loss of the Greenland ice sheet and the melting of Antarctica's glaciers (IPCC, 2019, p. 20). At the same time, the Arctic is warming at almost four times faster than the rest of the globe, primarily due to anthropogenic activities that did not originate in the region (Rantanen et al, 2021). The Arctic's strategic location and abundant natural resources, including oil, gas, and minerals, have long made it an attractive target for exploration and exploitation. Nevertheless, the increased attention to the Arctic means that it will soon, if not already, become a hotspot for additional human activities that include resource extraction, international shipping, and tourism.

In light of an emerging 'global' Arctic, many non-Arctic sovereign States and stakeholders from the Mediterranean region to Southeast Asia have introduced respective agendas (framed as Arctic 'strategies', 'policies' or

 | DOI:10.1163/9789004734685_005

'whitepapers') in order to contribute and get involved in the wider scape of Arctic Governance. This chapter seeks to explore the *status quo* of Greece's (officially the Hellenic Republic) relationship to the Arctic and explore trajectories that could be crucial for the State in further engaging with the region. Greece, a small coastal nation with immense maritime power, has at times made public its interest in becoming part of the Arctic reality. It is unquestionable that Greece will be impacted by what happens in the Arctic, predominantly when it comes to climate change and the State's maritime interests. Despite this, the State has not yet launched an official Arctic policy. This chapter posits that Greece should intensify its interest in delving into Arctic affairs by, *inter alia*, eventually developing a pertinent strategy, in a similar manner to other European Union (EU) and Mediterranean States. Against this background, the chapter first provides a retrospection of Greece's relationship to the region illuminating the existing Greek Arctic engagement (section 2). Subsequently, it sheds light on climate change's ramifications in the Mediterranean region which over the last few decades have been of paramount importance and has already driven several other Mediterranean nations' Arctic agendas (section 3). After setting the scene, section 4 explores strategic pathways for Greece to overcome ongoing barriers to participate in Arctic matters through three main avenues – participation in Arctic fora, international law of the sea, and research and innovation (subsections 4.1–4.3 respectively). Section 5 concludes with a summary of the main steps that the State could take in gaining a foothold in future Arctic matters.

2 Greece and the Arctic

Although Ancient Greeks were not particularly familiar with the region nowadays defined as 'the Arctic', the imaginary High North has been present in ancient Greek mythology and oral tradition from time immemorial. In ancient Greek mythology, the *Hyperboreans* (*Ὑπερβόρειοι*) were the peoples living in the northernmost part of the known world, in a peninsula or island named *Hyperborea*. Herodotus describes these peoples as being in contact with ancient Greeks in the island of Delos, a holy place for the gods Apollo and Artemis, by sending offerings there (Herodotus, n.d., IV, pp. 32–35). According to tradition, *Hyperborea* was a sacred and spiritual place where the god Apollo travelled on an annual basis (Gagnon, 2023).

In this context, the interest of the Greeks in exploring the High North has been expressed for over two millennia. In his piece *Meteorologica* written over 2,350 years ago, Aristotle (384–322 BCE) was the first thinker ever referring to the northern lights, explaining them as a light which resembles the flames of burning gas:

> Sometimes on a fine night we see a variety of appearances that form in the sky: 'chasms' for instance and 'trenches' and blood-red colours [...] For a weak light shining through a dense air, and the air when it acts as a mirror, will cause all kinds of colours to appear, but especially crimson and purple.
>
> ARISTOTLE, *Meteorologica*, Book I, V, 342

According to historians, Aristotle did not travel to the northern part of continental Europe, so there is only limited information about the philosopher's source of knowledge. Shortly before Aristotle's death, another ancient Greek astronomer and geographer, Pytheas of Massalia, became the first Mediterranean person to pursue a scientific expedition in the North Atlantic, and most possibly reached as far north as Iceland and the Arctic Circle (Tsiouvalas, 2022b). Pytheas introduced the idea of a distant 'Thule' to refer to a far more remote *terra incognita* – a geographic imagination denoting a place in the High North, much like previous thinkers have talked about the *Hyperborea*. There is no clear information on what region Pytheas was referring to, but recent interpretations relate the term to sub-Arctic regions such as Orkney, Shetland, northern Scotland, or even the island of Saaremaa (Ösel) in Estonia, and the Norwegian island of Smøla (Kleineberg et al., 2010). Following Pytheas's voyage to the North, Greek thinkers such as Strabo and Eratosthenes referred to the travels of Pytheas and the region that later meant to be named 'the Arctic', originating from the Greek word *ἄρκτος* (arktos = bear) derived from the northern constellation of Ursa Major (Large Bear) (Kleineberg et al., 2010).

Disregarding this premodern genuine interest in circumpolar exploration, in the contemporary political history of the modern State of the Hellenic Republic, which was established in continental Europe only after 1830 (when Greece achieved its independence from the Ottoman Empire under the London Protocol), interest in the Arctic has been minor, if not absent. During the first two centuries of developing as a nation, Greece's engagement with the polar regions has historically been minimal, with the modern State lacking an Arctic strategy that outlines national interests in the region or willingness to contribute to Arctic research. Greece never held a research station in the Arctic (neither in its geographic opposite), nor has it ever led systematized polar expeditions, as many neighbouring States have done in recent years, including Bulgaria, Italy, and Türkiye.

However, under ongoing geopolitical developments and given the major implications of the dramatic changes in the Arctic on the outside world, the State of Greece has more recently expressed an ever-increasing interest in Arctic (and not least Antarctic) matters. The Hellenic Republic is part of the EU which has been long now established as a significant geopolitical player in the High North, and many of its Member States have already demonstrated individual strategic concerns in the region (European Commission, 2021). Greece's Mediterranean neighbours Spain, Italy, and France are amongst the States that have expressed such concerns and have held a long history of active participation in Arctic research and exploration. They currently all hold observer status at the Arctic Council, the most prominent forum for Arctic collaboration. Greece has taken certain steps in order to increase its involvement in Arctic-related matters in recent years but is still lacking a coherent Arctic strategy. These will be discussed in detail in section 4 of this chapter.

3 The Changing Mediterranean

Similar to the polar regions, the Mediterranean Sea is also susceptible to rapid changes caused by climate change. The Mediterranean is warming up towards +1.54°C above pre-industrial values, and future forecasts indicate a warming of around +2.2°C, which is above the global average, a fact that has severe impacts on the biodiversity of the region (UNEP/MAP and Plan Bleu, 2020, p. 9). Many native fish species have started to move northward due to sea warming, while non-native and alien species, such as oceanic puffer (*Lagocephalus*) and lionfish (*Pterois*), have been introduced through the Suez Canal, a sea passage without barriers that supports both ship-mediated translocations and natural migration of species that have been proved to be disastrous for local ecosystems (Coro et. al, 2018, p. 37; Kuhlenkamp and Kind, 2018, p. 495).

Being in its very essence a coastal and maritime nation, environmental changes in Mediterranean waters have so far led to precarious consequences for Greece. While Greece has only 131,957 km^2 land area, its coastline, including the islands, is 13,676 km long and about one third of its population reside at a distance within only 2 km from the coast (Georgiopoulos and Papadimas, 2021). Greece produced 0.2 million metric tonnes of fish with a value of 794.4 million USD in 2018 only, while it is a net exporter of fish and fish products (OECD, 2021, pp. 1–2). Apart from residential areas, 90% of the country's tourism infrastructure is located on the coast (Georgiopoulos and

Papadimas, 2021), along with critical infrastructure for maritime transport not only within Greece but also for international trade.

Resultingly, Greece is already facing the impacts of global climate change which are connected with the rapid changes in both the Arctic and the Mediterranean Sea. The fisheries sector of Greece, even though predominantly based on aquaculture activities, is affected by the aforementioned introduction of alien and invasive species from warmer seas through the Suez Canal. Greece's critical infrastructure located in coastal regions will potentially experience coastal erosion with severe environmental, economic, and societal effects for the local communities (Georgiopoulos and Papadimas, 2021).

Heatwave events have increased in both the Mediterranean and the Arctic regions, along with forest fires and other extreme weather events that have dramatic results for the States' peoples, economies, and ecosystems (Copernicus, 2021; Arctic Council, 2023). Especially in the Arctic, forest fires have increased due to unusually hot and dry conditions, to which the Arctic States were ill-equipped to respond to due to the irregularity of the phenomenon (AMAP, 2021, pp. 16–17; Arctic Council, 2023). Simultaneously, forest fires in the Mediterranean, although they constitute a natural phenomenon, in contrast to the Arctic, are becoming more frequent and catastrophic due to anthropogenic climate change, prolonged droughts, and land abandonment (UNEP/MAP and Plan Bleu, 2020, p. 12; Turco et al. 2018, p. 2). As a result, the drying climate of the Mediterranean is estimated to not only adversely impact coastal communities but also communities in the mainland. The changes to the climate are affecting agricultural production in key areas such as Thessaly and Central Macedonia (Georgopoulos & Papadimas, 2021). The adverse effects caused by climate change and the impacts they have in both regions further underscore the need for Greece to contribute and collaborate in the wide international discussion on global warming and its effects on the polar regions. As various regions of the world undergo rapid and radical changes due to the effects of climate change, it becomes imperative for international cooperation and collaboration to increase, along with a heightened focus from coastal nations on the polar regions, often referred to as the planet's refrigerators.

4 Conceptualizing a Future Greek Arctic Policy

The need for international cooperation in response to global warming is only one among the different reasons for Greece to increase its engagement in Arctic governance. Arctic Governance is a complex system that includes a variety of governance arrangements, treaties, soft law instruments, and the involvement of both state and non-state actors (Koivurova, 2008, p. 16). The Arctic Council is considered the cornerstone of this complex governance system, as a high-level intergovernmental forum under the auspices of which a number of Arctic-related issues are discussed (Bloom, 1999, p. 715). The Arctic Council consists of the eight Arctic States (the USA, Canada, Iceland, Norway, Sweden, Finland, Denmark, and Russia) as Member States and six member organizations representing the Arctic Indigenous peoples as Permanent Participants. In addition, thirteen non-Arctic States have observer status in the Arctic Council, as well as a number of intergovernmental, interparliamentary, and non-governmental organizations. As of the time of writing, the EU does not hold observer status but "observes Arctic Council proceedings", with a final decision of the Ministers of the Arctic States about the EU's status pending (Arctic Council, n.d.; Stępień & Koivurova (2017), pp. 18 and 27.).

As mentioned earlier, and in contrast with other EU Mediterranean States, like Spain, France, and Italy, which have already obtained observer's status in the Arctic Council, Greece has not yet developed an Arctic strategy. Greece, along with Switzerland, Türkiye, and Mongolia, have also applied to obtain Observer Status in the Arctic Council – an application that was discussed during the 9th Ministerial Meeting of the Arctic Council in Iqaluit, Nunavut, in April 2015 (Knecht, 2015). The applications of the four States were initially denied, even though Switzerland attained the Observer Status later, at the 2017 Fairbanks Ministerial meeting (Fairbanks Declaration, 2017, para. 44). Even though the former Greek Prime Minister and Minister of Foreign Affairs reiterated Greece's interest in applying for the Observer Status in the Arctic Council in 2016 and 2017 (Tsiouvalas, 2022b), Greece has not made a new official submission to the Council since then.

Should Greece also decide to formalize a will to engage within Arctic Governance, certain premises need however to be met. In accordance with the Arctic Council's rules of procedure as revised at the 8th Ministerial Meeting in Kiruna, a State that wishes to attain observer status in the Arctic Council shall comply with several basic principles as reflected therein. These include, *inter alia*, the support of local and Indigenous peoples' traditions and cultures, the contribution to the sustainable development of the Arctic region, including economic and social development, and a commitment to the protection of the Arctic environment, including the health of Arctic ecosystems, maintenance or biodiversity in the Arctic region, and the conservation and sustainable use of natural resources (Arctic Council, 2013).

It is to be noted, however, that demonstrating interest in Arctic affairs and substantially implementing them constitute two different commitments. In these terms, three main areas of interest seem to be most promising in light of a forthcoming Greek Arctic Strategy: 1) Participation in Arctic fora and international treaties applicable in the Arctic; 2) Peace and collaboration in the sea; 3) Research and innovation.

4.1 *Participation in Arctic Fora and International Treaties Applicable to the Arctic*

The Arctic region is famously governed by a number of multilateral treaties and conventions which were either specifically negotiated in order to apply therein or have a more universal focus which naturally includes the Arctic. Greece, being a State with significant presence in international fora and willing to promote the rule of international law around the world, is a State Party to a number of treaties applicable to the Arctic and international organizations that have significant presence in the region. First and foremost, the Hellenic Republic has ratified the United Nations Convention on the Law of the Sea (UNCLOS) in 1995. UNCLOS has been famously described as the "constitution of the oceans" (Koh, 1985, pp. 11–16), a multilateral treaty that regulates uses of the oceans and the protection and preservation of the marine environment (particularly in Part XII of the Convention). In this regard, UNCLOS has further established an Arctic-related provision which is referring to ice-covered areas, namely Article 234, the wording of which was predominantly shaped by the two Cold War superpowers, along with Canada that always had a keen interest in the region (Tsiouvalas 2022a, p. 88). Article 234 has been described as the "Arctic exception" of UNCLOS (Bartenstein, 2011, p. 23), even if it does not refer to the Arctic per se and governs the navigational regime in ice-covered waters

> [...] where particularly severe climatic conditions and the presence of ice covering such areas for most of the year create obstructions or exceptional hazards to navigation, and pollution of the marine environment could cause major harm to or irreversible disturbance of the ecological balance [...].
>
> UNCLOS, Article 234

The Arctic coastal States have committed to the legal framework formulated by UNCLOS (Ilulissat Declaration, 2008). Even the US, which is not a Party to UNCLOS, considers certain provisions of it as customary international law (Rothwell, 2018, p. 12).

As for Arctic-specific treaties, Greece has ratified the Svalbard Treaty as early as 21 October 1925. According to Articles 2 and 3 of the Svalbard Treaty, "ships and nationals of all the High Contracting Parties shall enjoy equally the rights of fishing and hunting in the territories specified in Article 1 and in their territorial waters" and nationals of the contracting parties shall have equal liberty of access and "may carry maritime, industrial, mining and commercial operations on a footing of absolute equality" (Svalbard Treaty, 1920). Like most State Parties of the Svalbard Treaty, the Hellenic Republic has not made use of the rights that are provided therein, but its ratification of the treaty is rather seen as a recognition of the sovereignty of Norway over the archipelago in accordance with Article 1 of the Treaty.

Importantly, Greece is one of the 27 Member States of the EU. The EU has a foothold on the Arctic by virtue of Sweden and Finland which are also Member States, while Norway and Iceland are two of the three Member States of the European Economic Area (the third being Lichtenstein). The EU has famously tried to increase its involvement in Arctic governance. According to the new EU Arctic Policy that was introduced in October 2021, the EU aims to contribute to the peace and stability of the region, address the ecological, social, economic and political challenges arising as a consequence of climate change, take strong action to tackle climate change and environmental degradation, and support the inclusive and sustainable development of the Arctic region to the benefit of its inhabitants and future generations (European Commission, 2021, p. 2).

As an EU Member State, Greece also follows this EU Arctic Strategy and may in the future pursue a comprehensive Arctic policy. Furthermore, Greece is bound by the provisions of the 2018 Agreement to Prevent Unregulated High Seas Fisheries in the Central Arctic Ocean (Central Arctic Ocean Fisheries Agreement / CAOFA, 2018) ratified by the EU. The CAOFA was negotiated by the five Arctic littoral States along with China, Iceland, Japan, South Korea, and the EU. The EU has exclusive competence on the conservation of marine biological resources under its Common Fisheries Policy (CFP) and shared competence for fisheries, with the exception of the conservation of marine biological resources (TFEU, 2007, Arts. 3 and 4). Under its exclusive competence, the EU negotiated the CAOFA with the rest of its signatories in a process that aims to

> prevent unregulated fishing in the high seas portion of the central Arctic Ocean through the application of precautionary conservation and management measures as part of a long-term strategy to safeguard

> healthy marine ecosystems and to ensure the conservation and sustainable use of fish stocks.
>
> CAOFA, 2018, Art. 2

Not of least importance for the contribution of a non-Arctic State in the system of Arctic Governance is a State's approach to Arctic Indigenous peoples. The EU Arctic Strategy prioritizes people living in the Arctic and especially Indigenous peoples. It specifically intends on investing

> in the future of people living in the Arctic, stimulating better education, sustainable growth and jobs, including more involvement of young people, women and Indigenous Peoples in Arctic decision-making, on issues such as innovation and research, job creation, digital skills and education.
>
> EUROPEAN COMMISSION, 2021 p. 13

Recently, the Saami Council succeeded in its engagement through the EU consultation mechanism, which has helped the Saami people have their voice heard on key EU initiatives such as the EU Farm to Fork Strategy, the EU Biodiversity Strategy, the Just Transition Fund, and the European Climate Pact (DG MARE, 2022).

The Hellenic Republic does not have any populations recognized as Indigenous within its national territory. It has nevertheless voted in favor of the United Nations Declaration on the Rights of Indigenous Peoples (UNDRIP) in 2007 (UN DESA, n.d.). UNDRIP provides a comprehensive human rights framework for indigenous human rights and affirms that Indigenous peoples have the right to self-determination (Dorough, 2019, p.82). The UNDRIP is also considered an integral part of EU human rights policy, and as such, it is also acknowledged in the EU's Arctic Policy (EU Arctic Policy, 2021, p. 14). In addition to the soft law of UNDRIP, the 1989 Indigenous and Tribal Peoples Convention (No. 169) of the International Labour Organization (ILO) is directly relevant to Arctic Indigenous peoples. Due to the fact that there is not an indigenous population recognized in Greece, the State has not ratified the ILO Convention No. 169. It could thus further assure its support towards the rights of Arctic Indigenous peoples by ratifying the Convention in the same way as other EU States such as Denmark, Spain, Luxembourg, and most recently Germany – with the last three also not being home to any indigenous groups (ILO, 2022).

4.2 *Peace and Collaboration in the Sea*

The changing conditions of the Arctic and the melting of sea ice have contributed to the development new Arctic shipping routes with far-reaching geopolitical premises. The Northwest Passage and the Northern Sea Route (along with a potentially viable Transpolar Sea Route) are famous examples of passages that are utilized by the Arctic littoral States in order to attract more international trade (Rothwell, 2018, p. 17). For ships carrying commercial cargo, these previously inaccessible routes offer the chance to considerably reduce journey distances. In addition, the intensification of tourism, resource extraction, as well as expanding energy consumption in many areas around the Arctic region constitute different driving sources of maritime traffic (Deggim, 2018, p. 16). The 2009 ministerial meeting of the Arctic Council approved and published the Arctic Marine Shipping Assessment (AMSA) which was produced by the Protection of the Arctic Marine Environment (PAME) working group. According to the database established by PAME for the AMSA, there were approximately 6.000 vessels operating in the Arctic region in 2004, with almost 50% of which being fishing vessels (PAME, 2009, p. 72; Brigham, 2010, p. 163). Since then, the traffic of vessels entering Arctic waters has increased. Between the period 2013–2019 PAME has identified a 25% increase in traffic, a trend that is continuing to this day (PAME, 2020, p. 10).

While Greece is a relatively small country, the Greek shipping industry is undoubtedly the leading industry of the global maritime sector. According to the Union of Greek Shipowners (UGS), it is estimated that approximately 21% of global tonnage is owned by Greek shipowners, while Greece is the 8th largest ship registry in the world (UGS, 2019, p. 8). As such, Greek shipping is not only facilitating Greek interests, but also plays a major role in international trade and contributes heavily to the EU economy and maritime interests. As a major shipping State, Greece has been an important member of the International Maritime Organization (IMO) since 1958, when it became a Member State of the organization. Its presence in the IMO is important and follows its position as a global maritime power. For example, regarding the 2022–2023 biennium, the IMO Assembly elected Greece as a member of its Council (IMO, n.d.). The IMO Council is the executive organ of the Organization, and it mainly coordinates the work of the various IMO committees and organs, while it also performs the Assembly's functions when it is not in session, with the exception of the power to make recommendations (Chircop, 2015, p. 422). Greece was elected to the Council under its characterization as a "Category A State". Category A States are the ten

States with the largest interest in providing international shipping services (IMO, n.d.).

Greece's prominent position within the IMO ensures its involvement with those Arctic-related issues that are featured in IMO's work. Ever since 2002, the IMO has been working continuously to create a comprehensive regime for navigation and international shipping in the Arctic. The first step in that direction was the adoption of the non-binding IMO Guidelines for Ships Operating in Arctic Ice-Covered Waters (IMO, 2002; Symonides, 2015, p. 231). Afterwards, the IMO adopted the 2009 Guidelines for Ships Operating in Polar Waters that also included regulations on navigation in the waters surrounding Antarctica (IMO, 2009). Finally, on 1 January 2017, the International Code for Ships Operating in Polar Waters (Polar Code) entered into force as an amendment to the 1973/1978 MARPOL and 1974 SOLAS Conventions, while its provisions that amended the 1984 STCW Convention entered into force on 1 July 2018 (IMO, 2015; Williams, 2019, pp. 392–393). The Polar Code provisions are mainly containing construction, design, equipment, and manning standards aimed at ships navigating Arctic and Antarctic waters with the goal to ensure safety of navigation and the protection of the polar ecosystems. In case Greek-owned or Greek-flagged ships are navigating in the Arctic waters, they thus have to adhere to the Polar Code provisions applicable, in order to better protect and preserve the fragile marine environment of the region.

In this regard, the Union of Greek Shipowners (UGS) constitutes an important non-state actor that was recently involved with Arctic-related matters by becoming a member of the Arctic Economic Council (AEC) in 2018 (UGS, 2019, p. 18). The UGS was first established in 1916 and represents Greek-owned vessels of over 3,000 gross tonnage. Vessels represented may sail under Greek or other European and third country flags and are mainly bulk carriers, tankers, LNG/LPG carriers, or containerships (UGS, 2021, p. 30). While representing Greek-owned ships and shipowners, the UGS supports and fosters policies ensuring safety of life at sea in accordance with SOLAS, and environmental sustainability in accordance with IMO's environmental conventions, while at the same time it supports a dynamic and competitive business environment, and free trade facilitated by global rules and regulations (UGS, 2021, p. 30). The UGS closely follows developments within the IMO, as well as other international organizations such as the ILO, the Organisation for Economic Co-operation and Development (OECD), and the International Chamber of Commerce. It is also a member of the International Chamber of Shipping and the European Community

Shipowners' Associations and participates in the European Economic and Social Committee and the Economic and Social Council of Greece. In addition, it collaborates with the International Association of Classification Societies and individual classification societies. It is within this wide framework of international collaboration and advancement of sustainable practices for shipping, that the UGS was accepted as a member of the AEC in 2018 (UGS, 2021, p. 30).

The AEC on its part, was created during the Canadian chairmanship of the Arctic Council in 2013–2015 as an independent international business membership organization. Its stated goals are to "facilitate responsible business and economic development of the Arctic and its communities; share and advocate for best practices, technological solutions, and standards; support market accessibility; [and] provide advice and a business perspective to the work of the Arctic Council" (AEC, 2020, p. 4).

By joining the AEC, the UGS wished to contribute to the holistic approach of the organization towards the different issues affecting the Arctic by offering insights on ship operation and navigation, safety at sea, and the protection of the marine environment. The AEC welcomed this addition and acknowledged the importance of extending the geographical scope of the Council to Greece, a move that was seen as facilitating the sustainable economic development of the Arctic through collaboration and active engagement on a global level (AEC, n.d.). The participation of the UGS in the Arctic Economic Council can help achieve those goals and bring Greek policies and interests closer to the Arctic region by utilizing the leading sector of the country.

Greece's interest in maritime commerce and free trade is undisputed. In the same way, Greece is interested in a coherent and stable global ocean governance. As it was already noted, the Arctic coastal States have stated in the Ilulissat Declaration that the law of the sea is the primal tool that governs the Arctic Ocean (Ilulissat Declaration, 2008). Greece's official position is that all matters regarding maritime delimitation and uses of the sea should be solved on the basis of the international law of the sea (Hellenic Republic, n.d.). As such, its position is aligned with the position of the Arctic littoral States as expressed in the Ilulissat Declaration regarding the peaceful collaboration of States in accordance with international law, in order to better protect and preserve the fragile Arctic marine ecosystems.

In this regard, Greece is actively promoting the rule of international law in the Mediterranean. The geopolitical reality in the area, especially in the eastern Mediterranean, however, reveals existing barriers for the region's

States regarding maritime collaboration, security, and ocean governance. The maritime boundaries in the eastern Mediterranean are not fully delimited, in contrast with the Arctic where most maritime delimitation disputes have already been peacefully settled (Østhagen and Schofield, 2021, p. 11). Regarding Greece, a significant development in this direction was the 2020 delimitation agreement of a maritime boundary with Italy that settled the maritime boundary of the Exclusive Economic Zones of the two States (Agreement between the Government of the Hellenic Republic and the Italian Republic on the Delimitation of their Respective Maritime Zones, 2020). The resolution of the rest of the enduring disputes in the eastern Mediterranean, in particular in the Aegean Sea with its neighbouring State Türkiye, will be an important milestone for Greece, and not least Türkiye, to demonstrate their credibility and capacity to collaborate and engage in peaceful dialogue regarding ocean governance.

4.3 *Research and Innovation*

Over the last few decades, the Arctic has been of utmost importance to global scientific research that wishes to address these changes and provide potential solutions because of the rapid changes of the Arctic environment have repercussions not only for the region itself and its people but also globally. It is expected that innovative technologies, such as satellites, big data, artificial intelligence, and advanced modelling, are likely to transform the Arctic economy and societies by further enabling the different sectors to improve their sustainability or give rise to new sectors in the Arctic such as blue technologies, offshore renewable energy, hydrogen, and maritime security (European Commission, 2021, p. 12). As environmental and ecological changes in the polar regions have direct ramifications on the Mediterranean climate and ecosystems, another appropriate way for the Greek State to approach the region is thus by undertaking Arctic scientific research.

The Arctic States have themselves already recognized the importance of science and innovation in the area by signing the Agreement on Enhancing International Arctic Scientific Cooperation on 11 May 2017 (Arctic Scientific Cooperation Agreement, 2017). The Arctic Scientific Cooperation Agreement covers scientific activities relating to the Arctic as defined in its Article 1, promotes international cooperation in such activities and is applicable in the designated Arctic region as an integral area for the promotion of science, without distinguishing between land, sea, and airspace (Arctic Scientific Cooperation Agreement, 2017, Art. 1; Shibata, 2019, p. 207). As noted by Shibata (2019), albeit the Arctic Scientific Cooperation Agreement was not open for signing to other, non-Arctic States, it is nevertheless reflecting the necessity of scientific cooperation for the region. In its preamble, the Agreement still explicitly recognizes "the significant scientific expertise and invaluable contributions to scientific activities being made by non-Parties and specifically by the Arctic Council Permanent Participants and Arctic Council Observers" (Shibata, 2019, p. 217–218). Importantly, the Agreement is without prejudice to the rights and obligations of States regarding marine scientific research as stipulated in UNCLOS, thus promoting international cooperation in Arctic marine scientific research consistent with those rights and obligation of both coastal States and researching States, regardless of whether they are Arctic or non-Arctic States (Shibata, 2019, p. 214).

Scientific research such as marine scientific research activities regulated by the provisions of Part XIII of UNCLOS, facilitates a better understanding of the marine environment and ecosystems (UNCLOS, Part XIII). In a similar manner, climate research projects are vital in the efforts to identify the effect of human activities on the environment and tackle the effects of climate change in the Arctic and other regions of the globe. The EU's Arctic Strategy highlights this need for scientific research within the Arctic. The EU invested around EUR 200 million in Arctic-related research under its program 'Horizon 2020' between 2014 and 2020, and is supporting Arctic science via the Horizon Europe Programme for the period 2021–2027 (European Commission, 2021, p. 12) More recently, it intends to contribute EUR 2.4 million in order to develop scientific advice for fisheries beyond the EU Member States waters and develop and implement of the Joint Program of Scientific Research and Monitoring for High Seas Fisheries in the Central Arctic Ocean (UN DESA, 2023). Even though Greece at the time being is not undertaking any scientific research projects in the Arctic, future engagement with the development of transnational scientific collaboration in the protection of the marine environment and safety of life at sea could further increase Greece's credibility in Arctic fora.

Many persons from non-Arctic States, non-governmental entities, and institutions are currently conducting research in Arctic-related issues. In Greece, the Research and Innovation Centre in Information, Communication and Knowledge Technologies (ATHENA RC) is a partner to the International Network for Terrestrial Research and Monitoring in the Arctic (INTER-ACT), an EU-funded project that aims to build capacity for identifying, understanding, predicting, and responding to diverse environmental changes throughout the wide environmental and landuse envelopes of the

Arctic (Athena Research Center, n.d.). Furthermore, individual Greek researchers are active in Arctic and polar scientific research of various institutions outside Greece, while, since 2012, the Hellenic Polar Zones Society (ELEPOZ), has been active, bringing along Greek polar scientists representing a variety of scientific fields. ELEPOZ organizes annual scientific events with focus on circumpolar research, and increasingly engages in influencing governance instruments towards polar-oriented policymaking (ELEPOZ, n.d.).

However, coherent and institutionalized Arctic research efforts by State authorities remain – so far – underdeveloped and beyond the corresponding ministry's current agenda. As the vast amounts that have been invested by the EU in Arctic research show, conducting research in the region is highly priced. The Arctic is still characterized by harsh climatic conditions and vast remoteness that necessitate the use of modern technologies required for conducting research in compliance with the needs of the region's fragile ecosystems. In the aftermath of over a decade-long economic crisis that drastically impacted Greece's overall participation in international scientific collaboration, such initiatives necessitate political will and planning in a very prudent way.

5 Conclusions: Towards a Future Greek Arctic Policy

At first glance, it is arguable that Greece's present foreign policy has little to do with the Arctic region, due to its geographical distance and lack of a coherent strategy pertinent to issues affecting the polar regions. However, the popular proverb "what happens in the Arctic does not stay in the Arctic" holds true for many issues, inviting thus more non-Arctic States to get involved in Arctic governance. This chapter highlighted a threefold way forward for the Hellenic Republic to be involved in the Arctic. The first is to get involved in policy-making *fora* and international arenas that are facilitating Arctic governance. If Greece can demonstrate political will to contribute to the work of the Arctic Council, it could submit an updated application to obtain Observer Status therein. Although the Arctic Council had temporarily paused all official meetings of the Council and its subsidiary bodies due to the ongoing war in Ukraine during the period February 2022 - May 2023. At the time of writing, it has resumed its activities under the Norwegian chairmanship. Succeeding Russia, Norway took over the chairmanship of the Arctic Council from May 2023 for the following two years, and the Arctic States seem willing to re-engage with the Council's mandate. It can be asserted that in the future the imperative need for perpetuating co-operation in the Arctic may make room in the Council for additional non-Arctic observer States with a strong interest in Arctic dialogue.

In the same regard, being a Member State of the EU, Greece is already committed to European and global initiatives for the fight against climate change, echoing the EU's aspirations for an EU Green Deal and the interrelated EU Arctic Strategy. In support of the implementation of the EU's Arctic strategy, Member States should however demonstrate individual willingness to engage with the region in their own national policies and identify nuances that could render them important players in the North. Thus, the EU constitutes an open and easy-to-access foothold for Greece in the Arctic.

Greece is in a prominent position to also increase its involvement in issues of Arctic Ocean governance by taking advantage of its unique status as one of the strongest maritime nations in the world, as well as its constant devotion to the rule of law, and especially the law of the sea, as the backbone of ocean governance. The opening up of navigational routes in the Arctic gives great leeway for Greece to capitalize on its maritime sector and provide invaluable insights and knowledge on facilitating maritime trade within and through the Arctic Ocean.

Greece may further make use of research opportunities that are open for non-Arctic States in either its state capacity or by utilizing non-state actors that may wish to be involved in Arctic-related issues. Even though such projects may prove to be high-priced for a State, they remain necessary not only for an involvement in different regions and fields, like the Arctic, but also to facilitate a better understanding of climate change and issues of governance, the lessons of which may be applied both internationally and nationally. In a similar way to the polar regions, the Mediterranean remains one of the regions mostly affected by climate change, a situation that will surely be worsened in the decades to come.

With the local challenges of the Arctic becoming global, Greece would thus gain a lot by formalizing its engagement with Arctic matters. For a State like Greece without a polar tradition and missing an institutionalized unified approach to Arctic affairs, asserting its position on the Arctic stage necessitates strategic planning, economic investments, and constructive collaboration with actors already established in the region. International law, maritime navigation, science and collaboration, and support of the region's peoples and ecosystems may thus be key elements in justifying the formulation of a future 'Hellenic Arctic agenda'.

Bibliography

Agreement between the Government of the Hellenic Republic and the Italian Republic on the Delimitation of their Respective Maritime Zones (adopted 9 June 2020, entered into force 8 November 2021). https://www.un.org/depts/los/LEGISLATIONANDTREATIES/STATEFILES/GRC.htm

Agreement on Enhancing International Arctic Scientific Cooperation, (adopted 11 May 2017, entered into force 23 May 2018).

Agreement to Prevent Unregulated High Seas Fisheries in the Central Arctic Ocean (adopted 3 October 2018, entered into force 25 June 2021) [CAOFA 2018].

Arctic Council (n.d.). *List of Arctic Council observers*, Arctic Council. https://arctic-council.org/about/observers/

Arctic Council (1996). Declaration on the establishment of the Arctic Council [Ottawa Declaration]. http://hdl.handle.net/11374/85

Arctic Council (1998/2013). Arctic Council rules of procedure. http://hdl.handle.net/11374/940

Arctic Council (2017). Fairbanks Declaration 2017 on the occasion of the tenth ministerial meeting of the Arctic Council, http://hdl.handle.net/11374/1910

Arctic Council (2023). *Norwegian chairship launches initiative to address wildland fires in the Arctic.* Arctic Council. https://arctic-council.org/news/norwegian-chairship-arctic-wildland-fires-initiative/

Arctic Economic Council (AEC) (n.d.). *Press release: AEC welcomes two new members from Greece and Nunavut, Canada.* Arctic Economic Council. https://arcticeconomiccouncil.com/news/press-release-aec-welcomes-two-new-members-from-greece-and-nunavut-canada/

Arctic Economic Council (AEC) (2020), Rules of procedure (adopted as of September 2020, Amended at the Arctic Economic Council Governance Committee meeting in 2017, 2018, 2019 and 2020). https://arcticeconomiccouncil.com/wp-content/uploads/2020/10/AEC_-Rules-of-Procedure_FINAL.pdf

Aristotle (1951). *Meteorologica* (Book I, V). Harvard University Press.

Athena Research Center (n.d.), *International network for terrestrial research and monitoring in the Arctic.* Athena. https://www.athenarc.gr/en/projects/international-network-terrestrial-research-and-monitoring-arctic

Bartenstein, K. (2011). The "Arctic Exception" in the law of the sea convention: A contribution to safer navigation in the northwest passage? *Ocean Development and International Law* 42(1–2), 22–52. https://doi.org/10.1080/00908320.2011.542104

Bloom, E.T. (1999). Establishment of the Arctic Council. *The American Journal of International Law*, *93*(3), 712–722. https://doi.org/10.2307/2555272

Brigham, L.W. (2010). The Arctic Council's Arctic marine shipping assessment. In M. H. Nordquist, T.H. Heidar, & J. Norton Moore (Eds.), *Changes in the Arctic Environment and the Law of the Sea* (pp. 159–176). Martinus Nijhoff. https://doi.org/10.1163/ej.9789004177567.i-594.47

Chircop, A. (2015). The international maritime organization. In D.R. Rothwell, A.G. Oude Elferink, K.N. Scott, & T. Stephens (Eds.), *The Oxford Handbook of the Law of the Sea* (pp. 416–438). Oxford University Press.

Consolidated version of the Treaty on the Functioning of the European Union (adopted 13 December 2007, entered into force 1 December 2009), OJ L. 326/47–326/390. [TFEU 2007]

Copernicus (2021, October 21). *OBSERVER: Unprecedented mobilisation of Copernicus EMS during the 2021 Mediterranean wildfire crisis.* Copernicus. https://www.copernicus.eu/en/news/news/observer-unprecedented-mobilisation-copernicus-ems-during-2021-mediterranean-wildfire

Coro, G., Vilas, L.G., Magliozzi, C., Ellenbroek, A., Scarponi, P., & Pagano, P. (2018). Forecasting the ongoing invasion of *Lagocephalus sceleratus* in the Mediterranean Sea. *Ecological modelling, 371*, 37–49. https://doi.org/10.1016/j.ecolmodel.2018.01.007

Deggim, H. (2018). The international code for ships operating in polar waters (polar code). In L.P. Hildebrand, L.W. Brigham, & T.M. Johansson (Eds.) *Sustainable Shipping in a Changing Arctic* (pp. 15–35) (WMU Studies in Maritime Affairs, Volume 7). Springer. https://doi.org/10.1007/978-3-319-78425-0_2

Directorate-General for Maritime Affairs and Fisheries (DG MARE) (2022, July 26). *EU Helps the Sámi getting their voice heard.* European Commission https://oceans-and-fisheries.ec.europa.eu/news/eu-helps-sami-getting-their-voice-heard-2022-07-26_en

Dorough, D.S. (2019). Our homeland: Arctic indigenous people's perspectives on non-Arctic states. In A. Shibata, L. Zou, N. Sellheim, & M. Scopelliti (Eds.), *Emerging legal orders in the Arctic: The role of non-Arctic actors* (Routledge Research in Polar Law, pp. 69–90). Routledge.

European Commission, High Representative of the Union for Foreign Affairs and Security Policy (2021). *A stronger EU engagement for a peaceful, sustainable and prosperous Arctic*, Joint Communication to the European Parliament, the Council, the European Economic and Social Committee and the Committee of the Regions, 13 October 2021. https://www.eeas.europa.eu/sites/default/files/documents/Joint%20Communication%20on%20a%20stronger%20EU%20engagement%20for%20a%20peaceful%2C%20sustainable%20and%20prosperous%20Arctic.pdf.pdf

Gagnon, B.H. (2023, June 14). *In the Arctic, a 2500-year-old Greek myth is coming true.* Patheos. https://www.patheos.com/blogs/adventuresinecomythology/2023/06/in-the-arctic-a-2500-year-old-greek-myth-is-coming-true/

Georgiopoulos, G., & Papadimas, L. (2021, November 4) *After debt crisis, Greek economy faces climate change threats.* Ekathimerini. Retrieved 1 May 2023, from https://www.ekathimerini.com/society/1171121/after-debt-crisis-greek-economy-faces-climate-change-threats/

Hellenic Polar Zones Society (ELEPOZ) (n.d.), About us. Retrieved 1 May 2023, from https://www.elepoz.com/about

Hellenic Republic (n.d.), Greek-Turkish dispute over the delimitation of the continental shelf, Retrieved 5 August 2024, from https://www.mfa.gr/en/foreign-policy/foreign-policy-issues/issues-of-greek-turkish-relations/greek-turkish-dispute-over-the-delimitation-of-the-continental-shelf/

Herodotus (n.d.). *Ἱστορίαι* [Histories]. Αρχαία Ελληνική Γλώσσα και Γραμματεία [Ancient Greek Language and Literature]. Retrieved 12 December 2024, from https://www.greek-language.gr/digitalResources/ancient_greek/library/browse.html?text_id=30&page=100

Ilulissat Declaration (2008). 48 *ILM* 382 (2009).

Intergovernmental Panel on Climate Change (IPCC) (2019). *Special report on the ocean and cryosphere in a changing climate: Sea level rise and implications for low-lying islands, coasts and communities. Summary for policymakers.* https://www.ipcc.ch/srocc/chapter/summary-for-policymakers/

International Convention for the Prevention of Pollution from Ships as modified by the Protocol of 1978 (adopted 17 February 1978, entered into force 2 October 1983) 1340 UNTS 61 and 1341 UNTS 3. [MARPOL 1973/1978]

International Convention for the Safety of Life at Sea (adopted 1 November 1974, entered into force 25 May 1980), 1184 UNTS 278. [SOLAS 1974]

International Convention on Standards of Training, Certification and Watchkeeping for Seafarers (adopted 7 July 1978, entered into force 28 April 1984), 1361 UNTS 2. [STCW 1978]

International Labour Organization (ILO). Convention (No. 169) concerning Indigenous and Tribal Peoples in Independent Countries (adopted 27 June 1989, entered into force 5 September 1991). [ILO Convention No. 169]

International Labour Organization (ILO) (2022). Ratifications of C169 – Indigenous and tribal peoples convention, 1989 (No. 169).Retrieved 1 May 2023, from https://www.ilo.org/dyn/normlex/en/f?p=NORMLEXPUB:11300:0::NO::P11300_INSTRUMENT_ID:312314

International Maritime Organization (IMO) (n.d.). Council Members. Retrieved 1 May 2023, from https://www.imo.org/en/OurWork/ERO/Pages/Council-Members.aspx

International Maritime Organization (IMO) (2002). Guidelines for ships operating in Arctic ice-covered waters. IMO Doc. MSC/ Circ.1056– MEPC/ Circ.399.

International Maritime Organization (IMO) (2009). Guidelines for ships operating in polar waters. IMO Doc. A26/Res.1024.

International Maritime Organization (IMO) (2015). International code for ships operating in polar waters. IMO Doc. MSC 385(94) – MEPC 68/21/Add.1, Annex 10 [Polar Code].

Kleineberg, A., Marx, C., & Lelgemann, D. (2010). *Germania und die Insel Thule. Die Entschlüsselung von Ptolemaios' "Atlas der Oikumene"* [Germania and the island of Thule. The decryption of Ptolemy's "Atlas of the Oikumene"]. Wissenschaftliche Buchgesellschaft.

Knecht, S. (2015). *New observers queuing up: Why the Arctic Council should expand – and expel.* The Arctic Institute. https://www.thearcticinstitute.org/new-observers-queuing-up/

Koh, T. (1985). A constitution for the oceans. In M. Nordquist (Ed.), *United Nations Convention on the Law of the Sea 1982: A Commentary. Volume 1* (pp. 11–16). Martinus Nijhoff.

Koivurova, T. (2008). Alternatives for an Arctic treaty – Evaluation and a new proposal. *Review of European Community & International Environmental Law*, *17*(1), 14–26. https://doi.org/10.1111/j.1467-9388.2008.00580.x

Kuhlenkamp, R., & Kind, B. (2018). Introduction of non-indigenous species. In M. Salomon, & T. Markus (Eds.), *Handbook on marine environmental protection: Science, impacts and sustainable management* (pp. 487–516). Springer. https://doi.org/10.1007/978-3-319-60156-4_25

Marco, T., Rosa-Cánovas, J.J., Bedia, J., Jerez, S., Montávez, J.P., Llasat, M.S., & Provenzale, A. (2018). Exacerbated fires in Mediterranean Europe due to anthropogenic warming projected with non-stationary climate-fire models. *Nature Communications*, *9*, 3821. https://doi.org/10.1038/s41467-018-06358-z

Organization for Economic Co-operation and Development (OECD) (2021, January). *Fisheries and aquaculture in Greece.* Retrieved 1 May 2023, from https://www.oecd.org/agriculture/topics/fisheries-and-aquaculture/documents/report_cn_fish_grc.pdf

Østhagen, A., & Schofield, C.H. (2021). The Arctic Ocean: Boundaries and disputes. Arctic Yearbook, [*2021*], 1–17. https://arcticyearbook.com/images/yearbook/2021/Scholarly-Papers/1_AY2021_Osthagen_Schofield.pdf

Protection of the Arctic Marine Environment (PAME) (2009). Arctic marine shipping assessment. http://hdl.handle.net/11374/54

Protection of the Arctic Marine Environment (PAME) (2020, March 31). *The increase in arctic shipping 2013–2019: Arctic shipping status report* (*ASSR*) *#1*. PAME. https://pame.is/document-library/pame-reports-new/pame-ministerial-deliverables/2021-12th-arctic-council-ministerial-meeting-reykjavik-iceland/793-assr-1-the-increase-in-arctic-shipping-2013-2019/file

Rantanen, M., Karpechko, A.Y., Lipponen, A., Nordling, K., Hyvärinen, O., Ruosteenoja, K., Vihma, T., & Laaksonen, A. (2022). The Arctic has warmed nearly four times faster than the globe since 1979. *Communications Earth & Environment, 3*, 168. https://doi.org/10.1038/s43247-022-00498-3

Rothwell, D.R. (2018). *Arctic Ocean shipping: Navigation, security and sovereignty in the North American Arctic* (Brill Research Perspectives). Brill.

Shibata, A. (2019). The Arctic science cooperation agreement: A perspective from non-Arctic actors. A. Shibata, L. Zou, N. Sellheim, & M. Scopelliti (Eds.), *Emerging legal orders in the Arctic: The role of non-Arctic actors* (Routledge Research in Polar Law, pp. 207–225). Routledge.

Stępień, A., & Koivurova, T. (2017). Formulating a cross-cutting policy: Challenges and opportunities for effective EU Arctic policy-making. In N. Liu, E.A. Kirk, & T Henriksen (Eds.), *The European Union and the Arctic* (Publications on Ocean Development, Volume 85, pp. 9–39). Brill Nijhoff. https://doi.org/10.1163/9789004349179_003

Symonides, J. (2015). Problems and controversies concerning freedom of navigation in the Arctic. In L. del Castillo (Ed.) *Law of the Sea, from Grotius to the International Tribunal for the Law of the Sea: Liber Amicorum Judge Hugo Caminos* (pp. 225–242). Brill Nijhoff. https://doi.org/10.1163/9789004283787_016

Treaty concerning the Archipelago of Spitsbergen (adopted 9 February 1920, entered into force 14 August 1925) 2 LNTS 7. [1920 Svalbard Treaty]

Tsiouvalas, A. (2022a). Recalcitrant materialities of a liminal ocean: Deconstructing the 'Arctic Nomos'. *The Yearbook of Polar Law, 14*, 76–97. https://doi.org/10.1163/22116427_014010005

Tsiouvalas, A, (2022b, September 6). *Towards a Greek Arctic policy? The pathway for a Mediterranean state to the Arctic*. The Arctic Institute. https://www.thearcticinstitute.org/towards-greek-arctic-policy-pathway-mediterranean-state-arctic/

Union of Greek Shipowners (UGS) (2019). Greek shipping: A major EU export industry of strategic importance. https://www.ugs.gr/media/13634/eee_brochure.pdf

Union of Greek Shipowners (UGS) (2021). Annual report 2020–21, https://www.ugs.gr/media/13707/ugs_ar21_eng_lowres.pdf

United Nations Convention on Law of the Sea (adopted 10 December 1982, entered into force 16 November 1994), 1833 UNTS 3. [UNCLOS]

United Nations, Department of Economic and Social Affairs (UN DESA) (n.d.). *United Nations declaration on the rights of indigenous peoples. Historical Overview.* Retrieved 1 May 2023, from https://social.desa.un.org/issues/indigenous-peoples/united-nations-declaration-on-the-rights-of-indigenous-peoples

United Nations, Department of Economic and Social Affairs (UN DESA) (2023). *Implementing the joint program of scientific research and monitoring for high seas fisheries in the central Arctic Ocean.* Retrieved 5 August 2024, from: https://sdgs.un.org/partnerships/implementing-joint-program-scientific-research-and-monitoring-high-seas-fisheries#description

United Nations Environment Programme (UNEP) (2022, January). The shrinking Arctic sea ice (Foresight Brief No. 28). UNEP Science Division. https://wedocs.unep.org/bitstream/handle/20.500.11822/38414/FB028.pdf

United Nations Environment Programme (UNEP) / Mediterranean Action Plan (MAP) and Plan Bleu (2020). *State of the environment and development in the Mediterranean. Summary for decision makers*, UNEP https://planbleu.org/wp-content/uploads/2021/04/SoED_Summary.pdf

Williams, L.C. (2019). An Ocean between us: The implications of inconsistencies between the navigational laws of coastal Arctic Council nations and the united nations convention on the law of the sea for Arctic navigation", *Vanderbilt Law Review*, *70*(1), 379–411. https://scholarship.law.vanderbilt.edu/vlr/vol70/iss1/5

CHAPTER 5

Japan's Engagement with the Arctic after Russia's Invasion of Ukraine

Juha Saunavaara, Marina Lomaeva, Hiroki Takakura and Fujio Ohnishi

1 Introduction

Russia's invasion of Ukraine has had a significant spillover effect on the Arctic, causing turbulence in international relations and posing challenges to the structures of Arctic governance that have developed since the end of the Cold War. Besides the eight Arctic States, the new situation is affecting a variety of other state and non-state actors outside the Arctic. While Japan, as a State, is connected to Arctic governance and cooperation through its institutional bonds (e.g., having Observer status at the Arctic Council since 2013) and policy commitments, various other stakeholders, such as private companies, universities, subnational governments, and non-governmental organizations (NGOs), have invested resources, built networks, and committed themselves to long-term engagement and collaboration with a wide spectrum of Arctic actors. The existing situation forces all these actors to reconsider their attitudes toward the reformation of Arctic cooperation and take stock of their ongoing and future interactions with the Arctic. Although the invasion has complicated international collaboration, the need for global cooperative frameworks, such as the ones to mitigate the effects of climate change and biodiversity loss, are as important as ever. Furthermore, cross-border cooperation is needed in such fields as search and rescue.

This chapter seeks to answer the following questions to clarify and understand Japanese actors' current stance toward the Arctic: Who are (and have been) the most important Japanese actors vis-à-vis the Arctic? What kind of regulations, policies, structures, and objectives have guided Japanese actors' engagement with the Arctic? How have different levels of government and various Japanese non-state actors reacted to the outbreak of the war, and how has the war influenced their approach to and interaction with the Arctic? This research is based on reports, strategies, and other documents (including homepages) from relevant organizations, as well as newspaper articles, interviews conducted before and after the Russian invasion of

 | DOI:10.1163/9789004734685_006

Ukraine, and participatory observation. The first part of this chapter outlines the evolution of Japan's relations with the Arctic until the end of 2021. The second part provides a more detailed analysis elaborating on the reactions of the government, business community, academia, and other non-state actors in Japan. The final discussion summarizes the main findings and comments on the future of Japan's engagement with the Arctic.

2 Relationship between Japan and the Arctic: Historical Development

Accounts of Japan's engagement with the Arctic (Babin & Saunavaara, 2021; Ikeshima, 2016; Kossa et al., 2020; Lomaeva & Saunavaara, 2022; Ohnishi, 2016; Tonami, 2016; Tonami & Watters, 2012; Yennie-Lindgren, 2020) often trace the origins of its interactions and involvement back to the signing of the Svalbard Treaty (1920). While examples of activities and expressions of interest can be found both in the interwar period and the postwar decades, including the establishment of the National Institute of Polar Research (NIPR) as early as 1973, the major steps towards the diverse modern-day relationships were taken in the early 1990s. These developments included membership in the International Arctic Science Committee (IASC, 1990), the establishment of the NIPR Arctic Environment Research Center (1990) and the Ny-Ålesund research station (1991), and the launch of the International Northern Sea Route Programme (INSROP) with Norway and Russia (1993). Although the Japan Northern Sea Route Programme (JANSROP) followed INSROP in the early 2000s, Japan's application for observer status in the Arctic Council in 2009 and its eventual acceptance in 2013 marked a new phase of formal state-level ties.

In addition to the Ministry of Foreign Affairs (MOFA)'s involvement in matters concerning the Arctic Council, the Ministry of Land, Infrastructure, Transport and Tourism (MLIT), and the Ministry of Education, Culture, Sports, Science and Technology (MEXT) became active at the beginning of 2010s. References to climate change in the Arctic and the Northern Sea Route (NSR) had already been made in the Second Basic Plan on Ocean Policy (Cabinet Office of Japan, 2013). However, the announcement of Japan's first Arctic Policy in 2015 was an important milestone, reflecting the country's emphasis on science and technology, international cooperation, the environment and sustainable development, the respect of Indigenous peoples, the potential of the NSR, and a stable security environment (Babin, 2021; Bennett, 2014; Chuffart et al., 2020; Headquarters for Ocean Policy,

2015; Ohnishi, 2016). The Third Basic Plan on Ocean Policy, adopted in 2018, and the annual Diplomatic Bluebooks have further refined Japan's national framework for engagement in Arctic affairs (Cabinet Office, 2018; Ministry of Foreign Affairs of Japan, 2022a).

Japan has been an active contributor to the work of the Arctic Council for years, and it has participated in almost all Senior Arctic Officials' meetings and ministerial meetings since 2009 (even before its formal observer status and the creation of the position of Ambassador in Charge of Arctic Affairs). Japan has also regularly contributed to the work of the Arctic Council Working Groups (most actively in Arctic Monitoring and Assessment Programme (AMAP), Sustainable Development Working Group (SDWG), Protection of the Marine Environment (PAME), and Conservation of Arctic Flora and Fauna (CAFF)) and joined various expert groups and task forces. Outside the Arctic Council's framework, Japan was involved in the drafting and implementation of the 2014 International Code for Ships Operating in Polar Waters (Polar Code) and the 2018 Agreement to Prevent Unregulated High Seas Fisheries in the Central Arctic Ocean (Babin & Lasserre, 2019; Chuffart et al., 2020; Ohnishi, 2016). The Japanese government also collaborated with Iceland and hosted the Third Arctic Science Ministerial Meeting (ASM3, in a hybrid format, due to COVID-19-related travel restrictions) in May 2021. At the regional level, Japan has been involved in the Trilateral High-Level Dialogue (Trilateral Cooperation Secretariat, 2019) on Arctic issues with China and South Korea, and Arctic scholars from the same countries have also organized annual gatherings. However, high-level meetings involving Arctic Ambassadors, initiated in 2016, were not held during the COVID-19 pandemic (Lomaeva & Saunavaara, 2022; Yennie-Lindgren, 2020).

Japan has long-standing economic ties with various Arctic States. The trade and flow of investments has been considered part of the bilateral relations or of Japan's exchanges with the European Union (EU), for example. The trade statistics of Japan do not recognize "the Arctic" as a separate area, such as ASEAN, Central and Eastern Europe, or the Middle East (Trade Statistics of Japan, 2024). When increasing interest in the Arctic emerged in Japan in the late 2000s, along with related business opportunities, it stemmed from an earlier interest in the NSR. Over the past decade, the Arctic has also played an increasingly important role in Japan's energy policy as an alternative source of hydrocarbons to those imported from the Middle East. Although the Japan Organization for Metals and Energy Security (JOGMEC; until 2022, the Japan National Oil, Gas and Metals Corporation), an independent administrative institution, was involved in international projects to develop oil and natural gas fields in Greenland and Alaska in the early 2010s (Sinclair, 2014), large-scale projects in the Russian Arctic have attracted the greatest attention among Japanese stakeholders.

JOGMEC became involved in Russian hydrocarbon projects in the 1990s, and a greater number of Japanese stakeholders joined through the international oil and gas production projects in Sakhalin (Sakhalin 1 and 2) in the 2000s. In the case of the Yamal LNG (n.d.) project, Japanese companies were involved through engineering, procurement, and construction contracts as well as financing provided by the Japan Bank for International Cooperation (JBIC). Furthermore, Mitsui O.S.K Lines has been involved in the export of Yamal LNG, having operated three ice-breaking liquefied natural gas (LNG) carriers for the project since March 2018. In addition to these earlier steps leading to a situation whereby Russia supplied approximately 8.8 percent of the LNG and 3.6 percent of the crude oil imported to Japan in 2021, Japanese companies' involvement in the Arctic LNG 2 project and the planned construction of the LNG transshipment hubs in Kamchatka and the Kola Peninsula have demonstrated their readiness to participate in Arctic projects (Babin, 2021; Harada, 2022; JBIC, 2021; Lomaeva & Saunavaara, 2022).

Japan has also been envisioned as the East Asian landing for various trans-Arctic submarine fiber-optic cable projects, starting from the Russian Optical Trans-Arctic Cable system (ROTACS) and Canadian Arctic Fibre, which later became a project led by Alaska-based Quintillion subsea Holdings. Japanese companies became more involved and invested in the Arctic Connect project (Submarine Cable Network, n.d.), which was suddenly frozen by MegaFon, the Russian partner of the project, in May 2021. While the cable route through the Northeast Passage is currently part of the Russian state-led Polar Express project, Japanese Arteria Networks has formed Far North Fiber Inc. in cooperation with Cinia (Finland) and Far North Digital (US). This company is developing a cable system connecting East Asia, Northern Europe, and North America through the Northwest Passage (Saunavaara, 2022; Saunavaara & Salminen, 2023). Although economic aspirations are often described as important drivers of East Asian actors' interest in the Arctic, it is worth pointing out that none of the Japanese enterprises have joined the Arctic Economic Council (AEC).

According to Chuffart et al. (2020), Japan's Arctic identity-building relies on its scientific engagement, and science is the main driver of Japan's involvement in the region. Important structures forming the foundation of Japan's involvement in research and educational cooperation were created in 2011 when the Japan Consortium for Arctic Environmental Research

(JCAR) was established, MEXT launched the GRENE Arctic Climate Change Research Project (2011–2016) as Japan's Arctic flagship project, and Hokkaido University joined the University of the Arctic (UArctic). Four years later, in 2015, Japan hosted the Arctic Science Summit Week, Hokkaido University established the Arctic Research Center (HU ARC), and the Arctic Challenge for Sustainability (ArCS) project was launched (September 2015 to March 2020) under the leadership of NIPR, the Japan Agency for Marine-Earth Science and Technology (JAMSTEC), and Hokkaido University. This project integrated social sciences and humanities into the national Arctic studies project. ArCS was followed by ArCS II (June 2020 to March 2025), which promotes advanced research to understand the current status and processes of environmental changes in the Arctic, improve meteorological and climate predictions to assess the impact of rapid environmental changes in the Arctic on human society, and implement the results of this research into society. In addition, the Japan Arctic Research Network Center (J-ARC Net), administered by NIPR, JAMSTEC, and Hokkaido University, facilitated and funded interdisciplinary Arctic research between April 2016 and March 2022 (Saunavaara & Ohnishi, 2020). Finally, the influential role played by the Ocean Policy Research Institute (formerly Ocean Policy Research Foundation), a think tank of the Sasakawa Peace Foundation, should be mentioned. Since the implementation of the INSROP and JANSROP projects, the institute has participated in and organized international conferences, provided a forum for domestic discussions concerning Arctic matters, and offered policy recommendations (Lomaeva & Saunavaara, 2022; Ocean Policy Research Institute, n.d.).

In addition to private enterprises and epistemic communities, Japanese subnational governments have also engaged in cross-border cooperation in the circumpolar North. In particular, Hokkaido, which Foreign Minister Taro Kono (2018) described as "a gateway from Asia to the Northern Sea Route" in his 2018 keynote speech at the Arctic Circle Assembly (Reykjavik), has a long history of collaboration with northern entities. The Hokkaido Government and the City of Sapporo have played prominent roles in the Northern Forum (NF) and the World Winter Cities Association for Mayors (WWCAM), respectively. The NF was established in 1991, but its roots go back to the First International Conference on Human Environment in Northern Regions, organized in Hokkaido in 1974. The Northern Intercity Conference of Mayors, the precursor to WWCAM, was initiated in 1981 by the City of Sapporo, which currently hosts the association's secretariat. Hokkaido's active pursuit of collaboration with other northern regions has been institutionalized in the so-called 'Northern regions policy' and the Hokkaido Comprehensive Development Plans since the 1970s (Babin & Saunavaara, 2021; Tonami, 2020).

The 8th Hokkaido Comprehensive Development Plan (MLIT, 2016) recognized Hokkaido's potential to become the East Asian hub for the NSR, and thus reflected local discussions concerning the route, which intensified in the early 2010s. This interest prompted the Hokkaido Government to extend its regional ties beyond the Russian Far East and send a delegation to Murmansk Oblast in 2013, aiming to connect with the western end of the NSR (Hokkaido Government, 2016). Both subnational governments, aspiring to become hubs for the shipping route connecting Europe and East Asia, continued to exchange port- and trade-related information until the pandemic and war interrupted this exchange. The same geographical advantage (i.e., proximity to the Bering Strait, compared to other East Asian regions), which has supported hopes concerning Arctic shipping, has also been recognized as an asset in collaborations with trans-Arctic submarine fiber-optic cable projects (Kossa et al., 2020; Saunavaara, 2017).

Hokkaido has also played an important role in Japan's interactions with the Russian Arctic and Far East. This cooperation has been based on various agreements, such as the 1992 Memorandum to establish a permanent joint committee for economic cooperation between Hokkaido and the Russian Far East, the 2015 Memorandum of understanding between Hokkaido and Republic of Sakha (Yakutia), the 2018 regional program for cooperative development between the parties (6th term 2018–2022), and a 2019 Plan to promote friendship and economic exchanges by Hokkaido-Sakhalin (4th term 2019–2022), and frameworks (e.g., Hokkaido Council for Promoting Regional Exchanges with Russia, Hokkaido Platform for Cooperation with Russia, Hokkaido-Russian Far East Joint Committee on Economic Cooperation) (Hokkaido Government, 2023a; Hokkaido Government, 2019). Furthermore, Hokkaido recently hosted events promoting collaboration between Japanese and Russian actors (e.g., the 7th Japan–Russia Meeting on Cooperation Between Small and Medium Enterprises in 2019 and the opening ceremony for the Japan–Russia Year for Inter-Regional and Inter-City Exchanges in 2022) (Ministry of Economy, Trade and Industry of Japan, 2019; Ministry of Foreign Affairs of Japan, 2022b). However, it has often been difficult to draw a clear-cut distinction between Hokkaido's engagement with and policy concerning Russia and the Arctic.

The interaction between the Ainu (Indigenous people who have historically lived in northern parts of Japan and on disputed islands that are now part of Russia) and other northern Indigenous peoples represents (yet) another layer of Japan's engagement with the Arctic and the North. The Ainu

Museum (in Shiraoi), the Hokkaido Museum of Northern Peoples (in Abashiri), the Ainu Association of Hokkaido, and various researchers, for example, have actively engaged in cultural exchanges with circumpolar Indigenous peoples for decades. The opening of the Upopoy National Ainu Museum and Park (in Shiraoi) in July 2020 raised further hopes for both the revitalization of Ainu culture in Japan and international Indigenous cooperation (Mongkjargal, 2010; Sasaki, 2022; Sasakura, 2000).

3 Japan Facing the New Arctic Realities

3.1 *Japan, the New International Order, and Structures of Arctic Governance*

The Japanese government considers Russia's aggression toward Ukraine a threat to the very foundations of the rule-based international order, which the international community has built through hard work and many sacrifices over a long period of time (Ministry of Foreign Affairs of Japan, 2023a; 2023b). From the Japanese perspective, unilateral changes to the status quo by force are unacceptable, whether in Europe, East Asia, or elsewhere. Based on this perception, Japan's government made a major shift in its diplomacy toward Russia and committed to imposing strict sanctions against Russia (e.g., on financial institutions and their exclusion from the SWIFT system) in cooperation with the G7. Faced with the Japanese condemnation, on 7 March 2022, the Russian government designated Japan as one of the 48 countries and regions 'engaging in unfriendly activities toward Russia.' On 6 March 2022, the Japanese government raised its risk level estimation and warned its citizens to refrain from traveling to Russia. As in many other countries, the ongoing war, its spillover effects, and deteriorating relations with Russia have impacted discussions concerning Japan's Arctic policy.

Since the Arctic Council is the primary framework for Japan's engagement with the Arctic, the pausing of the Council's activities has been noticed in Japan. While emphasizing the importance of international collaboration and the work of the Arctic Council, Japan has followed the lead of the seven non-Russian Member States of the Council. Japan has neither questioned the decisions made by the so-called Arctic 7 States nor initiated any proposals concerning preferred actions in the future. Therefore, Japan's cautious approach has attracted less international attention than, for example, the comments made by China's Special Envoy for Arctic Affairs at the Arctic Circle Assembly in 2022 and the Arctic Circle Japan Forum in 2023 (Schreiber, 2022; Yennie-Lindgren & Lanteigne, 2023).

Japan regularly re-evaluates and amends its approach to the Arctic as part of the revisions to the Basic Plan on Ocean Policy. This process is based on the Basic Act on Ocean Policy (adopted in 2007) and led by the Headquarters for Ocean Policy. Therefore, the Fourth Basic Plan on Ocean Policy, which was announced in April 2023 (Cabinet Office of Japan, 2023), is the most important policy document for understanding Japan's Arctic policy, especially during what is sometimes described as a "post 'post-Cold War' era" (see The Japan Institute of International Affairs, 2023).

The Fourth Basic Plan reflects the Japanese government's cautious approach to the Arctic. While the prospects for the Arctic remain uncertain due to Russia's ongoing invasion of Ukraine, Japan is demonstrating its willingness to maintain its previous engagement in the Arctic through the three pillars of its Arctic policy: research and development, international cooperation, and sustainable use (Cabinet Office of Japan, 2023).

The first pillar, focusing on research and development, emphasizes the need to strengthen efforts related to Arctic research and data collection, the promotion of international scientific and technological cooperation, and the need to foster human resources that can contribute to solving different Arctic-related problems. This pillar is thus closely related to the research, observation, and human resource development objectives of the national Arctic flagship research project ArCS II and to the construction of an Arctic research vessel that is expected to be completed by autumn 2026.

The second pillar emphasizes the rule of law and active participation in international rulemaking, expansion of bilateral and multilateral cooperation, and further contributions to the activities of the Arctic Council. The Fourth Basic Plan on Ocean Policy consolidates Japan's commitment to strengthening its contributions to the Council's activities, expressing its interest in dispatching more representatives to relevant meetings and working groups, and its desire to be involved in discussions concerning the structure of the Council and role of observers. The new policy document also mentions other forums and frameworks supporting international collaboration. In other words, the Japanese government has identified various second-track forums, such as the Arctic Circle, Arctic Frontiers, and Arctic Science Ministerial Meetings, through which it can exchange and share its views, ideas, and scientific findings (Ministry of Foreign Affairs of Japan, 2023a, pp. 269–270). Although the activities of the Arctic Council were paused due to the outbreak of the war in Ukraine, the Arctic Ambassador of Japan actively attended the second-track forums (e.g., the Arctic Encounter Symposium in Anchorage in April 2022 and 2023; the Arctic Frontiers in Tromsø in May 2022; the Arctic Circle Forum in Nuuk, Greenland, in August 2022; the Arctic Circle Assembly in Reykjavik in 2022; and the Arctic Circle Forum in Tokyo in March 2023). Discussions among Japanese Arctic scholars have revealed that a few of them have participated in online meetings of AMAP and PAME since the winter of 2023–2024. The inactivity in other working groups reflects the slower reactivation of these groups rather than Japan's low interest in or incapability to contribute to their activities.

Although the Northern Sea Route still features prominently in the part of the document referring to the sustainable use of the Arctic, changes in details can be identified. In the Third Basic Plan, the utilization of the Northern Sea Route was emphasized more assertively by promoting conditions wherein Japanese shipping companies could utilize the route. However, the Fourth Basic Plan's emphasis on using satellites to gather ice observation data and sharing information among various public and private stakeholders suggests that large-scale commercial utilization of the NSR may not be anticipated in the near future. Other themes discussed include the conservation of the marine environment in the Arctic Ocean and the promotion of a sustainable marine economy in the Arctic.

The year 2023 marked the tenth anniversary of the several East Asian countries obtaining Observer status in the Arctic Council. As the existing structures of the Arctic governance have been shaken, the discussion concerning their post-conflict role in the Arctic has gained momentum. As part of this discussion, the possible revival of the Trilateral High-Level Dialogue on the Arctic between China, Japan, and South Korea has been discussed both among the Arctic Ambassadors joining public sessions in international events (most recently in Sapporo in August 2023) and among scholars (also including some of the authors) from the three East Asian countries. However, according to the informants and statements from previous high-level trilateral meetings, identifying concrete agenda and issues for cooperation among the three States regarding the Arctic has often been challenging (Ministry of Foreign Affairs of the People's Republic of China, 2018; Trilateral Cooperation Secretariat, 2019).

Finland and Sweden decided to apply for membership in NATO following the Russian invasion of Ukraine. Although the ratification process was slightly delayed in the case of Sweden, both countries have become Member States. The fact that seven out of the eight Arctic States are now NATO members has changed the security landscape of the region. Adaptation to the new situation has not, however, caused significant difficulties in Japan, which has simultaneously tightened its own collaboration with the political and military alliance, and the Prime Minister of Japan joined NATO leaders at the July 2023 meeting in Lithuania (Brumer & Yennie Lindgren, 2023; Murakami & Kelly, 2023).

Although the Arctic is not a top priority in foreign and security policy debate in Japan, the visible presence of Japanese decision-makers at the Arctic Circle Japan Forum (short remarks were delivered by four current or former ministers and members of the Parliamentary League of Arctic Frontier Study) at the beginning of March 2023 can be interpreted as a signal that Arctic issues are on the political agenda in Japan. Obviously, the presence of political leaders can also reflect their willingness to collaborate with the Nippon Foundation and the Sasakawa Peace Foundation, which served as the Japanese co-hosts of the event.

3.2 *Reconsidering Japanese Investments and Involvement in Arctic Business*

The role of JOGMEC, which provides equity financing and loan/liability guarantees to Japanese private companies involved in energy-related projects, has been significant in Japan's engagement with the Arctic. The recent revisions of the JOGMEC Act (e-Gov, 2023) have also given it greater leeway for involvement in projects in the Russian Arctic. Although other Japanese general trading houses have shown interest in Arctic projects, it was only Mitsui that eventually joined JOGMEC in the Japan Arctic LNG joint venture, purchasing a 10% stake in the Arctic LNG 2 project, which also received financing through JBIC. In general, Japan's involvement in Russian hydrocarbon projects is motivated by the desire to decrease its substantial dependence on energy imports from the Middle East (JOGMEC, 2019; Harada, 2023; Lomaeva & Saunavaara, 2022).

In early February 2022, just a few weeks before the Russian invasion of Ukraine, Mitsui O.S.K. Lines (MOL) announced its participation in cargo transport for the Arctic LNG 2 Project and signed a charter contract for an ice-breaking tanker with the project company, whose largest shareholder is PAO NOVATEK. The vessel was to be constructed in China and delivered in 2024. This contract followed the signing of charter contracts for three ice-breaking LNG vessels serving the same project in October 2020 (Mitsui O.S.K. Lines, 2022). While the delivery of the vessel has been delayed, MOL has faced serious difficulties due to the sanctions. As the company is unable to operate the vessel, it cannot provide the promised services to Arctic LNG 2. According to MOL's contracts with the project organization, it should sell its vessel to Arctic LNG 2 in case it is unable to comply with its obligations. However, the sanctions prevent this transaction (Humpert, 2024).

After the outbreak of the war, Japan followed the international movement in halting investments in the Russian energy sector and freezing new investments in the Arctic LNG 2 project. In practice, JBIC suspended the loan agreement made in November 2021. However, Japan has not suspended its entire participation in the Arctic LNG 2, and Japanese companies involved have not entirely withdrawn from Russia, unlike many other major international companies, such as BP, Equinor, ExxonMobil, and Shell. While the French TotalEnergies initiated a force majeure process on the Arctic LNG 2 project in Russia due to new sanctions in November 2023 (LNG Prime Staff, 2024), the loan contracts between Japan Arctic LNG and banks also became subject to a mandatory prepayment. JOGMEC fulfilled its loan guarantee and paid a total of around 814 million euros to banks on 30 January 2024 (Kumagai, 2024). Japan has announced only a gradual suspension of Russian coal imports, and has not joined the strictest international oil embargos. Simultaneously with the Arctic projects, Japanese stakeholders have re-evaluated their role in the Sakhalin-2 energy project, in which Mitsui owns 12.5 percent and Mitsubishi 10 percent equity (Harada, 2022, 2023; Thompson, 2022). According to the import and export data from fiscal year 2022, the total value of Japan's imports from Russia decreased by 6.3 percent, compared to the previous year. While the amount of LNG imported from Russia slightly decreased, its value increased significantly due to high prices. The amount of imported oil decreased by approximately 80 percent (Hokkaido Shimbun, 2023c).

Japanese actors have also been actively involved in efforts to develop hydrogen and ammonia production; carbon capture, utilization, and storage technologies; and renewable energy projects in Russia. Significant steps in this process were taken in September 2021, when PAO NOVATEK and the Ministry of Economy, Trade and Industry of Japan (METI) signed a Memorandum of Cooperation and JBIC and PAO NOVATEK signed a Strategic Cooperation Agreement (NOVATEK, 2021a, 2021b). PAO NOVATEK, which has attempted to reconfigure its Obsky LNG project in the Yamal Peninsula to produce ammonia, hydrogen, and methanol, has reportedly also engaged in negotiations with Mitsui. Although some media sources have reported on Mitsui's withdrawal from the project, it is unclear whether a formal agreement between the companies has been reached (Dyatel, 2023; Reuters, 2021; Staalesen, 2023).

Although it is difficult to evaluate the current status of the hydrogen, ammonia, and carbon capture projects, a representative of JOGMEC referred to their great long-term potential in a speech delivered at the Arctic Circle

Japan Forum at the beginning of March 2023. Since the Russian invasion of Ukraine, METI, JOGMEC, and JBIC, among others, have increasingly focused on the possibility of developing LNG production in North Slope, Alaska, and importing it to Japan. At the Alaska LNG Summit organized in Tokyo in October 2022, representatives of the US government emphasized the importance of fulfilling Japan's energy needs from reliable sources controlled by its allies (The Asahi Shimbun, 2023; Zia, 2022).

The ongoing war has also caused changes in the existing and planned connectivity and accessibility between Japan and Europe. As described above, Japan is strongly connected to the supply chains linked to LNG projects in the Russian Arctic. However, the collapse of trans-Arctic shipping activities between Europe and East Asia has been noticed in Japan. The closure of Russian airspace is another example of the spillover effects on Japan's logistical position and ties with Northern Europe in particular. Many flights between Japan and Europe have been rerouted over the North Pole and Arctic Ocean, increasing flight times, costs and emissions. In addition to business travel and tourism, the rerouting has had impacts, for example, on salmon and mackerel imports from Norway (Shinohara, 2022). In the case of trans-Arctic cable projects, a major shift happened before the outbreak of the Russian invasion of Ukraine, when the Arctic Connect project (envisioning a cable route through the Northeast Passage) was terminated. The ongoing war and conflicts between the US and China related to submarine cable development have increased interest in and overall awareness of this type of critical infrastructure. The possibilities related to the trans-Arctic cable projects have also been recognized in the interim report of the Japanese Government's expert group on digital infrastructure (Keizai Sangyōshō & Sōmushō, 2023).

The international turbulence has hindered Japanese companies' ability to establish a presence, dispatch staff, and maintain offices in the Russian Arctic and Far East. For instance, the Hokkaido Government and private companies from Hokkaido had to withdraw their employees from the Russian Far East, leaving all operations to local staff, and companies such as trading houses (*shōsha*) have started the procedure of liquidating their branch offices in the Far East. Companies that have made significant investments in Russia have demonstrated difficulties, and possibly also reluctance, in leaving the market. Japan Tobacco International, for example, has announced the suspension of investments in Russia, the company's most important foreign market, although recent reports have indicated that it has remained active and actually significantly increased its revenue in Russia during the war (B4Ukraine, 2023; JTI, 2022). The collapse of tourism from Japan to Russia

(Hokkaido Shimbun, 2023a) and Russia's termination of agreements reached in 1991 (between Japan and the Soviet Union) and 1999 (between Japan and the Russian Federation) regarding mutual visa-free visits by former inhabitants of the so-called 'Northern Territories' (the four disputed islands) and Russians (The Asahi Shimbun, 2022) have further accelerated the deterioration of people-to-people interactions.

However, it should be noted that interregional agreements between Hokkaido and the Russian Far Eastern regions have not been terminated, and informal contacts between regional officials have been maintained, according to our informant in the Hokkaido Government. Nevertheless, many areas of interregional cooperation, such as fisheries, have suffered. The fishing for Pacific saury, Pacific cod, and Japanese flying squid in the two countries' exclusive economic zones (EEZs), based on mutually allocated quotas, and for kelp harvesting around Signalny Island (Kaigarajima), based on an agreement between private actors, have continued. Japanese salmon fishing in the Russian EEZ was terminated in 2022 but resumed in 2024, and all Japanese fishing in the waters around the disputed four islands was terminated in 2023 (Hamada, 2023, pp. 11–12 and 17–18; Kimura & Imai, 2024). Meanwhile, the value of marine products (fish and seafood) exported from Russia to Japan has reached a record high since the collapse of the Soviet Union. The decision not to include marine products in the sanctioned products was reportedly due to pressure from Japanese companies dependent on imported products. Furthermore, it seems that the products formerly exported to North America and Europe (especially snow crab from the Bering Sea) are increasingly being sold to Japan (Hokkaido Shimbun, 2023b). Multilateral cooperation in the North Pacific on the conservation and management of marine living resources has continued, as evidenced by the participation of Russian representatives at the 7th annual session of the North Pacific Fisheries Commission (NPFC, 2023; Suisanchō, 2023) held in Sapporo in March 2023, at which both multilateral and Japan–Russia bilateral agreements on the catch were reached.

3.3 *Frozen Interregional Collaboration and Scientific Cooperation Navigating through Troubled Waters*

The Russian invasion of Ukraine has also had a direct impact on Arctic research conducted in Japan. While MEXT has urged universities to abstain from using governmental funding for collaborative activities involving Russian partners, Japanese scholars have participated both in domestic and international debate on whether scientific cooperation with Russian partners can be continued. Eventually, the dominant interpretation adopted by various universities and research institutions was that collaboration between individuals is possible but that institutional cooperation with Russian organizations cannot be continued. It has also been pointed out that since the start of the hostilities Russian academics have been "retreating from the central fora of global scientific collaboration," as suggested by a sharp drop in Russian participation at international conferences and in joint Russian papers with the colleagues from the 'unfriendly' States, due to the financial, logistical, and security-related constraints imposed on both sides (Matthews, 2023). The war in Ukraine has reportedly also triggered a surge in arrests of scientists who published internationally and collaborated with foreign colleagues and have been charged with high treason (alleged passing of state secrets to foreign countries) (Goryashko, 2024). The access to Russian governmental and other public institutions' websites from other countries have been restricted and only possible via Virtual Private Networks (VPNs) (Teraoka & Namiki, 2022), which further complicates research related to the Russian part of the Arctic. Meanwhile, new Russian students continued to arrive and be enrolled in Japanese universities after travel restrictions related to the COVID-19 pandemic were eased in spring 2022 (Lomaeva & Lyude, 2023).

After the invasion, various meetings and seminars were cancelled, and networks, such as those established under the Human Resource Development Platform for Japan–Russia Economic Cooperation and Personnel Exchange (HaRP), disintegrated. Furthermore, restrictions on the use of software developed by Western companies for online teaching and data sharing and the exclusion of Russian banks from the SWIFT system, for instance, have caused practical problems. After the Russian Union of Rectors, which represents the Russian side at the Association of Japanese and Russian Universities, expressed support for the Russian invasion in March 2022, the Embassy of Ukraine in Japan requested that Japanese universities cut their ties with Russian universities. This appeal did not, however, affect the stance adopted by most Japanese universities, which pledged support for faculty and students from both Ukraine and Russia in Japanese academia (Lomaeva & Lyude, 2023).

Scientific collaboration and research relying on field studies has faced severe difficulties. Since the late 1980s, Japanese academia has conducted cross- and inter-disciplinary joint projects in the areas ranging from linguistics and anthropology to geology and hydrology, mostly in the Sakha Republic and other Russian Far East regions. Although research focusing on the relation of permafrost land and people/culture, often within the framework of climate change (Hiyama & Takakura, 2018; Takakura et al., 2021), has received international recognition, it is not possible to conduct field research in the Russian Arctic at this moment. Therefore, long-term collaboration in anthropological fieldwork and the field observations at the Spasskaya Pad Scientific Forest Station in the Sakha Republic, for example, have been disrupted.

Although the nationwide ArCS II project has systematically collected data from Japanese researchers on the impact of the Russian invasion of Ukraine on their research activities, these findings have not been published. Similar questions have been discussed in smaller academic gatherings such as the closed roundtable discussion organized by the authors in Sapporo at the end of June 2024. At this event gathering Arctic researchers from various disciplines in social sciences and humanities, particular attention was paid to problems faced by younger researchers. The more experienced scholars have been able to keep at least some of their informal ties with Russian informants and partners dating back to the pre-COVID-19 pandemic era. However, the inauguration of new projects or establishment of new ties has been practically impossible for years. Some Japanese researchers have compensated for the lack of field studies in Russia by refocusing their research on people who have left Russia either before or during the ongoing war.

Despite these challenges, the relatively small Arctic research community in Japan has remained functional and even initiated new international collaboration with Arctic partners excluding Russia. Japanese scholars have maintained their research activities and contributions to the international Arctic studies community, which has been trying to adapt to the new situation. While events such as the UArctic Congress, planned to be held in Russia in autumn 2022, were cancelled, Japanese actors actively joined the Arctic Circle Assembly 2022 in Reykjavík, for example. Furthermore, in March 2023, the International Symposium on Arctic Research (ISAR-7) was organized by JCAR and NIPR in cooperation with other partners, concurrently with the Arctic Circle Japan Forum. Japanese Arctic researchers, under the auspices of JCAR, also completed a new version of the long-term plan entitled 'Arctic research: its current status and future plans' in January 2024. The massive publication (over 460 pages in Japanese), which outlines recent developments and offers various perspectives concerning the future of the Arctic research, is a strong testament to the vitality of the field, despite the problems related to international collaboration (JCAR, 2024a; JCAR, 2024b).

The ongoing Japanese project to build a new icebreaking research vessel and develop it into a platform for international cooperation has received great domestic and international attention and has not been affected by the recent turbulence. While such investment in infrastructure offers grounds for optimism regarding Japan's future contributions to Arctic research, scientific and educational cooperation have also been identified as potential channels for collaboration to be re-established once the current turbulence in international relations subsides.

3.4 *Other Channels of Interaction Equally Affected*

The ongoing war has affected Japanese subnational governments and other non-state actors' engagement with their Russian and Arctic partners. While Hokkaido Center, which was established in Yuzhno-Sakhalinsk in 2015 as a Russo-Japanese joint venture, has been deserted, and the dispatched Japanese staff of the Hokkaido Government have returned to Hokkaido, local staff have remained. The city of Wakkanai has postponed plans to resend its representative to Yuzhno-Sakhalinsk after the COVID-19 pandemic, and sister-city collaboration has practically stopped (Hokkaido Shimbun, 2023a). Although official meetings between the Hokkaido and Russian regional governments have been halted, and only a few cultural events have been conducted, all without government involvement, informants in the Hokkaido Government have referred to the existing informal personal correspondence with their Russian colleagues. Bilateral collaboration with other Arctic States and regions has continued. Furthermore, the informants have mentioned efforts to redirect efforts and resources formerly dedicated to collaboration with Russia in the Far East and the Arctic towards other regions, including Central Asian countries (the former republics of the Soviet Union, where Russian is still spoken).

Multilateral forums have also been affected. The WWCAM Mayors Conference was scheduled to take place in Norilsk in 2023, and although the conference dates and agenda were to be decided at the Working-Level Meeting in 2022 (WWCAM, 2022), they have not been announced. Furthermore, WWCAM has not published a newsletter since March 2022. Hokkaido's status within the NF is also ambiguous. The Hokkaido Government left the organization in 2013, along with several other non-Russian regions. When Alaska and Finnish Lapland re-joined the NF, Hokkaido did not follow them. However, the Hokkaido International Exchange and Cooperation Center (HIECC) remained at the NF as a business partner (Babin & Saunavaara, 2021). The new strategy, prepared by the NF after the outbreak of war and the withdrawal of most of the non-Russian members, aims at closer collaboration with Asian regions (Northern Forum 2023). However, the NF's pivot to Asia has not led to any action in Hokkaido. On the contrary, according to an informant, interaction with the forum secretariat in Yakutsk has been difficult, and payment of the membership fee, for example, has been impossible. Thus, repercussions from the invasion have not been limited to the bilateral level but also affected Hokkaido-based actors' collaboration with other northern and Arctic partners.

Although most regional exchange programs with Russia have been suspended, cooperation between actors from Japan and the Russian Far East still continued. Hokkaido–Sakhalin cooperation on the search for and recovery of the bodies of the passengers onboard the Kazu I tourist boat, which foundered near the Shiretoko Peninsula in April 2022, is an example of such cooperation. In addition, some Japan–Russia negotiations over annual quotas of the shared marine resources in 2022 were successful, although some failed. This outcome offers some hope for the future of regional environmental governance in the North Pacific, involving both state and non-state actors (Lomaeva et al., 2023).

Informants in both Finland and Japan have referred to the interest in developing collaboration between Upopoy and the Sámi Museum Siida (Inari, Finland), for example. However, the COVID-19 pandemic and the ongoing war, which have also affected Indigenous organizations in Russia, have hindered international cooperation, including among the Ainu and other northern Indigenous people. Although Upopoy has abstained from Russia-related collaboration since the outbreak of the war, the Hokkaido Museum of Northern Indigenous Peoples in Abashiri, for example, has carried out lectures, workshops, exhibitions, film screenings focusing on indigenous peoples of the Russian Arctic and Far East. As the museum is administered by the Hokkaido Board of Education, these activities are also listed among the collaborative efforts between the Hokkaido Government and Russia (Hokkaido Government, 2023b). Regardless of the international situation, cooperation between the new Upopoy organization and other Indigenous Ainu organizations will play a key role in developing successful collaboration between the Ainu and Arctic Indigenous peoples (Osakada, 2021).

4 Discussion

Since the 1990s, Japan has become closely integrated into post-Cold War Arctic cooperation. Although the Russian invasion of Ukraine is not the first test for the governance system anchored in the Arctic Council, the magnitude of the ongoing crisis cannot be compared to any of the previous challenges. When reacting and adapting to the changes in the circumpolar north, Japanese actors have taken a relatively cautious approach. Japan has expressed its support for the Arctic Council searching for a way forward, at least temporarily without Russia, and the recent (Fourth) Basic Plan on Ocean Policy has reaffirmed the pillars and objectives of Japan's Arctic policy. The country has joined several sanctions regimes against Russia, but it has not been in the vanguard of the movement aiming to cut off the Russian (Arctic) actors from international trade. While it is easy to argue with the benefit of hindsight that some of the investments and agreements made shortly before the outbreak of war were poorly timed, Japanese stakeholders have decided to freeze rather than terminate collaborative projects in the Russian Arctic. At the same time, new partnerships have been mapped out in North America and Europe. If the war is prolonged or escalates further, the approach based on "temporary" or "nonfixed time" suspension may be further questioned.

Japanese subnational governments and academic communities have also revised their activities. Many problems, and the actions taken to solve them, resemble the steps taken by other Arctic and non-Arctic States. Just as the Barents collaboration has been struggling at the western border of Russia, so have the eastern interregional partnerships involving Japanese subnational entities. Similarly, the approach banning institutional relationships while allowing the few remaining person-to-person exchanges with Russian researchers seems to be common in Japan and many other countries. The need for cooperation in Arctic research and education remains, so partnerships with other Arctic universities and research groups have continued and attempts to develop new initiatives have been observed.

Bibliography

Agreement to Prevent Unregulated High Seas Fisheries in the Central Arctic Ocean (adopted 3 October 2018, entered into force 25 June 2021). [2018 CAOFA] https://www.mofa.go.jp/files/000449233.pdf

B4Ukraine (2023, July 4). *The lucrative business of staying: Corporate foreign enablers of the Kremlin's war*. B4Ukraine. https://b4ukraine.org/what-we-do/business-of-staying

Babin, J. (2021). *Stretching the icecap: Japan's engagement and policy in the Arctic* [Doctoral Dissertation, Université Laval]. http://hdl.handle.net/20.500.11794/68753

Babin, J., & Lasserre, F. (2019). Asian states at the Arctic Council: Perceptions in Western states. *Polar Geography, 42*(3), 145–159. https://doi.org/10.1080/1088937X.2019.1578290

Babin, J., & Saunavaara, J. (2021). Hokkaido: From the "road to the northern sea" to "Japan's gateway to the Arctic. *Asian Geographer, 40*(1), 1–18. https://doi.org/10.1080/10225706.2021.1910525

Bennett, M. (2014). North by northeast: Toward an Asian-Arctic region. *Eurasian Geography and Economics, 55*(1), 71–93. https://doi.org/10.1080/15387216.2014.936480

Brumer, M., & Y.L., Wrenn (2023, July 10). *Anarchy is a bridge: Russian and China are pushing NATO and Japan together.* War on the Rocks. https://warontherocks.com/2023/07/anarchy-is-a-bridge-russia-and-china-are-pushing-nato-and-japan-together/

Cabinet Office of Japan (2013). *Basic plan on ocean policy, A provisional translation.* https://www8.cao.go.jp/ocean/english/plan/pdf/plan02_e.pdf

Cabinet Office of Japan (2018). *The basic plan on ocean policy.* https://www8.cao.go.jp/ocean/english/plan/pdf/plan03_e.pdf

Cabinet Office of Japan (2023). *Kaiyō kihon keikaku. Kakugi kettei, Reiwa 5 nen, 4 gatsu, 28 nichi* [Basic Ocean Policy, Cabinet Decision on April 28, 2023]. https://www8.cao.go.jp/ocean/policies/plan/plan04/pdf/keikaku_honbun.pdf

Chuffart, R., Hataya, S., Inagaki, O., & Arthur, L. (2021). Assessing Japan's Arctic engagement during the ArCS project (2015–2020). *The Yearbook of Polar Law, 12*(1), 328–348. https://doi.org/10.1163/22116427_012010020

e-Gov. (2023). *Dokuritsu gyōsei hōjin enerugii – kinzoku kōbutsu shigen kikō hō* [Act on the Japan Oil, Gas and Metals National Corporation, Independent Administrative Agency]. https://elaws.e-gov.go.jp/document?lawid=415CO0000000554_20230201_505CO0000000018

Goryashko, S. (2024, June 9). 'Spy mania': Why is Russia accusing its own physicists of treason? *BBC*. https://www.bbc.com/news/articles/c8001gvp4dpo

Hamada, T. (2023). Roshiagun no ukuraina shinkōka no nichiro gyogyō gaikou [Japan-Russia fisheries diplomacy under the Russian Invasion of Ukraine]. *Bosutōku, 53*, 9–12. https://file.www4.hp-ez.com/kyokutouken/file_20230413-014343.pdf

Harada, D. (2022). *Ukuraina jōsei: roshia ni yoru ukuraina shinkō ni tsuite* [The situation in Ukraine: On Russia's invasion of Ukraine]. JOGMEC. https://oilgas-info.jogmec.go.jp/info_reports/1009226/1009293.html

Harada, D. (2023). *Zenrei naki tairo seisai: kore made no keii, chūmoku sareru jishō to sono kage* [Unprecedented sanctions against Russia: Developments so far, key events, and their impact]. https://oilgas-info.jogmec.go.jp/_res/projects/default_project/_page_/001/009/608/202301_2a_009-060.pdf

Headquarters for Ocean Policy (2015). *Japan's Arctic policy*. https://www8.cao.go.jp/ocean/english/arctic/pdf/japans_ap_e.pdf

Hiyama, T., & Takakura, H. (Eds.) (2018) *Global warming and human-nature dimension in Northern Eurasia*. Springer. https://doi.org/10.1007/978-981-10-4648-3

Hokkaido Government (2016). *Hokkyokukai kōro no rikatsuyō ni muketa hōshin* [Policy for the utilization of the Northern Sea Route]. https://www.pref.hokkaido.lg.jp/fs/5/2/1/0/2/6/5/_/R01_feri.pdf

Hokkaido Government (2019). Kakushu bunsho [Various documents]. https://www.pref.hokkaido.lg.jp/fs/1/0/4/2/7/9/1/9/_/03_各種文書.pdf

Hokkaido Government (2023a). *Roshia to no chiikikan kōryū* (*Roshia kōryū kakari no peeji*) [Regional exchange with Russia (Russia exchange page)]. https://www.pref.hokkaido.lg.jp/ss/tsk/russia_new_top.html

Hokkaido Government (2023b). *Roshia kyōryū deetabeesu* [Russia Exchange Database]. https://www.pref.hokkaido.lg.jp/fs/1/0/4/2/7/9/2/0/_/04_交流の歴史データベース.pdf

Hokkaido Shimbun (2023a, February 1). *Nichiro todaeta kōryū* [The ceased Russo-Japanese exchanges].

Hokkaido Shimbun (2023b, May 6). *Roshia suisanbutsu yunyū saikō* [Record high imports of Russian seafood].

Hokkaido Shimbun (2023c, June 10). *Nichirō bōeki, chūkosha ya LNG zō* [Japan-Russia trade: increase in used cars and LNG].

Humpert, M. (2024, February 9). No Shipments from Russia's Arctic LNG 2 Until March as Sanctions Block Delivery of LNG Carriers. *High North News*. https://www.highnorthnews.com/en/no-shipments-russias-arctic-lng-2-until-march-sanctions-block-delivery-lng-carriers

Ikeshima, T. (2016). Japan's role as an Asian observer state within and outside the Arctic Council's framework. *Polar Science*, *10*(3), 458–462. https://doi.org/10.1016/j.polar.2016.07.006

International Maritime Organization (IMO) (2014). International code for ships operating in polar waters. IMO Doc. MSC 385(94) – MEPC 68/21/Add.1, Annex 10 [Polar Code].

JBIC (2021). *Project financing for Arctic LNG 2 project in Gydan Peninsula, Russia*. https://www.jbic.go.jp/en/information/press/press-2021/1201-015512.html

JCAR (2024a). *Arctic research: its current status and future plans. Executive summary*. https://www.jcar.org/longterm/executive_summary20240109.pdf

JCAR (2024b). *Hokkyokuiki no kenkyū: sono genjō to shōrai kōsō* [Research on the Arctic region: its current status and future prospects]. Kaibundo.

JOGMEC (2019). *Final investment decision for Arctic LNG 2 project in Russia*. https://www.jogmec.go.jp/english/news/release/news_15_000001_00002.html

JTI (2022). *JTI suspends investments in Russia and continues to prioritize the safety of its employees and their families.* https://www.jti.com/jti-suspends-investments-russia-and-continues-prioritize-safety-its-employees-and-their-families

Keizai Sangyōshō & Sōmushō (2023). *Dejitaruinfra (DC nado) seibi n ikan suru yūshikisha kaigō chūkan torimatome 2.0* [Expert meeting on the development of digital infrastructure (e.g., data centers) Interim summary 2.0.]. https://www.meti.go.jp/press/2023/05/20230530004/20230530004-a.pdf

Kimura, N., Imai, H. (2024, June 4). Roshia suiiki sake – masugyo – nichiro 3 nen buri daketsu [Agreement on salmon and trout fishing in Russian waters: Operations resume after 3 years starting in mid-month]. *Hokkaido Shimbun.* https://www.hokkaido-np.co.jp/article/1020152/

Dyatel, T. (2023, April 24). Iz ammiaka isparyayutsya nalogi. Vlasti obnulili NDPI dlya proyekta NOVATEK a [Taxes evaporate from ammonia: Authorities eliminate MET for NOVATEK's project]. *Kommersant.* https://www.kommersant.ru/doc/5952375

Kono, T. (2018). *Speech by H. E. Mr. Taro Kono, Minister for Foreign Affairs of Japan at the Arctic Circle 2018 Opening Session, 19 October 2018, Reykjavik, Iceland.* https://www.mofa.go.jp/files/000410409.pdf

Kossa, M., Lomaeva, M., & Saunavaara, J. (2020). East Asian subnational government involvement in the Arctic: A case for paradiplomacy? *The Pacific Review, 34*(4), 664–695. https://doi.org/10.1080/09512748.2020.1729843.

Kumagai, T. (2024, February 5). JOGMEC repays loan guarantee for Japan Arctic LNG before US sanctions waiver expiry. *S&P Global.* https://www.spglobal.com/commodityinsights/en/market-insights/latest-news/lng/020524-jogmec-repays-loan-guarantee-for-japan-arctic-lng-before-us-sanctions-waiver-expiry

LNG Prime Staff (2024, January 17). TotalEnergies issues force majeure over Novatek's Arctic LNG 2 project. *LNGPrime.* https://lngprime.com/asia/totalenergies-issues-force-majeure-over-novateks-arctic-lng-2-project/102579/

Lomaeva, M., & Lyude, A. (2023). Japan-Russia academic collaboration after Russia's invasion of Ukraine. In *Proceedings of the 37th International Symposium on the Okhotsk Sea & Polar Oceans 2023* (pp. 197–200).

Lomaeva, Marina, Mitani, Yoko, & Saunavaara, Juha (2023). Non-state actors and marine environmental governance in the North Pacific: The case of northern fur seal. In *Proceedings of the 37th International Symposium on the Okhotsk Sea & Polar Oceans* (pp. 23–26).

Lomaeva, M., & Saunavaara, J. (2022). Japan facing the Arctic and north: Interplay between the national and regional interests. In A. Likhacheva (Ed.), *Arctic fever: Political, economic & environmental aspects* (pp. 393–428). Palgrave Macmillan.

Matthews, D. (2023, November 14). Russian researchers disappear from academic conferences as isolation bites. *Science Business*. https://sciencebusiness.net/news/international-news/news-depth-russian-researchers-disappear-academic-conferences-isolation

Ministry of Economy, Trade and Industry of Japan (2019). *Tsūshō hakusho 2020. Dai 3 bu, dai 2 shō, dai 7 setsu. Roshia* [White paper on international economy and trade 2020. Part 3. Chapter 2. Section 7. Russia] https://www.meti.go.jp/report/tsuhaku2020/2020honbun/i3270000.html

Ministry of Foreign Affairs of Japan (2022a). *Foreign policy: Diplomatic bluebook*. https://www.mofa.go.jp/policy/other/bluebook/index.html

Ministry of Foreign Affairs of Japan (2022b). *Nichiro chiiki – shimaitoshi kouryuunen kaikaishiki no kaisai (kekka)* [The opening ceremony of Japan-Russia Interregional and Sister-City Exchange Year (Results)]. https://www.mofa.go.jp/mofaj/press/release/press3_000713.html

Ministry of Foreign Affairs of Japan (2023). *Kaigai anzen hōmupeeji: Roshia kiken・supotto・kōiki jōhō* [Overseas safety website: Russia: danger – spots – general information]. https://www.anzen.mofa.go.jp/info/pcinfectionspothazardinfo_178.html#ad-image-0

Ministry of Foreign Affairs of Japan (2023a). *Gaikō seisho: Dai 2 setsu: Nihon no kokusai kyōryoku (Kaihatsu kyōryokuto chikyūkibo kadai he no torikumi)* [Diplomatic bluebook: Section 2: Japan's international cooperation (development cooperation and efforts to address global Issues]. https://www.mofa.go.jp/mofaj/gaiko/bluebook/2023/pdf/pdfs/3_2.pdf

Ministry of Foreign Affairs of Japan (2023b). *Gaikō seisho: Tokushū: Roshia ni yoru Ukuraina shinkō to nihon no taiō* [Diplomatic bluebook: Feature: Russia's invasion of Ukraine and Japan's response]. *Foreign policy: Diplomatic bluebook*. https://www.mofa.go.jp/mofaj/gaiko/bluebook/2023/pdf/pdfs/1_3.pdf

Ministry of Foreign Affairs of the People's Republic of China (2018). *Joint statement the third trilateral high-level dialogue on the Arctic*. https://www.mfa.gov.cn/eng/zy/gb/202405/t20240531_11367362.html

Mitsui O.S.K. Lines (2022, February 9). *MOL signs charter contract for a newbuilding ice-breaking tanker to serve Russia's Arctic LNG 2 project – Participating in Japan's 1st condensate transport project using ice-breaking tanker*. https://www.mol.co.jp/en/pr/2022/22021.html

Mongkjargal (2010). Ainu no kaigai kōryū to minzoku no fukken. 1970 nendai no ainu chūgoku hōmon ga motarashita mono [Intercultural exchange and the restoration of indigenous rights: the Ainu delegations to China to the l970s]. Wakō daigaku gendai ningen gakubu kiyō dai 3 gō (2010 nen 3 gatsu), 117–135.

Murakami, S., & Kelly, T. (2023, July 7). Japanese PM heads to NATO to warn of East Asian risks. *Reuters*. https://www.reuters.com/world/japanese-pm-heads-nato-warn-east-asia-risks-2023-07-07/

NOVATEK (2021a, September 2). *NOVATEK and JBIC sign strategic cooperation agreement*. https://www.novatek.ru/en/investors/events/?id_4=4635

NOVATEK (2021b, September 2). *NOVATEK and Ministry of Economy, Trade and Industry of Japan sign memorandum of cooperation*. https://www.novatek.ru/en/press/releases/index.php?id_4=4633&mode_20=574&mode_5=pdrm&from_4=3

NPFC (2023, March 24). *Seventh commission session concludes hybrid meetings in Sapporo, Japan*. https://www.npfc.int/news/seventh-commission-session-concludes-hybrid-meetings-sapporo-japan

Ocean Policy Research Institute (n.d.). *History*. https://www.spf.org/opri-intl/about/history/

Ohnishi, F. (2016). Japan's Arctic policy development: From engagement to a strategy. In L. Lunde, J. Yang, & I. Stensdal (Eds.), *Asian countries and the Arctic future* (pp. 171–182). World Scientific Publishing. https://doi.org/10.1142/9789814644181_0011

Osakada, Y. (2021). An examination of arguments over the Ainu policy promotion act of Japan based on the UN declaration on the rights of indigenous peoples. *The International Journal of Human Rights*, *25*(6), 1053–1069. https://doi.org/10.1080/13642987.2020.1811692

Reuters (2021. June 24). *Russia's Novatek in talks with Japan's Mitsui on ammonia project, Kommersant says*. https://www.reuters.com/business/energy/russias-novatek-talks-with-japans-mitsui-ammonia-project-kommersant-says-2021-06-24/

Sasaki, S. (2022). Kokuritsu ainu minzoku hakubutsukan no setsuritsu to hatasu beki yakuwari [The establishment of the national Ainu museum: Process and expected roles]. *National Ainu Museum Journal*, *1*, 9–19. https://nam.go.jp/wp/wp-content/uploads/2022/10/005-shiro-sasaki_colour-comp.pdf

Sasakura, I. (2000). Hokkaidōritsu hoppō minzoku hakubutsukan no shozō shiryō to sono seiri ni tsuite [The collected materials of the Hokkaido museum of northern peoples and their organization]. *Bulletin of the Hokkaido Museum of Northern Peoples*, *9*, 85–104.

Saunavaara, J. (2017). The changing Arctic & the development of Hokkaido. *Arctic Yearbook*, [*2017*], 326–338). https://arcticyearbook.com/images/yearbook/2017/Scholarly_Papers/18_The_Changing_Arctic.pdf

Saunavaara, J. (2022). New marine communication cables in the Arctic. In J. D. Kim & C. E. Morrison (Eds.), *Science, technology and the path forward for a new Arctic. Papers from the 2021 North Pacific Arctic Conference* (pp. 165–173). Korean Maritime Institute & East-West Center.

Saunavaara, J., & Ohnishi, F. (2020). Arctic challenge for sustainability II: Japan's new Arctic flagship project. *Current Developments in Arctic Law, 8, 40–43*. https://lauda.ulapland.fi/bitstream/handle/10024/64478/Current%20developments%20in%20arctic%20law.pdf?sequence=1&isAllowed=y

Saunavaara, J., & Salminen, M. (2023). Geography of the global submarine fiber-optic cable network: The case for Arctic Ocean solutions. *Geographical Review, 113*(1), 1–19, https://doi.org/10.1080/00167428.2020.1773266

Schreiber, M. (2022, October 17). China will not recognize an Arctic Council without Russia, envoy says. *Arctic Today*. https://www.arctictoday.com/china-will-not-recognize-an-arctic-council-without-russia-envoy-says/

Shinohara, H. (2022, April 3). Sushi sticker shock: Ukraine was drives up salmon prices in Japan. *Nikkei Asia*. https://asia.nikkei.com/Business/Food-Beverage/Sushi-sticker-shock-Ukraine-war-drives-up-salmon-prices-in-Japan

Sinclair, J. (2014). Japan and the Arctic: Not so poles apart. *Sekiyu • Tennen gasu rebuy, 48*(2), 39–48. https://oilgas-info.jogmec.go.jp/_res/projects/default_project/_project_/pdf/5/5225/201403_039a.pdf

Staalesen, A. (2023, April 24). Moscow offers new subsidies for Arctic hydrogen. *The Barents Observer*. https://thebarentsobserver.com/en/new-energy/2023/04/moscow-offers-new-subsidies-arctic-hydrogen

Submarine Cable Network (n.d.). *Arctic Connect*. https://www.submarinenetworks.com/en/systems/trans-arctic/arctic-connect

Suisanchō (2023). *Kita taiheiyō gyogyō iinkai (NPFC) dai 7 kai nenji kaigō no kekka ni tsuite* [Concerning the results of the 7th Annual Meeting of the North Pacific Fisheries Commission (NPFC)]. https://www.jfa.maff.go.jp/j/press/kokusai/230324.html

Takakura, H., Fujioka, Y., Ignatyeva, V., Tanaka, T., Vinokurova, N., Grirorev, S., & Boyakova, S. (2021). Differences in local perceptions about climate and environmental changes among residents in a small community in eastern Siberia. *Polar Science, 27, 100556*. https://doi.org/10.1016/j.polar.2020.100556

Teraoka, A., & Namiki, R. (2022, March 4). Russia walls off government websites from nonfriendly countries. *Nikkei Asia*. https://asia.nikkei.com/Politics/Ukraine-war/Russia-walls-off-government-websites-from-nonfriendly-countries

The Asahi Shimbun (2022, September 6). Russia revokes agreements on visits to Northern Territories. *The Asahi Shimbun*. https://www.asahi.com/ajw/articles/14712176

The Asahi Shimbun (2023, March 8). Alaska's Qilak LNG targets Asia with $5 billion project to compete with Russia. *The Asahi Simbun*. https://www.asahi.com/ajw/articles/14856514

The Japan Institute of International Affairs (2023). *The 4th Tokyo Global Dialogue.* https://www.jiia.or.jp/TGD/tgd4/en/

The Northern Forum (2023). *Annual Report 2022.* https://www.northernforum.org/en/about-nf/annual-reports

Thompson, F. (2022). JBIC halts financing for Russian LNG project. *GTR Global Trade Review.* https://www.gtreview.com/news/global/jbic-halts-financing-for-russian-lng-project/

Tonami, A. (2016). *Asian foreign policy in a changing Arctic: The diplomacy of economy and science at new frontiers.* Palgrave. https://doi.org/10.1057/978-1-137-53746-1

Tonami, A. (2020). Hikokka akutā ni yoru paradipuromashī to kihan: hokkyokuiki ni tai suru Hokkaidō no torikumi wo rei ni [Paradiplomacy of non-state actors and norms: Hokkaido's approach towards the Arctic as an example]. In T. Oga, R. Nakano, & A. Matsumoto (Eds.), *Kyōsei shakai no saikōchiku III: kokusai kihan no kyōgō to chōwa* [Reconstruction of the inclusive society III: Conflict and coordination of international norms] (pp. 114–130). Hōritsu Bunkasha.

Tonami, A., & Watters, S. (2012). Japan's Arctic policy: The sum of many parts. *The Arctic yearbook* [*2012*], 93–103, https://arcticyearbook.com/images/yearbook/2012/Scholarly_Papers/4.Tonami_and_Watters.pdf

Trade Statistics of Japan (2024). *Trade statistics (Download) – Trade statistics of Japan.* https://www.customs.go.jp/toukei/info/tsdl_e.htm

Treaty concerning the Archipelago of Spitsbergen (adopted 9 February 1920, entered into force 14 August 1925) 2 LNTS 7. [1920 Svalbard Treaty]

Trilateral Cooperation Secretariat (2019). *Foreign affairs: Trilateral high-level dialogue on the Arctic.* https://tcs-asia.org/en/cooperation/mechanism.php?topics=3

WWCAM (2022). *World Winter City News, March 2022.* https://wwcam.org/wordpress/wp-content/uploads/2022/03/newsletter2022mar_en.pdf

Yamal. LNG (n.d.). *About the project.* http://yamallng.ru/en/project/about/

Yennie-Lindgren, W. (2020). Japan and Arctic security. In G. Hoogensen Gjørv, M. Lanteigne, & H. Sam-Aggrey (Eds.), *Routledge handbook of Arctic security* (pp. 324–336). Routledge.

Yennie Lindgren, W, & Lanteigne, M. (2023). Asia-Arctic diplomacy a decade later: What has changed? *The Diplomat.* https://thediplomat.com/2023/03/asia-arctic-diplomacy-a-decade-later-what-has-changed/

Zia, K. (2022). Japan, US join hands at Alaska LNG Summit. *The Diplomatic Insight.* https://thediplomaticinsight.com/japan-us-join-hands-at-alaska-lng-summit/

CHAPTER 6

Latvia in the Arctic: Towards Future Cooperation Opportunities

Gints Jegermanis and Pavel Tkach

1 Introduction

The Arctic is a vast region that brings together eight States located in the Far North, and the interests of non-Arctic States indicate their willingness to participate in discovering, developing, and protecting the Earth's northernmost region. The international political cycle in the Arctic is often characterized by the activities of the Arctic Council. The Arctic Council has positioned itself as a forum for debate about peace and science, as well as an appealing international arena in which non-Arctic States are able to participate. The principal subjects of debate in the Arctic Council were and continue to be climate change and preserving the Arctic's marine and terrestrial environments amongst others. Nonetheless, in recent years, and in parallel, representatives of Arctic Council Member States gradually included Arctic security into their official statements.

Latvia, a small country in the Baltic region with a population of 1,871,882, has grappled with numerous existential and pressing challenges since regaining independence in the 1990s subsequent to the dissolution of the Soviet Union (European Union, n.d.). It needed immense effort and energy to establish and expand democratic institutions and contemporary public services, to build defence forces and police, to reform the economy, to reshape education, and to provide various essential services. In addition to all of these monumental undertakings, Latvia pushed hard to re-establish itself on the international stage. It had to address several major challenges at once. Latvia had to focus on joining international and regional organizations as well as dealing with the Russian troop pull-out while gradually establishing its diplomatic service, reopening diplomatic missions, and expanding bilateral ties. Latvian diplomacy has also constantly been busy with countering the never-ending Russian misinformation campaigns (Pugliese, 2024). Since the beginning of the 2020s, Latvia's focus on joining international and regional organizations has included Arctic cooperation, emphasizing both the

 | DOI:10.1163/9789004734685_007

benefits of participating in Arctic cooperation and the challenges related to joining international Arctic fora.

Since Latvia is a small country with limited resources and a constant shortage of experts, Latvian universities and research institutions were unable to reach out to colleagues in the Nordic countries and establish long-term collaboration on Arctic issues during the first couple of decades of re-established independence. Meanwhile, the Baltic and Nordic countries' political dialogue and fruitful cooperation were strengthening. Although the importance of the Nordic-Baltic Eight (NB8) had grown in the region, particularly in the last 10 to 15 years, Arctic issues were not on its agenda (Šime, 2016).

The Arctic Council's observer State status allows non-Arctic States to contribute to the forum's operation. The observers' primary role is to observe the functioning of the Arctic Council, including by attending meetings and providing opinions on various topics, and participate in the work of the Arctic Council's subsidiary groups. As of late 2024, the Arctic Council has 13 non-Arctic States as observer States. Switzerland was the most recent observer State to be approved in 2017. In January 2021, Latvian authorities publicly expressed a willingness to join the Arctic Council as an observer State.

The goal of this chapter is to analyze EU Member State Latvia as the Arctic partner, NATO Member State Latvia as the Arctic partner, and independent State Latvia as the Arctic partner, as well as to examine Latvia's chances of receiving the status of observer State in the Arctic Council. The information presented in this chapter is derived from comprehensive desk research undertaken by the authors, alongside firsts-hand insights gained by one of the authors through their work with the Ministry of Foreign Affairs of the Republic of Latvia.

2 Latvia in the Arctic: Setting the Agenda

On 3–4 October 2019, Latvian Foreign Minister Edgars Rinkēvičs (as of 2024, President of Latvia) attended the EU Arctic Forum in Umeå, Sweden. Participation in this event hinted, for the first time, at the potential integration of the Arctic dimension into Latvian foreign policy.

Following Rinkēvičs visit to the Umeå Forum, the Latvian Foreign Ministry began analyzing national interests and options for Arctic cooperation. By the end of 2019, the Ministry had organized a separate workshop for Latvian ambassadors posted to Arctic Council Member States during the annual ambassadors' conference in Riga. At the beginning of 2020, the Foreign Ministry's European Department established a small informal unit to reach out to line ministries and expert communities, map national interests, and detect competence on Arctic issues in Latvia. The unit's analysis plainly demonstrated a lack of strong domestic and political interest (Ministry of Foreign Affairs of the Republic of Latvia, 2021a; Gints Jegermanis participated in the development of the analysis). Nonetheless, Foreign Minister Rinkēvičs stated in his annual speech to the Parliament during the foreign policy debate in January 2021 that Latvia would prepare and submit its application for the status of observer State in the Arctic Council (Ministry of Foreign Affairs of the Republic of Latvia, 2021c). An Estonian example could also have been at work. At the time, Estonia was actively pursuing its campaign in Arctic Council Member States and participating in numerous important Arctic forums to advance its prospects of becoming an Arctic Council observer State.

The Foreign Ministry was prompted by the Minister's political statement to begin the second round of national discussions with Latvia's line ministries, academic specialists, and research communities. The European Department also consulted with colleagues from other ministries as well as Latvian embassies accredited to Arctic Council Member States. Furthermore, the European Department contacted the Arctic or Polar Ambassadors in the Foreign Ministries of the Nordic countries, as well as several senior officials from the Arctic Council's observer States (the United Kingdom, the Netherlands, Switzerland, and Poland) (Celmiņš, 2021). In addition to that, the European Department maintained constant contact with its colleagues at the Estonian Foreign Ministry to learn from their experiences and discuss the Estonian approach towards the Arctic Council.

The Foreign Ministry's cooperation efforts and analyses of Latvia's Arctic interests were summarized in a report to the Government. It was approved in the Cabinet's meeting in July 2021. The paper provided context and explored the growing international and regional significance of Arctic challenges. According to the Foreign Ministry, Latvia's interests can be found in four areas: geopolitics, environment/climate, economy, and science (Ministry of Foreign Affairs of the Republic of Latvia, 2021a). The research emphasized that Arctic changes are politically, militarily, environmentally, and economically related to and have an impact on the Baltic Sea region. Therefore, it was advised that Latvia should pay attention to and understand the interests of Arctic countries by maintaining a continuous bilateral dialogue on these topics. The study detailed the history of the Arctic Council, how it operates, and what it would take for Latvia to be able to contribute to the Council's subsidiary bodies in the case of observer status application success. Finally, the Latvian Foreign Ministry proposed forming an Inter-Agency Working Group (IAWG) tasked with preparing and finalizing the national application and submitting it to the Arctic Council Secretariat by the end of 2022.

Even before reporting to the Government, Latvia's Foreign Minister sent a letter to Latvian universities, research institutes, the private sector, and non-governmental organizations informing them of the steps taken and asking if they are involved in activities that may be relevant to Arctic research, local culture, or if they can distinguish interests that may apply to Arctic Council's work. Responses and ongoing interaction enhanced the Ministry's understanding and aided in planning future measures.

In September 2021, the IAWG was formed. Following several meetings in the remaining months of 2021, the IAWG tasked Latvian embassies in Arctic Council Member States with reaching out to Indigenous peoples' organizations in Arctic countries in early 2022. The embassies were also urged to meet with the Arctic municipalities to examine potential collaboration opportunities. Despite the fact that Latvian embassies reached out and established contacts with several Indigenous organizations and municipalities in the Arctic, progress and efficiency were significantly impacted by the launch of a full-scale Russian invasion of Ukraine on 24 February 2022.

The IAWG resolved that Latvia should be more actively represented in Arctic regional and international conferences and forums. Among other things, the IAWG concluded that Latvia must develop a long-term Arctic policy. To foster knowledge and share experience in Latvia, the IAWG agreed that a special coordination and cooperation platform is needed. As a result, it was proposed that the Latvian Government assist in the establishment of a national Arctic Forum that would bring together a diverse range of experts from the government, academia, the research community, non-governmental organizations (NGOs), and businesses at least once a year to get to know each other, share information about daily work, discuss potential areas of interest, and decide on the next steps. The national Arctic Forum – Riga Forum – could also aid in developing cooperation with experts from Arctic Council Member States and outside. The conclusion of the IAWG deliberations was summarized and reported in the second report to the Government. The paper also identified possible areas and challenges for Latvian contribution to the activities of the Arctic Council working groups (Ministry of Foreign Affairs of the Republic of Latvia, 2021b).

Russia's war in Ukraine influenced and modified the activities of the Arctic Council and other Arctic organizations and forums. Cooperation with Russia was no longer acceptable, and as a result, Arctic governance and a number of professional networks suffered greatly. Russia technically continued to chair the Arctic Council until May 2023, but actual cooperation was only conceivable and acceptable among Nordic nations, the United States, and Canada, as well as indigenous peoples' organizations from these seven Arctic countries.

That has also influenced the plans of the Latvian Government. It was decided that Latvia would not submit the observer status application to the Arctic Council Secretariat before the end of 2022, as initially planned. Latvia will continue to develop its Arctic policy and consider national possibilities for contributing to the work of the Arctic Council working groups. The decision on the best time to apply for official observer status will have to be made later, after the Arctic Council full-scale resumes its regular work.

Prior to the commencement of the IAWG's endeavours, the Foreign Ministry commissioned Latvian research institutions to undertake comprehensive research on the Arctic and Latvia's role within the Arctic cooperation. In 2014, the Latvian Institute of International Affairs (LIIA), with the backing of the Konrad Adenauer Stiftung, curated an edited volume delving into the Arctic, titled 'Perceptions and Strategies of Arcticness in sub-Arctic Europe'. The book expounded upon the national interests and positions of Arctic Council Member States and observer States and showcased the advancements and substantive scientific and research contributions made by diverse Latvian academic and research institutes (Sprūds & Rostoks, 2014). In addition, several interviews were conducted with members of the Latvian research community. The study's overall finding suggested the presence of a few specific cases in Latvia that are pertinent to Arctic research. However, due to the lack of permanent funding and direct support by the Latvian universities, it is difficult to develop and continue meaningful research of Arctic issues.

Among several projects executed by Latvian researchers over the past decade, the polar exploration expeditions in the Arctic and the Antarctic stand out clearly. There is a small group of polar researchers in Latvia. They have travelled yearly to Iceland, Svalbard, and Greenland since 2014, and once to the Antarctic. These expeditions are mostly funded by the EU and private contributions in Latvia. Polar researchers have cooperated with several Latvian enterprises and have tested their specialized equipment and technologies in harsh climate conditions. They have been able to collect and analyze a unique set of data acquired during the expeditions. All of these efforts resulted in the establishment of the Polar Research Centre, which has been operating at the Faculty of Geography and Land Sciences of the University of Latvia since autumn 2021. Even though the University of Latvia approved the Polar Research Centre, it is not specifically funded.

On 14 December 2022, the Latvian Ministry of Foreign Affairs carried out a 'Latvia in the Arctic' seminar (Ministry of Foreign Affairs of the Republic of Latvia, 2022a). Andris Pelšs, State Secretary of the Latvian Foreign Ministry, emphasized in his opening remarks that this is only the first attempt to bring together Latvian stakeholders and foreign guests to learn from each other. He also stated that the Latvian Foreign Ministry aims to hold similar forums in the future. The seminar gathered experts from several Ministries, Latvian polar researchers, entrepreneurs, NGOs, musicians, and artists. They shared their experience of working in the Arctic. LIIA Deputy Director Mārtiņš Vargulis spoke about his research and reports on Latvia's options in the Arctic. Norwegian Ambassador Ine Måreng explained Norway's view on the actual situation in the Arctic and how the Arctic Council was continuing its work without Russia and talked about Norway's plans to chair the Arctic Council (Ministry of Foreign Affairs of the Republic of Latvia, 2022a). Peter Sköld, Latvia's Honorary Consul in Västerbotten County (Sweden) and professor at the Umeå University, spoke about the work of the Arctic Council and explained his long-standing expertise and experience on the Arctic issues (Ministry of Foreign Affairs of the Republic of Latvia, 2022a). He also indicated areas of potential cooperation among Latvian researchers and Arctic experts in the Nordic countries. Overall, the impression was that Latvian experts and practitioners had gained skills, gathered data, and were eager to continue investigating other opportunities for working in the Arctic and interacting with colleagues from Arctic countries. Their suggestion and appeal to the government are straightforward: for this activity to succeed, it must be permanently supported and adequately sustained. This seminar could be considered as an initial step toward indicating the Latvian interest in cooperating with the Arctic. Nevertheless, the seminar targeted mainly the domestic (national) audience and poorly disclosed mentioned interests to the international audience.

In the next section, the authors focus on Latvia's contribution to the Arctic partnership as an EU Member State – a vital actor in Arctic science, research, and diplomacy. That is important to address because the EU, as a union with extensive financial and knowledge resources, contributes to the Arctic on a daily basis.

3 Place of Latvia in EU–Arctic Relations: Supplementing the Agenda

3.1 *The Arctic in the EU Agenda*

The current EU's policy in the Arctic is built upon the principles set out in the United Nations Convention on the Law of the Sea (UNCLOS, 1982), the 2030 Agenda for Sustainable Development (United Nations General Assembly, 2015), as well as its involvement in the work of the Arctic Council, the Barents Euro-Arctic Council, and the Northern Dimension policy framework.

The Joint Communication to the European Parliament, the Council, the European Economic and Social Committee and the Committee of the Regions – A stronger EU engagement for a peaceful, sustainable and prosperous Arctic (EU Arctic Policy) emphasizes that as a significant geopolitical entity, the

> [European Union (EU)] has strategic and day-to-day interests, both in the European Arctic and the broader Arctic region. The EU also has a fundamental interest in supporting multilateral cooperation in the Arctic and in working to ensure that it remains safe, stable, sustainable, peaceful and prosperous. Being a major economic player, it shares the responsibility for global sustainable development, including in the Arctic regions, and for the livelihood of inhabitants, including Indigenous Peoples. The EU exerts a significant impact on the Arctic through its environmental footprint and demand for resources and products originating there.
>
> EUROPEAN COMMISSION, 2021

On May 1, 2004, Latvia joined the European Union. Daily, Latvian civil servants and experts participate in the working groups of the Council of the European Union by drafting the EU legislation and defending Latvia's interests (State Chancellery of Latvia, 2019). Latvia's Permanent Representation to the EU in Brussels is actively lobbying for Latvia's position in all EU institutions (State Chancellery of Latvia, 2019). Although Latvia initially played rather a role of an observer, over the years, Latvia's voice in the Council of the EU has become more audible, particularly regarding the EU's single market and its fundamental freedom, energy security and diversification of energy sources, digital development, and security (State Chancellery of Latvia, 2019).

3.2 *The Role of Latvia in the EU–Arctic Relations: Past, Present, Future*

The place of Latvia in the EU–Arctic relations can be evaluated from two perspectives: individual participation of Latvia in defining EU's Arctic-related policies and legislation and Latvian participation in EU's regional cooperation frameworks such as the Northern Dimension capable of directly and indirectly impacting the EU–Arctic agenda.

The individual participation of Latvia in defining the EU's Arctic-related policies and legislation can be characterized as not active, rarely impacting the setting of the EU–Arctic agenda. Thus, Latvia has been commenting on the EU Arctic Policy drafts twice – in 2016 and 2021. The comments, which are not publicly available, have been discussed within the Council Working Party on Eastern Europe and Central Asia (COEST) and presented by the Ministry of Foreign Affairs of Latvia. Conversely, in September 2014, the Directorate-General for Maritime Affairs and Fisheries (DG MARE) launched a public consultation on streamlining EU funding in the Arctic and extensively announced the call for opinions from Member States and research institutions based in Member States (Šime, 2016, p. 162). The Baltic States or research institutions based in the Baltic States have not contributed to the public consultation, indicating a lack of involvement from this region in the consultation process (Šime, 2016, p. 171).

In the context of Arctic research in the Baltic States, Zane Šime posits that one explanation for the infrequent engagement of Baltic States in EU-Arctic affairs is the reluctance of national institutions to prioritize policy initiatives that do not align with their top priorities (Šime, 2016, p. 171). Apparently, both Latvian and Lithuanian Ministries of Education focused during the mid-2010s mainly on their engagement in the Joint Baltic Sea System Research Programme (Šime, 2016, p. 171). The absence of the Arctic partnership and research in the top research priorities reflects the limited involvement of the Baltic States, particularly Lithuania and Latvia, in the Arctic agenda.

On 1 January 2015, Latvia took over the Presidency of the Council of the European Union for six months. Among legislative and non-legislative acts that the Member States agreed on under the Latvian Presidency of the EU Council was a draft regulation, which transposed the latest, at that moment, North-East Atlantic Fisheries Commission (NEAFC) recommendations into the EU Law (Latvian Presidency of the Council of the European Union, 2015). Reached consensus resulted in the amendment of Regulation (EU) No 1236/2010 of the European Parliament and of the Council laying down a scheme of control and enforcement applicable in the area covered by the Convention on future multilateral cooperation in the North-East Atlantic fisheries (Latvian Presidency of the Council of the European Union, 2015). The mentioned regulation provided for an appropriate framework for multilateral cooperation on the rational conservation and management of fishery resources in areas within those parts of the Atlantic and Arctic Oceans and their dependent seas, which lie north of 36°N latitude and between 42°W longitude and 51°E longitude (Regulation (EU) No 1236/2010, 2010). One of the regulated resources is the Arctic skate that lives near the seabed between 140 and 2,500 m deep in the Arctic Ocean and in the waters around Canada and northern and northwestern Europe and is an important part of marine biodiversity in the North Atlantic and Arctic Oceans (FishBase, n.d.). The amendment to the regulation adopted under the Latvian presidency was a significant step in combating illegal, unregulated, and unreported fishing, as well as trust-building with regional fisheries management organizations functioning in the Arctic region.

The Northern Dimension (ND) is a common policy of the EU, Russia, Norway, and Iceland, established as the EU's external policy with its own action program in 1999. The cooperation within the ND mainly takes place in the form of partnerships (Northern Dimension, 2020a). In March 2022, the European Union, Iceland, and Norway suspended until further notice all activities of the Northern Dimension policy which involve Russia and Belarus (European External Actions Service, 2022). Latvia is represented in all four sector-oriented partnerships. In two of them, Latvia is a founding partner – ND Partnership in Public Health and Social Wellbeing (NDPHS) and ND Partnership for Transport and Logistics (NDPTL) (Ministry of Foreign Affairs of the Republic of Latvia, 2021d). Participation in the Northern Dimension (ND) policy framework, until the suspension of its full-scale activities in 2022, used to be one of the ways for the EU to keep involved in the Arctic agenda and one of the directions in the foreign policy of Latvia for promoting the competitiveness of the Baltic Sea Region.

The European Commission Joint Staff Working Document – 'The inventory of activities in the framework of developing a European Union Arctic Policy' issued in 2012 put a special emphasis on activities of NDPTL aimed at establishing trans-European (multi-modal) connections in Europe's High North, that in conjunction with the EU regional development policy and its transport and infrastructure modernization projects are crucial tools to developing the Arctic region (European Commission, High Representative of the European Union for Foreign Affairs and Security Policy, 2012). The NDPTL's steering committee's latest road map for 2019–2024 paid extensive attention to the Arctic region and noted that well-developed infrastructure for transport and logistics is a prerequisite for sustainable Arctic development (Northern Dimension Partnership on Transport and Logistics, 2018). It is important to mention that Latvia is a founding partner in the respective partnership and signatory of the Memorandum of Understanding setting out the modalities of establishing the Northern Dimension Partnership on Transport (2008), which completed numerous transport and infrastructure projects, including in the Arctic region.

The partnership in which Latvia is one of the observers – ND Environmental Partnership (NDEP), has claimed its usefulness for the Arctic region. Particularly, the NDEP projects on nuclear and hazardous waste treatment on the nuclear fleet support ship *Lepse* and the spent fuel storage facility at Andreeva Bay have considerably reduced radiological and environmental risks in the Arctic and contributed to developing methodologies applicable also in the Baltic Sea (Northern Dimension, 2020b).

In general, the developers of the EU Arctic Policy, in its working documents, recognized that the Northern Dimension was "a useful umbrella to facilitate cooperation between the *Four Councils of the North*, i.e. the Arctic Council, the Barents Euro-Arctic Council, the Council of the Baltic Sea States and the Nordic Council of Ministers" (European Commission, High Representative of the European Union for Foreign Affairs and Security Policy, 2012, p. 29). As a regional cooperation framework within the EU, the Northern Dimension appeared to be an efficient connector of the EU and the Arctic in development projects involving Arctic States or implementing in the territories of the Far North.

To summarize, Latvia's role in defining the EU–Arctic agenda is slight, and among the Baltic States, Latvia demonstrates less initiative than Estonia in terms of contributing to the EU–Arctic engagement. Arctic affairs were not included among the top priorities of Latvian foreign policy, research, science, and education for a long time. Nevertheless, Latvia's interest in the Arctic has been steadily strengthening. In the mid-2010s, Latvia aligned with the EU's interests in the Arctic, particularly in the areas of climate mitigation, marine biodiversity preservation in the Arctic Ocean, North Atlantic Ocean, and adjacent seas, as well as the development of new transportation networks from the Baltic to the Far North. The significance of developing new transportation networks for both the Baltic and Arctic regions has been extensively emphasized in the European Parliament resolution of 7 October 2021, on the Arctic: opportunities, concerns, and security challenges. The European Parliament remarked that "new northern rail links would stimulate the economies of the northern and Baltic States and improve the North-South dimension of market access [and called] on the Commission, therefore, to address northern transport issues and identify opportunities in the context of the [NDPTL]" with special emphasis on the fact "that better links are needed within the Northern Dimension region to reduce remoteness and ensure connectivity in response to global development" (European Parliament, 2021, para. 28). The realization of the Rail Baltica project (Rail Baltica, n/d.) could be a great start in ensuring connectivity of the Arctic region for the EU.

At present, Latvia in its potential application for observer status in the Arctic Council can not reference to active involvement in shaping EU Arctic Policy. Nevertheless, Latvia can underscore its engagement in the ND partnerships, particularly NDPTL and NDEP, as evidence of its capacity to indirectly address Arctic-related matters. Also, it is worth mentioning that the EU highly evaluates its cooperation in the Baltic Sea region for defining the Arctic agenda. Thus, the Opinion of the European Committee of the Regions on the 'new EU Arctic strategy' in 2021 emphasized that the EU cooperation in the Baltic Sea region is also linked to the Arctic cooperation package, implying that cooperation in the Baltic Sea region will not disappear from the EU–Arctic agenda (European Committee of the Regions, 2021). Therefore, it is up to Latvia to strengthen its own presence in EU projects in the Baltic that can have an impact on the Arctic region, such as biodiversity conservation projects that help create methodologies applicable to both Baltic and Arctic water areas and initiatives assuring the connectivity of the Arctic region.

Russia's war in Ukraine highlighted the need to pay attention to security issues in the North-East region, including the Baltic Sea region and the Far North with the Arctic Ocean. In the next section, the authors examine Latvia's role in reforming regional security arrangements and how the topic of security circulated in Nordic and Baltic States throughout the decades.

3.3 *The Place of Latvia in Transforming Regional Security Arrangements: Modifying the Agenda*

For a long time, the Nordic and Baltic countries developed their security posture and carried out national defence based on various political realities and history (Piotrowski, 2018). After surviving the Winter War in 1939–40, Finland strengthened its neutrality and carefully managed relations with the Soviet Union (Hannikainen, 2020). Simultaneously, Finland was heavily investing in its regular army and defense to withstand Soviet bullying on its own (Hannikainen, 2020). Since 1814, Sweden has successfully avoided military conflicts, developed sophisticated defense capabilities, and maintained a strong military industry after World War II (Brommesson, 2022).

Denmark, Norway, and Iceland joined NATO and were organizing their defense with their transatlantic political and military allies. Despite the fact that the Nordic countries have been quite innovative and forthright in establishing and evolving strong political and economic ties within the Nordic cooperation framework and joint institutions since the 1950s, they have been unable to discuss regional security and military developments due to Finland and Sweden's neutrality (Strang, 2016). This gradually began to change after 1995 due to Finland and Sweden's accession to the European Union. In 2009, five Nordic countries signed a Memorandum of Understanding in Helsinki, agreeing to the formation of Nordic Defence Cooperation (Nordefco).

The Soviet Union occupied the Baltic countries in 1940, effectively erasing them from the European political map for the next fifty years. With cautious and limited aid from the West, Estonia, Latvia, and Lithuania had to create their own organizations and armies, buy weapons, and train soldiers after regaining independence in 1991. Since the mid-1990s, the Baltic countries have sought NATO membership, eventually becoming full members of the Alliance in 2004.

Many factors contributed to the slow pace of Nordic and Baltic military and defense cooperation over the last three decades. The opposition of Finland and Sweden to joining NATO was one of many impediments to forging deeper military connections in the region. Since the 1950s, the Nordic countries have been strengthening their already strong links. Faced with increasing danger from Russia, the Baltic countries focused on determining the best means to defend themselves and work out sustainable conditions for the Baltic Sea's regional security in collaboration with NATO allies.

When Finland and Sweden eventually resolved to apply for NATO membership in May 2022, the major regional transformation began. Finnish and Swedish contribution to regional and NATO defense and security will open up new avenues and pose new questions. Even though military planning will eventually be shaped and carried out within NATO structures in Brussels and elsewhere, the Nordic and Baltic countries will need to rethink their political, economic, and military strategic cooperation. This discussion will bring to light some previously neglected topics. For example, Finland and Sweden's NATO membership will enable the establishment of defense arrangements for the Nordic and Baltic regions as a single military theatre for the first time. NATO allies will have to combine two images: developments in the High North and the Baltic Sea.

Over the last two to three decades, security policy experts and military strategists in the Nordic countries have been able to develop a certain understanding of the security developments in the Baltic Sea (Westgaard, 2023). This notion will need to be updated. However, colleagues in the Baltic countries have very limited experience and understanding of the High North's dynamic, context, and changes in military and security buildout. A new political and security conversation between the Nordic and Baltic countries will be required to bridge the gap and strengthen Nordic and Baltic partners' awareness of each other, as well as to answer crucial concerns about how to safeguard NATO's North-East flank cooperatively. Finally, it will necessitate more funding as well as an increase in human resources within the Baltic governments and think-tank groups.

Although the Arctic Council is not supposed to deal with military security issues, it is safe to assume that the new geopolitical situation in the Nordic and Baltic regions will significantly impact the Arctic debate in Latvia and other Baltic countries.

In developing its Arctic policy and seeking appropriate answers, the Latvian Government, in collaboration with national stakeholders, will most likely prioritize military and security components of Nordic and Baltic cooperation. Latvia's Foreign Ministry, in collaboration with the Ministry of Defence, will be a driving force and will continue to nudge line ministries, academia, the research community, and Arctic experts toward developing the Arctic agenda in the coming years.

3.4 *Latvia as a Potential Observer State of the Arctic Council: Realizing the Agenda*

The Nuuk Declaration, issued on the occasion of the Arctic Council's seventh ministerial meeting on May 12, 2011, in Nuuk, Greenland, established new criteria for admitting observers to the Arctic Council (Arctic Council, 2011). These criteria have since been incorporated into Annex 2, paragraph 6 of the Arctic Council Rules of Procedure (Arctic Council, 1998/2013). The procedural document states that an applicant for observer status must *inter alia*, accept and respect the Arctic Council, its principles, and procedures, demonstrate willingness, as well as political, scientific, and financial capability, and preparedness to cooperate with other Arctic Council members, Arctic Indigenous peoples, and Arctic inhabitants, and fully recognize Arctic State sovereignty, sovereign rights, and jurisdiction in the Arctic (Arctic Council, 1998/2013). In addition, the applicant should fully recognize that an extensive legal framework applies to the Arctic Ocean (Arctic Council, 1998/2013).

The work of IAWG demonstrates that Latvia recognizes the Arctic Council's values and objectives as outlined in the Declaration on the Establishment of the Arctic Council (Ottawa Declaration) (Arctic Council, 1996). This is also expressly stated in IAWG's first work report (Ministry of Foreign Affairs of the Republic of Latvia, 2021a). Latvia is a Party to UNCLOS and fully supports the international law of the sea and its importance in Arctic Ocean governance (Ministry of Foreign Affairs of the Republic of Latvia, 2021a). Furthermore, Latvia has a trilateral agreement with Sweden and Estonia on the Common Maritime Boundary Point in the Baltic Sea and has not been in disagreement with these countries on this arrangement.

The manifestation of intent and readiness to contribute to the work of the Arctic Council and to be a part of Arctic cooperation under the auspices of this international forum is expected to be done in a way that is visible to other Arctic Council members, Permanent Participants, and Arctic people in general. For example, Alar Karis, President of the Republic of Estonia, delivered a speech at the Arctic Circle Assembly 2022 in Reykjavik, and the Estonian Ministry of Foreign Affairs organized a session at the same forum titled 'Small States in Arctic science: Estonia – Where technology meets tradition' (Arctic Circle Assembly, 2022). Furthermore, on 14 January 2021, Kersti Kaljulaid (former President of Estonia) discussed what Estonia could give the Arctic at the Arctic Circle Virtual webinar series. The purpose of the Estonian participation in the Arctic Circle events was to demonstrate Estonia as a trustworthy State in Arctic cooperation and science.

As a potential observer candidate, Latvia should demonstrate its collaboration and research objectives similarly by actively participating in international conferences and assemblies. Thus, the Latvian glaciology specialist from the University of Latvia – Kristaps Lamsters – presented the Latvian expertise in glaciological studies at the Arctic Circle Assembly 2021 in cooperation with Poland, i.e., an Arctic Council observer State (Arctic Circle Assembly, 2021). Participation in such high-level conferences helps potential observer status applicants by providing visible facts to a broad audience about existing competencies in science and research, as well as intentions and capacities to collaborate with other Arctic Council participants in science and research.

Organizing an Arctic Circle Assembly session and bringing persons from Latvia to Iceland to deliver presentations or speeches can, however, cost over a thousand euros per person (including entrance fees, logistics, and housing). Arctic Frontiers, a large conference in Tromsø, Norway, costs much more, as does Arctic Encounter, a major conference in Alaska. In addition to organizing and participating in Arctic-related events and forums, observer States should, under Annex 2, paragraph 6, subparagraph e) of the Arctic Council Rules of Procedure, contribute to the operations of Arctic Council working groups and Permanent Participants (Arctic Council,

1998). This includes sending delegates to the working sites of the aforementioned stakeholders to participate in their activities and, in some cases, contribute to the events themselves. The undertaking of delegation travel to the Far North carries significant costs. When factoring in supplementary expenditures, it becomes apparent that a prudent annual provision from the national budget is necessary to substantiate Latvia's representation as an observer State within the Arctic Council. Regrettably, Latvia's historical commitment to this end has been notably modest.

Determining whether Latvian science and research can effectively contribute to Arctic science and research, particularly in the Arctic Ocean, is critical. Individual academics and scientific groups in Latvia have conducted Arctic research with funding from the state budget for scientific activities as well as the support of private companies (Ministry of Foreign Affairs of the Republic of Latvia, 2021b). Several expeditions led by geologists and researchers from the University of Latvia's Faculty of Geography and Earth Sciences to study glaciers in Iceland, Greenland, and Svalbard have produced internationally significant results, as highlighted by Latvia's participation in the Arctic Circle Assembly in 2021 (Ministry of Foreign Affairs of the Republic of Latvia, 2021b). It is important to note that Latvia is a Baltic Sea coastal State, and Latvian science and research capacities in the Baltic Sea can provide a comparative perspective in studying the Arctic Ocean, particularly the effects of climate change on marine biodiversity and fish migration patterns. Moreover, climate change has been identified as the top priority of national science and research by Latvian authorities, and it is expected that the country will fund research activities on the subject, indicating Latvia's willingness to participate in climate science and research on a global scale (Ministry of Foreign Affairs of the Republic of Latvia, 2021b).

The Latvian scientific and research community's direct and indirect contribution to Arctic studies goes beyond its interest in climate change. Thus, on 1 May 2021, the Institute of Solid State Physics of the University of Latvia, in collaboration with institutions from Iceland and Lithuania, began the implementation of a project co-funded by the European Economic Area (EEA) and Norway grants and the Ministry of Education and Science of the Republic of Latvia titled 'Aluminium recycling for hydrogen production – from waste through hydrogen energy to alumina – AliCE-Why' (Institute of Solid State Physics of the University of Latvia, 2021). The primary objective of the project is to design and implement an innovative technological solution that will streamline the recycling process for aluminum waste (Institute of Solid State Physics of the University of Latvia, 2021). This will not only improve overall recycling efficiency but also lead to the generation of hydrogen for energy purposes. Additionally, the project aims to develop new low-emission alumina products, thereby contributing to a more sustainable and environmentally friendly industrial landscape (Institute of Solid State Physics of the University of Latvia, 2021). The implementation of the project is not directly targeting the Arctic region itself. Still, it is being implemented in collaboration with Iceland, and the project's outcomes could be very beneficial to the Arctic.

In their second work report, the IAWG outlined potential directions and thematic areas for science and research collaboration (Ministry of Foreign Affairs of the Republic of Latvia, 2021b). However, the implementation of outlined plans could be slowed down or postponed because of ongoing Russia's war against Ukraine and existing uncertainties about the future of the Arctic Council. Nevertheless, Latvia appears to be signaling its political commitment to contribute to the work of the Arctic Council, with the intention of demonstrating its potential usefulness through the identification of best practices in glaciological and climate change studies, as well as the development of recycling methodologies. It is vital to acknowledge that these aspirations are speculative at this juncture and will require validation in the coming years. This, however, is highly hypothetical at this stage and needs to be verified at some point in the coming years.

To demonstrate compliance with the requirement to respect the values, interests, culture, and traditions of Arctic Indigenous peoples and other Arctic inhabitants, Latvia and its officials should actively promote the work of the Livonian Institute of the University of Latvia, as well as their collaboration with institutions already involved in Arctic research cooperation, namely Uppsala University, the University of Helsinki, and UiT The Arctic University of Norway (Ministry of Foreign Affairs of the Republic of Latvia, 2022b; Livonian Institute of the University of Latvia, 2019). As of 2024, the Livonian Institute has received little attention at the international Arctic level, with only individual communication from Latvian embassies in the Nordic countries, as mentioned earlier. In the third working report of IAWG, it has been noted that the Ministry of Culture of Latvia indicated the need to allocate the Livonian Institute 6,000 euros annually until 2025 to organize visits to Arctic States and Indigenous organizations to participate in knowledge exchange and 800 euros to organize online seminars (Ministry of Foreign Affairs of the Republic of Latvia, 2022b).

The criterion of recognition of Arctic States' sovereignty, sovereign rights, and jurisdiction in the Arctic has always been difficult due to disputable areas that did not have a clear answer even from Arctic Council Member States, such as the Beaufort Sea, which is shared by the United States and

Canada. The United States and Canadian Coast Guards have signed a pollution prevention and response agreement (Lockett, 2022). However, in the event of a jurisdictional conflict in the specified area, the voting for application within the Arctic Council may be influenced, notwithstanding Latvia's position. Moreover, Arctic States such as Canada, Denmark, Norway, Russia, and the US (whose capacity to submit to the Commission on the Limits of the Continental Shelf (CLCS) is debatable (Keating-Bitonti, 2024, p.2)), have declared in the past and can declare in the future an extension of their outer continental shelf, and it is always a question of which attitude non-Arctic States should take before these applications are approved by the CLCS.

All of these considerations will make sense only after the Arctic Council resume its day-to-day operations at a full-scale. Until 2022, the Russian Federation was an active member of the Arctic Council. Because all decisions in the Arctic Council are made by consensus of the Member States or, in case of the absence of a particular Member State, by consensus of present Member States and confirmation in writing by the absent States within 45 days after receiving notice of the decision, consensus cannot be obtained without Russia (Arctic Council, 1998/2013). But, more importantly, under the current circumstances, Latvia is not prepared and will not be prepared to cooperate with Russia – a State sponsor of terrorism, as recognized by the Latvian Parliament (Saeima, 2022), and with the Russian Indigenous peoples' organization RAIPON, which has an indirect affiliation with the Kremlin (Lackenbauer, Sidorova, & Sukhankin, 2023).

As of 2024, it is difficult to say that Latvia meets the conditions for acquiring observer State status in the Arctic Council. Despite Latvia's demonstrated political commitment to engage in Arctic Council activities and establish advantageous bilateral relationships with Member States on Arctic matters, this commitment is currently not receiving prioritization by the authorities in comparison to other regional and international security concerns. Thus, the Foreign Minister did not mention the Arctic issues in his annual foreign policy address to the Parliament in 2023 and 2024. Even though the Foreign Ministry has been able to establish a national procedure and IAWG produced three reports on Latvia's Arctic policy to the government, these tangible steps were not mentioned in the annual Foreign Minister's report either. In turn, the Ministry of Education and Science – co-chair of the IAWG, did not take part in the 'Latvia in the Arctic' seminar that the Foreign Ministry organized in December 2022.

Intentions to collaborate with Indigenous organizations have yet to be discovered, as communication regarding such cooperation has been only delegated to Latvian embassies. At the same time, the Latvian authorities' interest in developing the Livonian Institute of the University of Latvia gives some hope that future institutional engagement with Indigenous peoples in the Arctic will be secured. Nonetheless, there are no clear instances of joint activity between Latvia or the Livonian Institute of the University of Latvia and Indigenous peoples in the Arctic that may be attached to the observer status application. Latvia's financial capacity to finance the operations of the Arctic Council and its permanent participants is not clearly defined at this stage. In its third working report, the IAWG stated that the Ministry of Foreign Affairs will apply for a cross-sectoral budgetary allocation of 16,500 euros for 2023, 2024, and 2025 to ensure the cooperation of the Livonian Institute of the University of Latvia and Indigenous communities in the Arctic, as well as the organization of Arctic events in Latvia (Ministry of Foreign Affairs of the Republic of Latvia, 2022b). This amount includes only Latvian participation in the Arctic cooperation; however, the potential observer State should be ready to contribute financially to the work of Permanent Participants. Therefore, the Latvian financial commitment must be eventually increased.

The primary obstacle in delivering observer status applications is the lack of agreed-upon solutions in the Arctic Council on approving new observers without Russia's participation in the processes. In this context, there are uncertainties regarding accepting new observers until the rules and procedures are clarified. Thus, Latvian authorities should be prepared to withhold from applying until uncertainties of the Arctic Council functioning are solved. Nonetheless, despite existing complications, Arctic cooperation did not stop, and Latvian intentions, capacities, and competencies must be represented on the international stage, as well as pioneering cooperation opportunities with Arctic institutions and Indigenous organizations, to demonstrate that interest in Arctic cooperation is genuine so that the Arctic Council could take this into account.

4 Conclusions

From 2019, when Edgars Rinkēvičs participated in the EU Arctic Forum in Umeå, Sweden, to 2023, when Norway assumed the Arctic Council chairmanship, a series of significant events occurred that altered the geopolitical agenda. These events included the global impact of the COVID-19 pandemic and the ongoing conflict in Ukraine. These circumstances highlighted the importance of strong regional and international cooperation, careful security considerations, and strict border control. Latvia's unwavering commitment to bolstering relations with its Nordic neighbours prompted its decision to apply for the status of observer in the Arctic Council when the circumstances allow. Despite encountering substantial obstacles both on the international and domestic fronts from 2021, the Latvian Foreign Ministry, for a long time, remained resolute in its pursuit of these goals. After careful examination of Latvia's interests in Arctic cooperation, the authors determined the following:

The war in Ukraine has clearly emphasized the pressing need for robust NATO collaboration, specifically in the High North. As NATO member countries have been carefully considering a stronger presence in the Arctic Ocean, Latvia, with its extensive experience in the Baltic Sea, is well-positioned to play its part in facilitating NATO's conversation about the High North. Furthermore, Russia's full-scale invasion of Ukraine has prompted Finland and Sweden NATO membership. These developments have brought military security agenda into Arctic international cooperation, although the Arctic Council is designed to avoid security issues.

Latvia's role in defining the EU–Arctic agenda has been modest so far, and among the Baltic States, Estonia has surpassed Latvia in expressing its interest in contributing to the EU–Arctic partnership. Questions related to potential Arctic cooperation were not included among the top priorities of Latvian foreign policy, research, science, and education for a long time. Latvia has been a reliable partner in the Northern Dimension partnerships, especially in the ND Partnership in Public Health and Social Well-being and the ND Partnership for Transport and Logistics, where Latvia is one of the founding partners.

Latvia has established productive partnerships with all Arctic Council Member States except Russia. The cooperation has been centered around crucial issues like improving regional and global security within the EU and NATO, tackling the adverse effects of climate change, and executing significant projects like Rail Baltica. These efforts have resulted in mutual benefits for all parties involved.

Latvian participation in international public events in and on the Arctic remains minimal, making it difficult for foreign audiences, notably Arctic residents, and Indigenous peoples, to comprehend Latvian objectives in joining high-level Arctic cooperation.

At the moment, it appears that Latvia is not prepared to provide sufficient financial resources for participating in Arctic international forums, fieldwork, and supporting Arctic Council Permanent Participants.

Latvia has developed research capacities and expertise on various Baltic Sea environment and marine issues, as well as the ability to offer a valuable comparative perspective in Arctic research. However, limited funding has prevented the development and prioritization of thematic Arctic research in Latvian science and research institutions.

The changing regional and global security agenda, the increased need to invest more in strengthening national defence, security of the Baltic Sea and NATO's Eastern flank, and the uncertainties about the future of the Arctic Council within and beyond this international forum temporarily slowed down the commitment of the Latvian public authorities in pursuing the goal of joining the Arctic Council.

To advance Arctic cooperation, Latvia should continue internal deliberations involving both governmental and non-governmental stakeholders and extend the external dialogue to not only Member States of the Arctic Council but also its observer States. The first seminar, which was organized by the Foreign Ministry in December 2022, should become an annual forum on the Arctic issues in Latvia. The continuous debate should lead to a national policy document – Latvia's Arctic or Polar Strategy. Currently, Latvia's position and aspirations are only outlined in three working reports from the IAWG.

From all of the aforementioned reasons, one fundamental conclusion can be drawn: Latvia has proven to be a reliable EU, NATO, and Baltic-Nordic partner, but applying for the position of observer State in the Arctic Council appears to be unachievable in the short-term future. Nonetheless, Latvia's interest in developing mutually beneficial Latvia-Arctic cooperation should remain consistent and be declared in future thematic national policy documents.

Bibliography

Arctic Circle Assembly (2021). *Program 2021*. https://prismic-io.s3.amazonaws.com/arctic-circle-www/4b5186fb-e081-4113-94d3-7ad5502a72c9_2021+Assembly+Program.pdf

Arctic Circle Assembly (2022). *Program 2022*. https://prismic-io.s3.amazonaws.com/arctic-circle-www/786c4152-ee51-4e5f-bf53-70f15c4f1844_B%C3%A6klingur_2022_web_v2.pdf

Arctic Council (1996). *Declaration on the establishment of the Arctic Council*. http://hdl.handle.net/11374/85 [Ottawa Declaration]

Arctic Council (1998/2013). *Arctic Council rules of procedure.* http://hdl.handle.net/11374/940

Arctic Council (2011). *Nuuk declaration on the occasion of the seventh ministerial meeting of the Arctic Council (12 May 2011, Nuuk, Greenland).* http://hdl.handle.net/11374/92

Brommesson, D., Ekengren, A.-M., & Michalski, A. (2022). Sweden's policy of neutrality: Success through flexibility? In C. de la Porte, G.B. Eydal, J. Kauko, D. Nohrstedt, P. Hart, & B.S. Tranøy (Eds.). *Successful public policy in the Nordic countries: Cases, lessons, challenges* (pp. 284–305). Oxford University Press. https://doi.org/10.1093/oso/9780192856296.003.0014

Celmiņš, K. (2021). ES Arktikas politika: kur vieta Latvijai? [EU Arctic policy: where is the place for Latvia?]. In *Latvijas intereses Eiropas Savieniba 2021/2. [Latvia's interests in the European Union 2021/2]* (pp. 52–66). https://www.mfa.gov.lv/lv/media/4623/download

European Commission (2012, June 26). *Joint Staff Working Document. The inventory of activities in the framework of developing a European Union Arctic Policy.* https://eur-lex.europa.eu/legal-content/EN/TXT/PDF/?uri=CELEX:52012SC0182

European Commission (2021, October 13). *Joint Communication to the European Parliament, the Council, the European Economic and Social Committee and the Committee of the Regions. A stronger EU engagement for a peaceful, sustainable and prosperous Arctic.* https://eur-lex.europa.eu/legal-content/EN/TXT/?uri=CELEX%3A52021JC0027

European Committee of the Regions (2021). Opinion of the European Committee of the Regions on 'The new EU Arctic strategy'. *Official Journal of the European Union C 375/15.* https://eur-lex.europa.eu/legal-content/EN/TXT/PDF/?uri=CELEX:52021IR6509

European External Actions Service (2022, March 8). *Northern dimension policy: Joint statement by the European Union, Iceland and Norway on suspending activities with Russia and Belarus.* https://www.eeas.europa.eu/eeas/northern-dimension-policy-joint-statement-european-union-iceland-and-norway-suspending_en

European Parliament and the Council of the European Union (2010). Regulation (EU) No 1236/2010 of the European Parliament and of the Council of 15 December 2010 laying down a scheme of control and enforcement applicable in the area covered by the convention on future multilateral cooperation in the north-east Atlantic fisheries and repealing Council Regulation (EC) No 2791/1999. *Official Journal of the European Union L 348/17.* https://eur-lex.europa.eu/legal-content/EN/TXT/PDF/?uri=CELEX:32010R1236&from=en

European Parliament (2021). European Parliament resolution of 7 October 2021 on the Arctic: Opportunities, concerns and security challenges (2020/2112(INI)) (2022/C 132/10). *Official Journal of the European Union C 132/113.* https://eur-lex.eu

ropa.eu/legal-content/EN/TXT/PDF/?uri=CELEX:52021IP0413&qid=1674125098166&from=EN

European Union (n/d). *Latvia.* Retrieved 23 December 2024, from: https://european-union.europa.eu/principles-countries-history/eu-countries/latvia_en

FishBase (n/d). *Amblyraja hyperborea (Collett, 1879). Arctic skate.* FishBase. Retrieved 23 December 2024, from: https://www.fishbase.us/summary/SpeciesSummary.php?genusname=Amblyraja&speciesname=hyperborea

Hannikainen, L. (2020). Finland's Continuation War (1941–1944): War of aggression or defence? War of alliance or separate war? *Baltic Yearbook of International Law,* 17(1), 77 –121. https://doi.org/10.1163/22115897_01701_006

Institute of Solid State Physics of the University of Latvia (2021). *Aluminium recycling for hydrogen production – from waste through hydrogen energy to alumina – AliCE-WHy (Aluminium in a circular economy – from waste to hydrogen energy to alumina "-AliCE-WHy)* https://www.cfi.lu.lv/en/research/projects/eea-and-norway-grants/aluminium-recycling-for-hydrogen-production-from-waste-through-hydrogen-energy-to-alumina-alice-why-aluminium-in-a-circular-economy-from-waste-to-hydrogen-energy-to-alumina-alice-why/#

Keating-Bitonti, C. (2024, February 7). *Outer limits of the U.S. extended continental: Background and issues for congress* (CRS Report No. R47912). Congressional Research Service. https://crsreports.congress.gov/product/pdf/R/R47912

Lackenbauer, W.P., Sidorova, E., & Sukhankin, S. (2023, July 21). *RAIPON, Russian indigenous peoples, and the war in Ukraine: Pro-Kremlin narratives and voices of dissent.* (Policy Primer. North American and Arctic Defence and Security Network (NAADSN). https://www.naadsn.ca/wp-content/uploads/2023/07/23jul-RAIPON-Russian-Indigenous-PWL-ES-SS-NAADSN-policy-primer.pdf

Latvian Presidency of the Council of the European Union (2015). *Results of the Latvian Presidency of the Council of the European Union.* https://eu2015.lv/images/news/EU2015LV_results_en.pdf

Lockett, M.S. (2022, June 13). *US, Canadian coast guards update joint pollution response plans.* Juneau Empire. https://www.juneauempire.com/news/u-s-canadian-coast-guards-update-joint-pollution-response-plans/

Ministry of Foreign Affairs of the Republic of Latvia (2020). *Northern Dimension.* https://www.mfa.gov.lv/en/northern-dimension

Ministry of Foreign Affairs of the Republic of Latvia (2021a). *Informatīvais ziņojums "Par starpinstitūciju darba grupas izveidi Latvijas pieteikuma Arktikas padomes novērotājvalsts statusam gatavošanai un iesniegšanai".* [First informative report "on Latvia's further actions in the preparation and submission of the application for Arctic Council observer state status]. https://tap.mk.gov.lv/doc/2021_07/AMIzz_290621_Arktikas%20padome.1699.docx

Ministry of Foreign Affairs of the Republic of Latvia (2021b). *Informatīvais ziņojums "Par Latvijas gatavību Arktikas padomes novērotājvalsts statusam".* [Second informative report "on Latvia's further actions in the preparation and submission of the application for Arctic Council observer state status]. https://tapportals.mk.gov.lv/attachments/legal_acts/document_versions/285fd557-ddb7-4931-ab2c-beb872908d35/download

Ministry of Foreign Affairs of the Republic of Latvia (2021c). *Speech by Foreign Minister Edgars Rinkēvičs at the annual foreign policy debate in the Latvian Parliament (Saeima), 28 January 2021.* https://www.mfa.gov.lv/en/article/speech-foreign-minister-edgars-rinkevics-annual-foreign-policy-debate-latvian-parliament-saeima-28-january-2021-0

Ministry of Foreign Affairs of the Republic of Latvia (2021d). *Ziemeļu Dimensija* [Northern dimension]. https://www.mfa.gov.lv/lv/ziemelu-dimensija

Ministry of Foreign Affairs of the Republic of Latvia (2022a). *Experts discuss the rising importance of the Arctic region and Latvia's role in the Arctic.* https://www.mfa.gov.lv/en/article/experts-discuss-rising-importance-arctic-region-and-latvias-role-arctic

Ministry of Foreign Affairs of the Republic of Latvia (2022b). *Informatīvais ziņojums "Par Latvijas tālāko rīcību Arktikas padomes novērotājvalsts statusa pieteikuma gatavošanā un iesniegšanā"* [Third informative report "on Latvia's further actions in the preparation and submission of the application for Arctic Council observer state status]. https://tapportals.mk.gov.lv/attachments/legal_acts/document_versions/f04f4d3e-61c9-4919-ab7e-ac17e8e4cbc5/download

Musanovic, A. (2022, May 17). *Latvia's Arctic connections: Interview with Mārtiņš Vargulis.* The Polar Connection. https://polarconnection.org/martins-vargulis-interview/

Northern Dimension (2020a). *Exploring the northern dimension.* https://um.fi/documents/35732/0/Northern_dimension_fact_sheet_A4+%282%29.pdf/d889c953-dd2d-aa3b-f769-04cb0cf77f8b?t=1613129222310

Northern Dimension (2020b). *Northern dimension: Towards a more sustainable future.* https://um.fi/documents/35732/0/Northern_dimension_tulevaisuusesite.pdf/3f86b027-f960-1485-f9a6-5410d104e7dc?t=1613128536253

Northern Dimension Partnership on Transport and Logistics (2018). *Northern dimension partnership on transport and logistics steering committee: Draft road map for 2019–2024.* https://ndptl.org/wp-content/uploads/2021/12/NDPTL-Road-Map-2019_2024.pdf

Northern Dimension Partnership on Transport and Logistics (2008). *Memorandum of understanding setting out the modalities of establishing the northern dimension partnership on transport and logistics.* https://ndptl.org/wp-content/uploads/20

21/10/Memorandum-of-Understanding-setting-out-the-modalities-of-establishing-the-Northern-Dimension-Partnership-on-Transport-and-Logistics.pdf

Piotrowski, S. (2018). Security policy of the Baltic states and its determining factors. *Security and Defence Quarterly, 22*(5), 46–70. https://doi.org/10.5604/01.3001.0012.7586

Pugliese, D. (2024, January 18). *Russian propaganda campaigns in Latvia flopped, Canadian military says.* Ottawa Citizen. https://ottawacitizen.com/news/national/defence-watch/russian-propaganda-campaigns-in-latvia-flopped-canadian-military-says

Rail Baltica (n.d.). *Rail Baltica – Project of the century.* https://www.railbaltica.org/about-rail-baltica/

Saeima (2022, August 18). *Saeima adopts statement declaring Russia a state sponsor of terrorism.* Saeima https://www.saeima.lv/en/news/saeima-news/31309-saeima-adopts-statement-declaring-russia-a-state-sponsor-of-terrorism

Šime, Z. (2016). Arctic research across the Baltic states: Re-integrated in the Northern Europe, getting closer to the Arctic frostbites. *Arctic Yearbook*, [*2016*], 162–180. https://arcticyearbook.com/images/yearbook/2016/Briefing_Notes/4.Zane.pdf

Sprūds, A., & Rostoks, T. (Eds.). (*2014*). *Perceptions and strategies of arcticness in sub-Arctic Europe.* Latvian Institute of International Affairs. https://www.liia.lv/en/publications/perceptions-and-strategies-of-arcticness-in-sub-arctic-europe-367?get_file=1

State Chancellery of Latvia (2019). *The diligent teenager: Latvia's 15 years in the European Union.* https://www.mk.gov.lv/en/media/8834/download

Strang, J. (2016). *Nordic political and economic cooperation: Context, history and outlook* (Forum Paper). ASEAN Energy Market Integration (AEMI). https://www.asean-aemi.org/wp-content/uploads/2016/03/AEMI-Forum-November-2015-Strang-Feb2016.pdf

Thatcher, I (2022, September 7). *The EU and the future of Arctic cooperation in the northern dimension.* Polar Points. https://www.wilsoncenter.org/blog-post/no-14-eu-and-future-arctic-cooperation-northern-dimension

United Nations Convention on the Law of the Sea (adopted 10 December 1982, entered into force 16 November 1994) 1833 UNTS 3. [UNCLOS]

United Nations General Assembly (2015). Transforming Our World: the 2030 Agenda for Sustainable Development. 25 September 2015. A/RES/70/1.

Westgaard, K. (2023, December 21). The Baltic sea region: A laboratory for overcoming European security challenges. *Carnegie Endowment for International Peace.* https://carnegieendowment.org/research/2023/12/the-baltic-sea-region-a-laboratory-for-overcoming-european-security-challenges?lang=en

CHAPTER 7

The Netherlands in the Arctic: From Exploration to Exploitation to Preservation

Eline Lüschen

1 Introduction

When the Dutch explorer Willem Barentsz sailed to Novaya Zemlya in 1596, he had already been defeated by the sea-ice twice. As his ship sailed through the icy waters of the sea that would later come to bear his name, he remained convinced that if he could *just* break into the Kara Sea, he would be able to find that illustrious open passage to the riches of the East. When his crew returned nearly a year later, without riches, knowledge of a northern passage to the east, and most crucially without Barentsz, they brought back to the Netherlands tales of the Arctic winter and how they had miraculously managed to survive it. They had built their own shelter, fought polar bears, and braved the endless Arctic night (Degroot, 2015, pp. 478–480). Ultimately, they had nothing but a few new maps of the regions to show for it.

To some adventurous Dutch explorers and merchants, the tales of hardship brought back by Barentsz's crew did not serve as a deterrent when it came to further expeditions and ventures in the Arctic region. Over the 400 years following Barentsz's last journey there have been many different instances of Dutch presence in the Arctic from expeditions to business ventures to research efforts. These instances of Dutch presence have not been independent from Dutch national policy. On the contrary, each of these instances have been inextricably connected to policies back home.

This chapter aims to place Dutch presence in the Arctic in the context of Dutch policy throughout the past 400 years. At the same time, it seeks to investigate the basic driving forces and motivations at the heart of Dutch presence in the Arctic. It will do so by providing a general historical overview of Dutch activities in the Arctic and the accompanying policies that have supported that presence. By placing the various expeditions, business ventures, research efforts, and government representations in this historical context some trends in the development of motivations and driving forces may be pointed out.

 | DOI:10.1163/9789004734685_008

Section 2 of this chapter will be dedicated to the history of Dutch Arctic policy from the 16th century to today. It will discuss the most prominent developments in Dutch presence in the Arctic, together with their context within Dutch politics. Section 3 of this chapter will be dedicated to the official Polar policies published by the Dutch ministry of Foreign Affairs from 2010 onwards. The whole chapter is based on historical research, study of policy documents, and interviews with Eelco Leemans of the Dutch Arctic Circle and Liz ter Kuile of the Dutch ministry of Foreign Affairs. These interviews were conducted in the first half of 2023.

2 The Sixteenth Century to Today

2.1 *Willem Barentsz's Journeys*

In the 16th century the main focus of Dutch exploration was to find a route to the Far East. A hundred years earlier, the fall of Constantinople had closed Europe off from the lucrative trade with the east, spurring various European attempts to find sea-routes to India, Indonesia, and China. The Dutch were among those looking for a route, and preferred to find one unbothered by the Spanish and Portuguese (Kennedy, 2021, p. 126). Before finding out that the most convenient route was around the Cape of Good Hope, early attempts set off in wildly different directions, including northwards. One of the most memorable of these attempts was the one undertaken by Willem Barentsz, whose route passed north of North Cape and into the Arctic seas above Siberia.

Willem Barentsz made a total of three journeys to the Arctic, the first two of which were state funded. At this time there was already a small Dutch presence in the region; in 1560 Dutch merchants had founded a trading post on the Kola peninsula (Hacquebord, 1995, p. 249). During Barentsz's first two explorations he had been halted by the sea-ice above Novaya Zemlya and forced to return empty-handed. All seven of his ships had gotten stuck in sea-ice. They broke loose after a while and drifted back into the Yugorsky Strait (Hacquebord & van Leunen, 1996, p. 11). One of Barentsz's partners had been more successful; he had managed to break through into the Kara Sea, passing under Novaya Zemlya. This partner became convinced that this sea would not freeze over, and, when traversed, it would prove to be an open passage to China. They turned around after a strong wind discouraged them from going further, but they surmised that the passage was possible. (Degroot, 2015, p. 469). The explorers returned to the Netherlands without having found the exact route (later research would show that 1594, the year in which this expedition took place, was an unusually warm year with less ice than normal: Degroot, 2015, p. 471). Unfortunately, this guess alone was not enough. The Republic saw the first two journeys as a failure and refused to fund a third. It did, however, promise a large reward for the person who could discover a northeastern passage to the Pacific Ocean (Schilder, 1984, p. 496). The possibility of obtaining this reward was enough for Barentsz to convince new investors to support his explorations, among which the city of Amsterdam (Schilder, 1984). This led to the third and final journey of two ships led by Barentsz (Hacquebord & van Leunen, 1996, p.75).

In 1596 two ships left from the island of Texel, above Holland, with the goal of finding a northeastern passage to the Pacific Ocean. On board were the usual crews of sailors as well as cartographers. Initially a different route was chosen when compared to the previous two journeys. The ships passed sharply to the North, discovering and charting Bear Island in the Barents Sea (Schilder, 1984, p. 496; Degroot, 2015, p. 475). From there they pressed further into Arctic waters, until the ice forced them to turn southwards. Navigating along the ice, they saw one of the islands of the Svalbard Archipelago in the south. The peaks of the mountains on the island pierced through the clouds, so they named the land *Spitsbergen,* which means 'pointy/pointed/sharp mountains' in Dutch (Degroot, 2015, p. 476). The ships' cartographers drew the western coast of the island. After this the two ships decided to separate. On one of the ships, the pilot decided to try going straight north, hoping to find a passage through the ice over the pole. Barentsz, taking the other ship, decided to try to break through to the Kara Sea again, and so turned back to Novaya Zemlya (Schilder, 1984, p. 497). He managed to sail around the northern tip of Novaya Zemlya, but then the ship was beset by ice and it got stuck. The winter had crept up around them.

As the ice closed in on the ship over the span of a week, Barentsz's crew was forced to abandon ship. This meant they needed shelter on the ice. They built the *Behouden Huys,* or the 'Saved House' from trees they found on Novaya Zemlya's shore as well as parts of their ship (Degroot, 2015, p. 478). The crew spent the winter in this house, from 11 September 1596 to 14 June 1597. After their stay on Novaya Zemlya, the crew built two open boats from the remains of the house, managed to find the Kola River, and returned to the Netherlands (Schilder, 1984, p. 497). Barentsz died *en route,* reportedly from scurvy (Degroot, 2015, p. 479). The rest of the crew faced ice, bears, walruses and navigational blunders before finally finding their way to Amsterdam on 1 November of that year (Degroot, 2015, p. 479).

Barentsz was not the first Dutchman in the Arctic, nor was he the last. But it is his journey specifically that has sparked the imagination of the Dutch people since the return of his crew. What happened to Dutch Arctic exploration afterwards is less well known. After Barentsz's death, the Dutch government would hire the English captain Henry Hudson to try to find the Northeast passage again. Hudson quit his attempts to find the Northeast passage in 1609 and decided to go the other way around, trying his luck at finding a Northwest passage. He ended up in the Americas, where he sailed up a river that would later come to bear his name (Kennedy, 2021, p. 126). In 1619 the Russian Empire would close off the Northeastern passage to outsiders to protect trade colonies in Siberia (Bobrick, 1992, p. 56). This was the end of Dutch attempts to find the Northeastern passage.

2.2 *Smeerenburg*

Less than 30 years after Barentsz's final journey a whaling industry was established on the island of Svalbard. A town called Smeerenburg was established on the island of Amsterdam (Amsterdamøya) to the far northeast of Svalbard (Birkhold, 2019). The name of the town may be interpreted as 'Blubbertown' or 'Filthytown' depending on the use of the word *smeer*. 'Smeer' may refer to a type of oil or blubber, or to *smerig*, meaning dirty or filthy. The town consisted of six Dutch try-works, which are oil extraction facilities, as well as a single Danish facility (Hacquebord & Avango, 2009, p. 26). As opposed to the facilities of nearby English whalers, who kept their encampment provisional, these settlements consisted of wooden houses (Hacquebord & Avango, 2009, p.28). In Smeerenburg, they would process the recently caught bowhead whales into a substance called *walvistraan*, which was used for lamp oil or to make candles and soap. In the period from 1614 to 1642, this endeavour was carried out by the *Noordsche Compagnie* (hereinafter: *Compagnie*), a cartel that had obtained permission from the Dutch government to maintain a monopoly on whale hunting and the surrounding industry (Ministerie van Buitenlandse Zaken, 2010, p. 22). The Dutch presence would still at times clash with English or Danish sailors, who would be hunting the same whales. To protect Dutch hunters and interests, the government would even send warships (Jong, 1972, p. 222). Nearing the end of the government-given monopoly the *Compagnie* had grown enough to establish a second settlement in Greenland (Ministerie van Buitenlandse Zaken, 2010, p. 22). The monopoly ran out in 1642, after which a set of other Dutch companies joined the *Compagnie* in the whale hunt, causing a shift in the organization of Dutch whale-hunt (Hacquebord & Avango, 2009, p. 35).

The monopoly running out would prove the end of the Dutch whaling industry. With a multiplicity of different companies in Smeerenburg, the whale-hunt became a small-scale effort. This coincided with changes in ice cover around Svalbard and a slow decline in the whale population in the region. In 1670, there were so few bowhead whales left that whale hunters had to relocate to other regions (Schokkenbroek, 2008, p. 29). The Dutch abandoned shore-based whale-hunt for pelagic whale-hunt. Smeerenburg deteriorated, and by the 18th century it was abandoned (Birkhold, 2019). Amsterdamøya would remain uninhabited. By the 19th century the whales, too, had left the region completely (Hacquebord, 2001, p. 379). Interestingly, Smeerenburg would go on in legend as a thriving Arctic metropolis complete with shops and brothels, despite only ever having housed less than 500 men in about nineteen actual buildings (Birkhold, 2019).

2.3 *NESPICO*

In 1920, representatives of the Netherlands were present at the signing of the Spitsbergen Treaty (Treaty concerning the Archipelago of Spitsbergen, including Bear Island, 1920). Afterwards it was the first state to ratify the treaty, moving quickly to establish a mining company on the island (De Nederlandsche Bank, 2019). This was the *Nederlandsche Spitsbergen Compagnie*, also known as NESPICO, which was made by a shipping company called N.V Van der Eb & Dresselhuys from Rotterdam (Nationaal Archief, 2024a). This same company had acquired land on Svalbard before the treaty, which now allowed them to exploit the area. There would be a Dutch coal mine on Svalbard. In order to accommodate the 500 men who would work that mine, the towns of Rijpsburg and Barentsburg were built. However, this venture did not last. After coal prices went down in the mid-1920s, the mine became unprofitable. The effort was abandoned in 1925, after which the mine was to be sold. The company called the Svalbard mining effort a concatenation of expensive disappointments (Nationaal Archief, 2024b). Selling the mine was harder than expected. Not even the Norwegians wanted to buy it (Teal Jr., 1951, p. 269). Around this time, the Russians got an interest in Svalbard. Development of the northern Russian territories needed a supply of coal (Teal Jr., 1951, pp. 269–270). In 1932, the NESPICO mine was sold to a Russian coal mining company, *Arktikugol* (De Nederlandsche Bank, 2019). To this day, the town of Barentsburg still exists, housing around 450 Russian and Ukrainian speaking people (Hacquebord & Avango, 2009, p. 32).

2.4 *Early Research Efforts*

After the sale of NESPICO's assets to the Soviet Union there was relatively little Dutch involvement with the Arctic until the 1990s, save for the occasional research projects. Among these was the Netherlands Spitsbergen Expedition and Foundation for Arctic Biological Research, which started a series of research projects on Svalbard from 1968 to 1988 (Boschman & Hacquebord, 2004, p. 11). There were a few different expeditions. The first was completely privately funded. During this first expedition biological data on polar bears was gathered. This data contributed to the Agreement on the Conservation of Polar Bears (1973), which went into force in 1976, and prohibits killing Polar Bears, with exceptions (Boschman & Hacquebord, 2004, p. 5). Later expeditions would focus on tundra birds, Svalbard reindeer, and Arctic seals, as well as the effects of oil drilling on the tundra of Edgeøya. In the late 1970s, a research station called Kapp Lee station was established, from which more research was conducted. In 1987, a polar bear attacked one of the researchers, causing some non-fatal but severe injuries. The year after the station was sold to the Norwegians for a symbolic sum and subsequently completely demolished. It was the last medium-size research facility on the west coast of Svalbard (Boschman & Hacquebord, 2004). In 1990 a new station was established in Ny-Ålesund.

2.5 *The Arctic Council and Predecessors*

The Arctic became more relevant for Dutch politics with the development of regional cooperation mechanisms. After the establishment of the Arctic Environmental Protection Strategy (AEPS) in 1991, the Netherlands joined the Arctic Monitoring and Assessment Programme (AMAP) working group in 1993 (Arctic Council, 2019). When the Arctic Council was established in 1996, the Netherlands were present at the signing (Arctic Council,2020; Nieuwe Commissievoorstellen en initiatieven van de lidstaten van de Europese Unie, 2011). It received observer status at the Iqaluit Ministerial meeting in 1998 (Arctic Council, 1998, p. 1). The Netherlands also joined the Barents Euro-Arctic Council (BEAC) as an observer for the first time in 1994 (Barents Council, 1994). It is still active as observers in both organizations.

2.6 *Modern Day Presence*

Nowadays, the Netherlands is involved in the Arctic in two major ways, i.e., through the presence of Dutch companies in the Arctic, and through cooperation with Arctic States in Arctic Council working groups. Aside from this, the Netherlands maintains bilateral relations with various Arctic states. For a majority of these states, the relations are very good. The exception to this is the bilateral relationship between the Netherlands and the Russian Federation, which has been directly affected by the annexation of Crimea and downing of flight MH17 in 2014 (van der Togt, 2016). After the Russian invasion of Ukraine in 2022, this relationship has worsened.

The private interest in the Arctic is focused mostly on shipping, dredging, and offshore infrastructure (i.e., support for oil and gas installations) in the Scandinavian and Russian region. Notable companies include Royal Boskalis, Royal Wagenborg, Royal van Oord, and Mammoet. Royal Boskalis is a dredging and salvaging company which was responsible for the raising of the *Kursk* submarine after it sank in the Barents Sea in 2001, through its subsidiary enterprise Smith Salvage.[1] Royal Wagenborg operates icebreakers which support maritime operations (through towing, icebreakers, and supply runs), and Royal van Oord does dredging and builds oil infrastructure (Geurts & Keyzer, 2022, Royal Wagenborg, n.d.). Mammoet is a heavy lift company involved with Russian state-owned oil companies in the Arctic, which had earlier received a billion-dollar contract for oil projects near Murmansk. All of these larger companies have existed for over a century. With the exception of Mammoet, they have also received the title 'Royal' from the Dutch monarch as a testament to their reputation, age, and expertise (Het Koninklijk huis, n.d.).

There is also an increase in the presence of smaller, younger Dutch companies at work in the Arctic, for example in tourism or in the development of instruments for scientific research (Medusa, 2023). As the Arctic becomes more accessible due to the melting sea ice and local development, it is likely more entrepreneurs will seek to establish themselves there. A significant number of Dutch tourism companies are members of the Association of Arctic Expedition Cruise Operators (AECO), which seeks to protect the Arctic environment through imposing strict guidelines for conducting tourism in the area (Ministerie van Buitenlandse Zaken, 2020, p.37).

The cooperation in the Arctic Council working groups is partly done through providing experts to various working groups, such as the Arctic Monitoring and Assessment Programme (AMAP, which it had joined in the

1 At the time this was the largest salvage operation ever conducted, despite being carried out only four months after the contract between Smit, Mammoet, and the Russian government was signed. The operation cost USD 65 million, a significant part of the yearly budget of the Russian Navy at the time. The timeframe of the operations was this tight in order to adhere to Russian Orthodox funeral practices, since the salvage was at the same time the recovery of the 118 bodies of the *Kursk* crew. The whole incident marks as one of the first great scandals of the Putin era, as well as the first operation to cover up his mistakes (Barany, 2002).

1990s), Conservation of Arctic Flora and Fauna (CAFF), and Sustainable Development Working Group (SDWG). As of 2017, the Dutch association of scientists was considering joining a fourth one, Protection of Arctic Marine Environment (PAME) (Coppes, 2017). This ambition was still relevant in 2020, when Liz ter Kuile wrote in the Netherlands Arctic Council observer report that the Dutch aimed to get more involved with the shipping expert group (ter Kuile, 2021). Dutch scientists are especially represented in the fields of glaciology, oceanography, biology, international law, human sciences, and social sciences (ter Kuile, 2018). The Netherlands also promotes a focus on studies into the causes and consequences of climate change. Oddly prominent within Dutch research is the focus on Arctic migratory birds, which migrate south from the Arctic to the Dutch Wadden Sea to spend the winter (Coppes, 2017). For example, the Arctic Migratory Birds Initiative (AMBI), which is part of CAFF, is supported by the Netherlands through funding and research efforts (Conservation of Arctic Flora and Fauna, 2021).

The other part of Dutch presence in the Arctic Council happens through activity in the Council itself, which is attended by government officials who represent the Netherlands in its observer status. It is in this effort that the Dutch Arctic policy, as decided by the Dutch government, is actually enacted.

3 Modern Dutch Arctic Policy: From 2010 Onwards

3.1 *Drafting Dutch Arctic Policy*

The Dutch Arctic policy is usually published in documents that describe the entire Dutch Polar policy for the coming five years. This timespan is not written into law, but rather reassessed every so often according to need. The past three documents have maintained this pattern consistently, having been published every fifth year since 2010. Because policies on national and European level may still be changed in that time, small parts of the published documents on Dutch Arctic policy may become outdated. However, the policies are usually written with this in mind, and are intended to last the entire five-year period.

The process of drafting Dutch Arctic policy is labor-intensive. The employees of the Ministry of Foreign Affairs (MFA, Dutch: *Ministerie van Buitenlandse Zaken*) tasked with compiling the strategy or policy documents take great effort to maintain a realistic view of the Arctic. They maintain frequent contact with any parties that could have interests in the Arctic, which ranges from other ministries such as the Ministry of Justice and Security, the Ministry of Infrastructure and Water Management, or the Ministry of Economic Affairs, to representatives of Dutch companies in the Arctic and researchers. In the run-up to a publication of a policy document or letter to Parliament these parties meet once every two months in a so-called polar discussion. They are further informed by independent research by local experts on subjects such as security, as well as independent networks representing companies, such as the Dutch Arctic Circle (DAC). The DAC acted as a network opportunity for companies, environmental organizations, researchers, and other parties interested in the Arctic. In 2017, it became an advisory group within the MFA, which allowed for a close collaboration between the MFA and other Dutch parties with interests in the Arctic.

There are a few levels to Dutch Arctic policy. Generally, Arctic policies are decided on a national level. Then, the Netherlands also has to contend with an overarching European Union Arctic policy. The relationship between the EU and Dutch Arctic policies is complicated. While the Netherlands is an observer in the Arctic Council, the European Union as a whole is not. Some parts of Dutch Arctic policy happen on a bilateral basis, such as cooperation preservation and "green recovery" (Ministerie van Buitenlandse Zaken, 2020, p. 17).

At the same time, the Netherlands adheres to decisions made at the EU level as well. Dutch Arctic Policy and EU Arctic policy tends to align, although the Netherlands at times encourages EU policy to be more involved and better informed when it comes to ecological issues (Tweede Kamer der Staten-Generaal, 2011). At other times, EU decisions with regard to the Arctic are more progressive than the Dutch national policy. For example, in 2021 the European Commission started pursuing a moratorium on the extraction of Arctic gas and oil, which did not yet exist in Dutch Arctic policy, but which was then supported fully by the Dutch government (Rijksoverheid, 2021; European Commission, 2021).

3.2 *Dutch Arctic Policy from 2011 to 2015*

The 2011–2015 document marks the first time the Arctic receives more attention than the Antarctic within Dutch Polar policy (Ministerie van Buitenlandse Zaken, 2010, p. 3). It was put together under the supervision of Vincent van Zeijst. This particular document makes a clear distinction between the Dutch polar programme and the Dutch polar policy. The former is the structure through which Dutch polar research is organized and funded. The policy, on the other hand, describes the strategy the Netherlands wishes to maintain in order to protect Dutch interests in the area. The Netherlands Polar Programme has a budget for the funding of various projects, but there is no budget associated with the Polar policy. Instead, all of the goals stated in the document are set to be attained through negotiation in meetings that had already been planned, such as those within bilateral talks with Arctic states as well as participation in the Arctic Council.

In 2010, the Dutch government immediately took a stance on a couple of key issues in the Arctic region. For example, the United Nations Convention on the Law of the Sea (UNCLOS) was taken to be the primary legal structure of the maritime dimension of the Arctic, both for the purpose of solving legal disputes and environmental protection (Ministerie van Buitenlandse Zaken, 2010, p. 54; Ilulissat Declaration, 2008). The Arctic Council was, and still is, considered to be the primary forum of the region. In the same spirit, the Netherlands actively supports the European Union in its application to obtain observer status in the Arctic Council. The 2011–2015 Dutch Arctic policy aligned almost completely with the broader European Union Arctic policy (Tweede Kamer, 2011). However, according to the Dutch government, more Arctic matters would have to be addressed at an EU level as opposed to a national level, since the European Union has far more regulatory power than a single Member State alone (for more information on the EU's interaction with the Arctic, see Bailes & Ólafsson, 2017).

The Netherlands also encouraged other states to become more involved with the Arctic. According to the 2011–2015 policy, the regions that lay outside the sovereignty and jurisdiction of the Arctic states are deserving of protection in order to preserve them for future generations. Because the problems that exist in this area originate in part from outside the Arctic region, non-Arctic states should also be responsible for, and involved with, the protection of this common area. According to the policy, this could be achieved by creating additional international agreements on environmental protection.

The security of the region was also addressed. The 2011–2015 document reveals that there is little reason to actually worry, but that the geopolitical, human, and ecological security of the region must nonetheless be monitored. As to the geopolitical aspect of Arctic security, the Netherlands stated that it desires a transparent cooperation between Arctic states, the EU, the North Atlantic Treaty Organization (NATO, of which the Netherlands is one of the founding members), the Arctic Observers, the Nordic Council, and the Permanent Participants of the Arctic Council. Because the Arctic has an important geopolitical position, it is necessary to keep the area stable. According to the policy, the Netherlands was willing to come to assist Arctic states when called upon for disaster prevention, though 'disasters' are not very well defined in the document. The document makes a distinction between ecological and humanitarian disasters but does not elaborate on what those could be. Nonetheless, assistance is offered. Measures to prevent such vaguely defined disasters are also part of the Dutch Arctic policy. It argues for a stronger governance of the Arctic region, which would enable stricter environmental management. It also looks for binding and stringent environmental rules that would regulate sustainable retrieval of various minerals in the maritime areas of the Arctic (Ministerie van Buitenlandse Zaken, 2010, p. 39).

The economic dimension of the Arctic is a more complicated matter. For the Netherlands, the economic opportunities of this region lie on the edge of ecological preservation and economic exploitation. The document emphasizes the Dutch ability to provide services that could lessen the effects of climate change in the area. Dutch expertise when it comes to sustainability could be used to mitigate the negative consequences of shipping or the extraction of natural resources, should they occur. In order to actually achieve these goals, the Netherlands emphasized that non-Arctic states should have the ability to access the Arctic economy, without tariffs or other obligations. It furthermore presses for the possibility of free passage of ships through areas that were previously ice-infested.

Lastly, the 2011–2015 Arctic policy document considers matters of tourism and fishing. In doing so, the relationship between the Netherlands and Svalbard is discussed. The Netherlands is keeping a close eye on tourism in the area, including how Norway supervises tourism. Fishing is a more complicated matter. Article 1 of the 1920 Spitsbergen Treaty grants sovereignty over the archipelago and territorial waters to Norway. Citizens of countries that signed the Spitsbergen Treaty, like the Netherlands, would be allowed equal rights in the exploitation of various natural resources, among which mining and fishing (Treaty concerning the Archipelago of Spitsbergen, including Bear Island,1920, Art. 3). However, the Spitsbergen Treaty only mentions territorial waters around the archipelago and does not explicitly grant any rights to the area outside the territorial sea (such as an area claimed for fishing beyond the territorial sea, which is allowed through UNCLOS) (Churchill & Ulfstein, 2010). According to the 2011–2015 Arctic policy, the Netherlands is of the opinion that the non-discrimination clause of the Spitsbergen Treaty also applies to the areas outside the territorial waters that Norway has or could claim through UNCLOS. The policy paper admits that this opinion is not shared by Norway. However, it also admits that discussion, supervision, or dispute resolution on this matter is difficult to achieve, as no structure for this was established by the Spitsbergen Treaty itself (Ministerie van Buitenlandse Zaken, 2010, p. 29). In later policy documents, the Netherlands started considering involving the European Commission to settle the issue (Ministerie van Buitenlandse Zaken, 2020, p. 27).

3.3 *Between the Publication of the 2011–2015 Policy and the 2016–2020 Policy*

In 2013, the Netherlands got involved with a conflict between the environmental organization Greenpeace and the Russian Federation. The Greenpeace vessel *Arctic Sunrise*, which sails under the Dutch flag, was boarded and impounded in the Russian Exclusive Economic Zone after a protest against Arctic oil extraction. Two activists had boarded the oil rig *Prirazlomnaya*, one of the first offshore installations to extract oil from the bottom of the Arctic Ocean. At the time, the *Prirazlomnaya* rig was still being prepared for oil extraction, but the project was regarded as risky. The rig itself was called 'rickety' by environmental organizations and the Russian Federation had barely any infrastructure to prevent or clean up a potential oil spill in the Arctic (Bellona, 2014a). The two activists who had boarded *Prirazlomnaya* were taken aboard a coast guard vessel immediately (Permanent Court of Arbitration, 2015, paras. 90–92; BBC, 2013a). Later on, a helicopter with Federal Security Service officers (*Federal'naya Sluzhba Bezopastnosti Rossiskoi Federatsii,* or FSB) boarded and impounded the *Arctic Sunrise*, and arrested the 28 remaining crewmembers (Permanent Court of Arbitration, 2015, para. 101; Brown, 2013). Early on, the crew of the *Arctic Sunrise* faced charges of piracy, but these were later changed to charges of hooliganism (Permanent Court of Arbitration, 2015, paras. 113 and 123; BBC, 2013b).

The Netherlands considered the act of seizing the vessel as illegal under UNCLOS and filed a case against Russia to the International Tribunal for the Law of the Sea (ITLOS). The Russian Federation proceeded to decline to participate in the court case. ITLOS then ruled in favor of the Netherlands, though the tribunal admitted that Greenpeace had similarly broken the law of the sea by entering the safety zone of an oil rig (Käpylä & Mikola, 2015). The Russian government was ordered to pay damages to the Netherlands (Permanent Court of Arbitration, 2015, paras. 388–397). The Russian State also had to release the vessel and all persons detained on bond (International Tribunal for the Law of the Sea, 2013, p. 2). The crew of the Arctic Sunrise (then known as the Arctic 30) ultimately received amnesty from the Parliament of the Russian Federation in late 2013 (BBC, 2013c).

This incident is more indicative of the Dutch insistence on complying with international law than strong support of climate activists. A year later, when Greenpeace's vessel *Rainbow Warrior* prevented the *Mikhail Ulyanov*, a Russian oil tanker, from entering Rotterdam harbor in protest against the fact that it was carrying oil extracted from *Prirazlomnaya*, the Dutch police arrested the Greenpeace activists (Bellona, 2014b, BBC News, 2014; Greenpeace NL, 2014).

Also in 2014 the Dutch organization *Adviesraad Internationale Vraagstukken* (AIV) published 'De toekomst van de Arctische Regio: Samenwerking of Confrontatie?' [*The Future of the Arctic Region: Collaboration or Confrontation?*], a report on the geopolitical reality of the Arctic (de Hoop Scheffer et al., 2014). The AIV is an organization that provides advice about questions concerning international policy to the Dutch government. It consists of a college of experts on different aspects of international relations. This particular document was commissioned by Frans Timmermans, the then Minister of Foreign Affairs, and Jeanine Antoinette Hennis-Plaschaert, the then Dutch Minister of Defence. It was published just as relations between the Russian Federation and the West were deteriorating due to the recent annexation of Crimea. As such, a good part of the report considers the relationship between the Russian Federation, other Arctic States, and the rest of the world. According to the predictions of the AIV, Russian political developments under Putin could reinvigorate the need for NATO presence in the region. At the same time, the Russian Federation turning away from the West could be disastrous for international cooperation in the Arctic. Arctic cooperation relied on good relations amongst Arctic and Non-Arctic states. So, while there was increasing animosity towards the Russian Federation in other dimensions (going as far as to impose various sanctions on the Russian Federation), the Netherlands was still in favor of cooperating with the Russians in the Arctic (de Hoop Scheffer et al. 2014, p.8).

Another aspect of the Arctic that was geopolitically interesting to the Netherlands was the possibility of the Northern Sea Route (NSR) that would pass above Siberia towards the Pacific Ocean. Climate change was (and still is) warming up the Arctic Ocean, possibly allowing for a passage through the decreasing ice. At the same time, the AIV report admitted that climate change may similarly cause a dangerously unpredictable environment in the Arctic. The idea of a NSR presented an attractive possibility to the Netherlands. The port city of Rotterdam, which is one of the largest in Europe, and which traditionally supplies the German hinterland, was perfectly located to profit from the shipping possibilities presented by such a new route (Coppes, 2017). At the same time, the NSR was complicated by practical consideration and Russian ambition. While the NSR could open up for use as a trade route between Europe and the Far East, it would only be open for a few months a year. Complex weather patterns, a lack of infrastructure on the Russian Arctic coast, a lack of maps, shallow waters, and high insurance costs make passing through the Northern Sea Route very difficult, at least for the next few years. Containerships would have to be ice-class or require icebreaking assistance. Because of this, Russian President Putin stated in 2014 that he would prefer that the majority of ships in the Northern Sea Route fly the Russian flag, and thus, fall under Russian jurisdiction. Non-Russian ships could be forced to sail with a Russian icebreaker escort, out of concerns for the safety of the ships. This would effectively allow the Russian state a great amount of control over traffic in the NSR (de Hoop Scheffer et al., 2014).

After the publication of the AIV report, in July 2014, Dutch relations with the Russian Federation went from cautiously amicable to outright strained. The Dutch and Australian government alleged that Russian soldiers were responsible for the downing of the MH17 flight, which killed 200 Dutch citizens, among many other victims. As the Russian Federation has refused to cooperate with efforts to bring the alleged perpetrators to justice, Russian-Dutch relations are not likely to ever return to the 'normal' established before 2014. Despite these developments, Dutch diplomatic efforts to keep correspondence with Russia in order to maintain mutual understanding and collaboration are continued (van der Togt, 2020).

The Netherlands kept cooperating with the Russian Federation within the activities of the Arctic Council. In 2015, the Royal Dutch Shell company retreated from its operations in the Alaskan Arctic, citing "challenging and unpredictable federal regulatory environment in offshore Alaska" (Shell, 2015; Greenpeace, 2015). At this time, oil prices were going down, and the USD 9 billion investment in the infrastructure associated with oil extraction was not showing any signs of returning profit any time soon (Shell, 2015). This retreat collapsed the small sector of Dutch companies surrounding oil extraction in the Alaskan Arctic, such as geological surveyors, shipping companies, and infrastructural engineers for the oil platforms. To this day, this industry has not returned to the region.

3.4 *Dutch Arctic Policy from 2016 to 2020*

The next Polarpolicy document was published in 2015. It detailed the Dutch plan for the period from 2016–2020. It bore the title *Samen voor Duurzaam*, which translates to 'together for sustainability' (Ministerie van Buitenlandse Zaken, 2015). With regards to the Arctic, this document had less background information, but more concrete plans to be carried out (as opposed to goals to be met during previously scheduled meetings). Because the previous document established a lot of long-term plans and stances, the 2016–2020 document only had to denote notable changes to those plans and stances. The policy document was action-oriented, meaning that the Dutch government sought to move beyond the passive stance it had taken in the previous Arctic policy. With the changing Arctic environment, it was time to make more effort to protect Dutch interests in the region.

This document introduced the three keystone concepts of Dutch Arctic policy. These were (and still are) international cooperation, scientific research, and sustainability. While these concepts were indeed present already in the 2011–2015 document, it is only now that they are elevated to the keystone concepts on which the entirety of Dutch Arctic Policy is built. The concepts themselves are broad but widely applicable. They were meant to remain relevant even in future policy documents. International cooperation can be used both as a strategy to maintain a geopolitically stable Arctic (as it was proposed in the document published by the AIV in 2014), but also as a method to improve the Arctic overall, whether through the framework of international law or through various initiatives to carry out the work that is needed to preserve the Arctic environment. Scientific research is elevated to a keystone concept both for its inherent worth and for its importance to Dutch interests. It can be used to provide expertise to assist in the protection of the Arctic environment. Sustainability is the one keystone concept that needs some further clarification; it does not refer to sustainable *development*, but rather to the sustainability of the Arctic overall. The Netherlands prefers the Arctic to stay untouched. The policy, therefore, is to be reluctant towards development, especially in the areas of oil and gas extraction, and to ensure that those projects that cannot be prevented are carried out in a sustainable manner.

Following a trend of increasing worry about the global climate and depreciation of the Arctic environment specifically, the Netherlands affirms in this document an apprehensive stance towards oil and gas extraction in the Arctic. While it is not outright forbidden or condemned, the document emphasizes the need to keep the necessary extraction of resources as sustainable and environmentally friendly as possible. Those resources that are extracted could still become relevant for the Dutch economy. Dutch companies could provide their expertise in developing more sustainable methods for the extraction of resources. The port city of Rotterdam could receive ships carrying the liquefied natural gas (LNG) and oil from the Russian Arctic, and transfer them onto different vehicles such as trains, trucks, and smaller ships for further export to the European mainland

At this time, the situation in the Arctic had changed quite a bit from the situation in 2010. Royal Dutch Shell had left its Arctic enterprise behind, six new states had obtained observer status in the Arctic Council (China, India, Italy, Japan, Korea, and Singapore), and relations between the Russian Federation and the West had deteriorated. The 2016–2020 document addressed these changes. The new Arctic Council observers are warmly welcomed. A special note is made of increasing Chinese involvement in Arctic matters. According to the Dutch Arctic Policy, the Netherlands does not seem to be particularly worried about this development, remarking that there was still very little mention of the Arctic in the 13th five-year-plan of the Chinese government.

As to the Dutch relationship with the Russian Federation, the sanctions following the 2014 annexation of Crimea affected the Arctic mostly with regards to deep water oil exploration and production, arctic oil exploration and production or shale oil projects (European Council, 2014a; European Council, 2014b). At this time, the Russian Federation was also increasing its military presence in the Arctic. Military restructuring in 2010 had seen the forces in the northern regions at a higher level of readiness, a new naval base on Kotelny was established, and, in 2014, the process of opening fourteen new airfields in the Arctic region was started (Kjellen, 2022). The 2016–2020 policy document expresses concern about these developments.

3.5 *Between the Publication of the 2016–2020 Document and the 2021–2024 Document*

Although the official Dutch policy was not to actively support oil and gas drilling in the Arctic region, a Greenpeace report from 2020 proved that various Dutch companies were still involved with the retrieval of Arctic oil through investing in and providing loans to companies such as Exxon, Rosneft, Gazprom, and BP (Greenpeace, 2020). An investigation by independent journalists writing for *Follow the Money* later revealed that the Dutch government themselves was at this point still involved with talks between various European states and Gazprom (Keyzer, 2021). At this time, the Netherlands was still dependent on Russian gas and was partly supportive of the Nord Stream 2 project (Slingerland, 2019). Not all the gas collected by companies like Gazprom comes from the Arctic, but a significant amount of it does (Mcgee, 2020).

3.6 *The 2021–2025 Document*

The 2021–2025 Polar policy document was named *Beslagen ten Ijs*, a saying that means something along the lines of 'to be prepared', combined with a convenient ice-related pun (Ministerie van Buitenlandse Zaken, 2020). Specifically, it refers to the need to equip a horse with sharpened horseshoes to allow them to walk on the ice. It may similarly mean 'to acquire the right skills before starting the task'. As of writing, it is the most recent Dutch Arctic Policy. The drafting process started in 2019 and it was published in 2020. This document presents again the same three keystone concepts of international cooperation, scientific research, and sustainability as the foundational pillars of the policy as a whole (Ministerie van Buitenlandse Zaken, 2020, p. 6). As was the case with the 2016–2020 policy, this document only lists notable changes to established plans and stances.

At the time of publication, the situation in the Arctic had once again changed in the five years since the publication of the last policy document. The Trump presidency in the United States had kicked off an era of global distrust that reached into the Arctic region. President Trump's Secretary of State Mike Pompeo came to Rovaniemi, Finland, at the occasion of the 2019 Arctic Council Ministerial Meeting. There, he gave a speech in which he warned Arctic Council members as well as observers of the dangers of Chinese involvement in the region. He projected an Arctic far more susceptible to economic exploitation than had been the case in the previous decade (Pompeo, 2019). The 2021–2025 document reflects this stance. As opposed to the previous document, in which the new observers were welcomed, in this document the Dutch appear to be more worried about increasing Chinese involvement. The apparent Chinese disregard to sustainable development directly opposes the Dutch preference for limiting ecological damage in the region.

In 2020, the Arctic policy starts paying even more attention to the security dimension of the Arctic. The document divides the Dutch Arctic security policy into three separate parts. These are economic, ecological, and military security. Economic security becomes more important as the Arctic opens up for new industries such as fisheries and tourism. At the same time, climate change makes it more important to make attempts to preserve the regional environment through sustainable practices and legal structures. These processes make the Arctic politically increasingly important. Because the Netherlands is of the opinion that the Arctic should stay as apolitical as possible, it aims to use its observation status in the Arctic Council to promote increasing cooperation between the Arctic States (as well as between Arctic States and observers). Military security, however, is not the purview of the Arctic Council. Instead, the Netherlands opts to keep a close view on especially the developments in the Russian Arctic, opting to act through NATO if the need for it arises.

The three dimensions of security in the Arctic cannot be considered to be entirely separate from each other. While they are different dimensions, each aspect informs and is changed by the other two. Yet, by making this distinction, the reasons for insecurity in the Arctic region can be more accurately identified and targeted. This method of separating three different dimensions has proven to be an effective way of talking about Arctic security. According to an interview with Liz ter Kuile (2023), the then Dutch representative at the Arctic Council, this method has inspired the Finnish government in its own Arctic policy.

The Netherlands proposes various strategies to emphasize the importance of curbing climate change, protecting the maritime and terrestrial Arctic environments, protecting local fauna, and preventing pollution, among which nuclear waste. Different parts of the government are getting involved with this effort. For example, *Rijkswaterstaat*, the infrastructural office of the Netherlands, has been in charge of monitoring ambient noise in the North Sea, techniques that can similarly be applied to the Arctic Ocean. The efforts to protect the Arctic environment are directly tied in with an increase in Dutch participation in Arctic Council working groups (Ter Kuile, 2018; Ter Kuile, 2021, Ter Kuile, 2023; Ministry of Foreign Affairs, 2021). The information gathered in such groups has clearly made its way back to the Netherlands in order to inform Dutch policy- this particular document mentions a very wide array of interest points, each of which gets its own plan of attack.

3.7 *After the Publication of the 2021–2025 Document*

One part of the policy document is already out of date; this being the Dutch stance on drilling for oil and gas in the Arctic. In 2021, the European Commission introduced a full moratorium on new Arctic oil and gas sources (European Commission, 2021). Specifically, while old sources could still be accessed, exploring for, preparing, and making use of, new sources would be prohibited. The Netherlands agreed with this decision and has adopted this stance into its national policy (Rijksoverheid, 2021).

In 2021, the European Commission published a document that promoted sustainable development in the Arctic (European Commission, 2021). It calls for investment in a so-called sustainable blue economy in the Arctic, as well as a future-proof Arctic. In this dimension, the Dutch Arctic policy seems to diverge from the EU policy once more, since the Netherlands has been focusing on a sustainability that does not see the Arctic environment altered any further.

The Russian invasion of Ukraine in 2022 brought some significant changes to world politics. The Arctic has not remained unaffected. Sanctions have made cooperation between Western companies and counterparts in the Russian Federation difficult, for example by disallowing gas storage and banning the exports of industrial goods (European Commission, 2024). In the Arctic, this has affected gas exports, and sanctions on industrial goods have prevented Russia from obtaining icebreakers they had ordered from Korean shipyard Deawoo Hanwha back in 2014 (Arbeloa, 2024). In 2022, the Russian Federation had the chairmanship of the Arctic Council. Due to a general opposition to Russian actions in Ukraine, the other seven Arctic States have refused to cooperate with the Russian Federation within the structure of the Arctic Council, although they were willing to continue cooperation amongst themselves (Government of Canada, 2022). The Arctic Council paused most of its activities for a major part of 2022 and 2023, slowly resuming activities upon Norway taking the chairmanship of the Council (Arctic Council, 2024). Political level meetings have not yet been resumed as of the writing of this document. Since the Dutch Arctic policy at the political level is based in part on participation in such meetings, the Netherlands has not been able to carry out that part of its Arctic policy.

Also affected by the Russian invasion of Ukraine were various research projects that were being conducted by Dutch scientists in the Arctic, including those projects that fell under the umbrella of AC working groups. It has become a lot harder to physically travel to the Russian Federation because of a lack of direct flights, lack of payment services, and lack of insurance (Verbond van Verzekeraars, 2017). The then-Minister of Education, Culture, and Science Robbert Dijkgraaf called for cooperation between universities in the Netherlands and Russia to be frozen (Rijksoverheid, 2022). This caused data, knowledge, and financial exchange to cease (Bakker, 2022). In the Arctic, this affected various projects, from observations of migratory birds to the monitoring of radioactive waste in the region. These were either halted or canceled altogether.

Some Dutch companies have suffered under the current circumstances. There were a few companies, mostly in the marine sector, that were very active in the Russian Arctic. Between the sanctions and moral opposition to the actions of the Russian government, there is no more cooperation between those companies and any Russian actors (Geurts & Keyzer, 2022). The Delta Group, which previously brokered cooperation between various Dutch companies and the Russian state-owned oil company Gazprom, has stated that the basis for collaboration with the Russian Federation has been compromised by the invasion of Ukraine (Project Delta Group, n.d.). It is unlikely to resume unless there is significant reason to lift the sanctions. Should this happen, however, it is very likely Dutch companies will try to return to the Russian Arctic. In a 2023 interview, Eelco Leemans of the Dutch Arctic Circle maintained the hope that work there could one day be resumed.

4 Conclusion: Policy to Protect and Economy to Add

So far, this chapter has discussed a general history of Dutch presence in the Arctic as well as the policies that accompanied that presence. It has seen the goals of the Dutch go from exploration to exploitation to finally preservation. This general history, when viewed as a whole, reveals two interplaying driving forces throughout time: the possibility for economic gain and ecological considerations.

Economic gain starts out as the only major driving force. The earliest explorations were spurred onwards by the spirit of (future) commerce. Barentsz's crew included mapmakers tasked with recording the Arctic region and hopefully, if discovered, the Northeast passage. Later on, the whalers in the Arctic Ocean and the miners on Svalbard sought to make a profit of the natural resources of the Arctic, without much regard for the ecological effect of their whaling and mining respectively. These exploitative efforts were not very successful. Barentsz was not able to discover his route, nor did he get very far into the seas above Siberia. Hudson ran into similar obstacles in the west. The whalers hunted their game nearly to extinction and when their monopoly ran out, they competed each other out of business. The mine on Svalbard would fail and be sold within a decade.

From the latter half of the 20th century onwards, possibilities of economic gains were still present in the Arctic, but the type of possibility had changed. Dutch companies promote their knowledge of sustainable engineering, hoping to participate in large development projects such as dredging to allow larger ships to reach Russian Arctic ports, building LNG-towers in Russian gas fields, and building wind parks on the Kola peninsula (Geurts & Keyzer, 2022). As the Arctic opens up, more opportunities are likely to arise for such companies. The Netherlands keeps a wary eye on the developments of Arctic shipping routes and development projects in Arctic regions, constantly reassessing what it could mean for the Dutch economy. This type of economic gain, however, can be distinguished in one significant manner from the Arctic exploits of the past: the economy of the Dutch now seeks not to be one of exploitation, but rather one of addition. Dutch companies export products of knowledge *to* the Arctic, as opposed to returning Arctic materials to the Netherlands. Foreign companies extracting resources in the Arctic to bring them to the Netherlands are slowly losing favor, both due to deteriorating relations with their country of origin (Russia) and due to concerns for the Arctic environment. Royal Dutch Shell retreated from the Arctic due to the fact that profits were hindered by restrictive regulations, again intended to preserve the Arctic environment.

The second driving force is ecological consideration. This became relevant far later, around the last two decades of the 20th century when the foundations of Dutch Arctic policy, such as scientific research and participation in regional fora were established. Where, in the time of early exploration, the Arctic started out as an area that was ripe for limitless exploitation, the current perspective acknowledges that the Arctic cannot bear such industry without consequence. Modern Dutch policy thus seeks to preserve as much of the Arctic as possible, both for the sake of the Arctic itself as well as to avoid the effects a deteriorating Arctic will have on the rest of the world. Throughout the policy documents, there are goals and initiatives that would allow for greater protection of the Arctic from the effects of exploitative industries. In the 2011–2015 Arctic policy document, the argument for stronger Arctic governance is explicitly connected to a more effective protection of the Arctic environment. Later on, the 2016–2020 and 2021–2025 documents show that the Netherlands became increasingly apprehensive of the extraction of Arctic oil and gas. The Arctic policies of the Netherlands state a clear interest in the protection of the Arctic environment. This position is mostly idealist. While the Netherlands could benefit in the long term from the protection of the Arctic environment by containing the effects of climate change, there is no direct economic benefit from preserving the Arctic environment to the Netherlands.

These driving forces are constantly interplaying. As time goes on, the possibilities for economic benefit are increasingly hindered by ecological considerations. Where NESPICO didn't even pay any regard to the possible negative effects of mining on Svalbard, Royal Dutch Shell had to retreat from the Arctic partly due to the complicated rules around Arctic oil extraction. The Dutch government makes it clear it sees almost no benefit in the extraction of Arctic resources. At the same time, it carefully watches for other possibilities for economic benefit. For example, the possibility of exporting Dutch knowledge to the Arctic through the companies that help dredge harbors, salvage sunken ships, or build the infrastructure for resource extraction in such a way that damage to the Arctic environment is minimized. Or through the possibility of a Northeast passage above Siberia, which would directly benefit the port of Rotterdam. While these endeavors are *additive*, that is to say, they bring Dutch products to the Arctic instead of taking Arctic resources back to the Netherlands, they may still be harmful to the environment. Shipping and dredging can disturb wildlife and introduce pollutants into the water, and oil extraction may still be the cause of oil spills. As this continues, new Dutch Arctic policies may be introduced in order to contain these harmful effects. Whether this happens is of course dependent on the relative benefit of Arctic protection versus economic gain.

Economic gain and ecological consideration are the most important driving forces nowadays, but they might not be the only ones in the future. Over the past thirteen years, the Dutch and European Union Arctic policy documents have increasingly begun to mention the strategic dimension of the Arctic. This strategic dimension is mostly concerned with Russian military presence in its own Arctic region. In the 2011–2015 document, the Netherlands stated that it were adamant that any security-related issues in the Arctic region should be handled through NATO. In the 2016–2020 document, worries are expressed about the development of Russian military installations in its own Arctic region. In the 2021–2025 document, these developments are once again closely regarded. While the Netherlands does not show any intention for its own military presence in the Arctic (instead consistently insisting matters of security should be handled by NATO), this concern over the strategic dimension of the Arctic only seems to grow. Yet, there is no indication that any conflict is actually expected. In Dutch Arctic policy documents, the Netherlands displays wariness, but not readiness. The Netherlands seems to remain insistent on maintaining a neutral and apolitical Arctic, and looks towards diplomacy to achieve this. As such, it is not infeasible that a Dutch presence aiming for international cooperation (and, in the worst-case scenario, de-escalation) may be driven to the Arctic in the future.

Bibliography

Agreement on the Conservation of Polar Bears (adopted 15 November 1973, entered into force 26 May 1976) 2898 UNTS 243.

Arbeloa, I.U. (2024, June 27). *Western sanctions on icebreakers stall Russia's Arctic LNG expansion*. Elcano Royal Institute. https://www.realinstitutoelcano.org/en/analyses/western-sanctions-on-icebreakers-stall-russias-arctic-lng-expansion/

Arctic Council (1998). *The Iqaluit Declaration*. http://hdl.handle.net/11374/86

Arctic Council (2019). *Observer regular reporting 2018 compilation.* http://hdl.handle.net/11374/2348

Arctic Council (2020) *Interview with Arctic Council observer: The Netherlands.* Arctic Council. https://arctic-council.org/news/interview-with-arctic-council-observer-the-netherlands/

Arctic Council (2024, May 16). *One year into the 2023–2025 Norwegian chairship: A Q&A with SAO chair Morten Høglund.* Arctic Council. https://arctic-council.org/news/one-year-norwegian-chairship/

Bailes, A.J.K., & Ólafsson, K.Þ. (2017). The EU crossing Arctic frontiers: The Barents Euro-Arctic Council, Northern Dimension, and EU-West Nordic relations. In N. Liu, E.A. Kirk, & T. Henriksen (Eds.), *The European Union and the Arctic* (Publications on Ocean Development, Volume 85, pp. 40–62). Brill. https://doi.org/10.1163/9789004349179_004

Bakker, M. (2022, May 26). *De oorlog in Oekraïne is ook een klap voor de kanoet in de poolcirkel (en de wetenschap in het algemeen)* [The war in Ukraine is also a problem for the Red Knot (and science in general)]. De Volkskrant. https://www.volkskrant.nl/wetenschap/de-oorlog-in-oekraine-is-ook-een-klap-voor-de-kanoet-in-de-poolcirkel-en-de-wetenschap-in-het-algemeen~ba5ee96c/

Barany, Z. (2004). The tragedy of the *Kursk*: Crisis management in Putin's Russia. *Government and Opposition, 39*(3), 476–503. https://doi.org/10.1111/j.1477-7053.2004.00131.x

Barents Euro-Arctic Council (1994). *Joint statement Barents Euro-Arctic Council. Second session.* https://barents-council.org/document/499_doc_Tromsocommunique_1994_e.pdf

BBC News (2013a, September 18). *Greenpeace assails oil rig in Russian Arctic.* BBC News. https://www.bbc.com/news/world-europe-24141667

BBC News (2013b, October 2013). *Russia drops piracy charges against Greenpeace group.* BBC News. https://www.bbc.com/news/world-europe-24645300

BBC News (2013c, December 18). *Russia parliament approves amnesty for prisoners.* BBC News. https://www.bbc.com/news/world-europe-25433426

BBC News (2014, May 1). *Greenpeace Russian tanker activists held in Netherlands.* BBC News. https://www.bbc.com/news/world-europe-27236750

Bellona (2014a, April 23). *Russia opens oil sluices in Arctic as rickety Prirazlomnaya platform begins production.* Bellona. https://bellona.org/news/arctic/2014-04-russia-opens-oil-sluices-arctic-rickety-prirazlomnaya-platform-begins-production

Bellona (2014b, May 5). *Activists in Rotterdam arrested and released for trying to block Russian Arctic oil tanker from docking.* Bellona. https://bellona.org/news/arctic/2014-05-activists-rotterdam-arrested-released-trying-block-russian-arctic-oil-tanker-docking

Birkhold, M.H. (2019, July 10). *The Myth of Blubber Town, an Arctic metropolis*. The Public Domain Review. https://publicdomainreview.org/essay/the-myth-of-blubber-town-an-arctic-metropolis/

Bobrick, B. (1992). *East of the sun: The epic conquest and tragic history of Siberia*. Poseidon Press.

Boschman, N., & Hacquebord, L. (Eds.) (2004). *Permanence in diversity: Netherlands ecological research on Edgeøya, Spitsbergen*. Barkhuis Publishing. https://pure.rug.nl/ws/portalfiles/portal/37075462/permanence-complete.pdf

Brown, J. (2013, September 24). *Russia arrests 30 environmental activists during Arctic protest*. The Independent. https://www.independent.co.uk/news/uk/home-news/russia-arrests-30-environmental-activists-during-arctic-protest-8830165.html

Churchill, R., & Ulfstein, G. (2010). The disputed maritime zones around Svalbard. In M. Nordquist, J. Norton Moore, & T.H. Heidar (Eds.), *Changes in the Arctic environment and the law of the sea* (Center for Oceans Law and Policy, Volume 14, pp. 551–594). Brill Nijhoff. https://doi.org/10.1163/ej.9789004177567.i-594.156

Conservation of Arctic Flora and Fauna (2021) *Arctic migratory bird initiative (AMBI): Mid-term evaluation 2017 and 2021*. http://hdl.handle.net/11374/2634

Coppes, M. (2017, February 9). *The Dutch beef up their Arctic engagement*. High North News. https://www.highnorthnews.com/en/dutch-beef-their-arctic-engagement

De Nederlandsche Bank (2019). *Inventaris van het archief van de Nederlandse Spitsbergen Compagnie (Nespico), 1921 – 1948 (1958) (De Nederlandsche Bank)* [Inventory of the archive of the *Nederlandse Spitsbergen Compagnie (Nespico) 1921–1948 (1958) (De Nederlandsche Bank)*]. Nationaal Archief, Ministerie van Onderwijs, Cultuur en Wetenschap. Versie: 25-02-2019. https://www.nationaalarchief.nl/onderzoeken/archief/2.25.77.30/download/pdf

Degroot, D. (2015). Testing the limits of climate history: The quest for a northeast passage during the little ice age, 1594–1597. *The Journal of Interdisciplinary History*, *45*(4), 459–484. https://doi.org/10.1162/JINH_a_00755

Dutch Arctic Circle (2022). *Verslag Dutch Arctic Circle bijeenkomst 3 jaar vernieuwde DAC in het Arctische landschap* [Report of the Dutch Arctic Circle meeting 3 years of renewed DAC in the Arctic landscape]. https://www.dac-netwerk.nl/wp-content/uploads/2023/03/Verslag-Dutch-Arctic-Circle-bijeenkomst-8-december-2022.pdf

European Commission (2021). *Joint communication to the European Parliament, the Council, the European Economic and Social Commission and the Committee of the Regions: A stronger EU engagement for a peaceful, sustainable, and prosperous*

Arctic. https://www.eeas.europa.eu/eeas/joint-communication-stronger-eu-engagement-peaceful-sustainable-and-prosperous-arctic_en

European Council (2014a) *Council Regulation (EU) No 960/2014 of 8 September 2014 amending Regulation (EU) No 833/2014 concerning restrictive measures in view of Russia's actions destabilising the situation in Ukraine*. http://data.europa.eu/eli/reg/2014/960/oj

European Council (2014b) *Council Regulation (EU) No 1290/2014 of 4 December 2014 amending Regulation (EU) No 833/2014 concerning restrictive measures in view of Russia's actions destabilising the situation in Ukraine, and amending Regulation (EU) No 960/2014 amending Regulation (EU) No 833/2014*. http://data.europa.eu/eli/reg/2014/1290/oj

European Council (2024). *Timeline – EU sanctions against Russia*. Council of the European Union. https://www.consilium.europa.eu/en/policies/sanctions-against-russia/timeline-sanctions-against-russia/

Geurts, O., & Keyzer, T. (2022, March 31). *Russische oorlogszucht verpest Nederlands succesverhaal in Noordpoolgebied* [Russian warmongering spoils Dutch success-story in the Arctic region]. Follow The Money – Platform Voor Onderzoeksjournalistiek. https://www.ftm.nl/artikelen/noordpool-lonkt-nl-exploitatie-olierijk-arctisch-gebied

Government of Canada (2022). *Joint statement on limited resumption of Arctic Council cooperation (8 June 2022)*. https://www.canada.ca/en/global-affairs/news/2022/06/joint-statement-on-limited-resumption-of-arctic-council-cooperation.html

Greenpeace NL. (2014, May 1). *Greenpeace verhindert aanmeren tanker met Noordpoololie in Rotterdam* [Greenpeace hinders the mooring of a tanker with Arctic oil in Rotterdam]. https://www.greenpeace.org/nl/algemeen/5554/greenpeace-verhindert-aanmeren-tanker-met-noordpoololie-in-rotterdam/

Greenpeace (2015, September 30). *You did it! Shell abandons Arctic drilling*. https://www.greenpeace.org/international/story/7022/you-did-it-shell-abandons-arctic-drilling/#:~:text=And%20in%20Shell's%20own%20statement,You%20challenged%20them

Greenpeace (2020, February 6). *Oliewinning bij de Noordpool: Betrokkenheid van Nederlandse financiële instellingen* [Oil extraction in the Arctic: Involvement of Dutch financial institutions]. https://www.greenpeace.org/static/planet4-netherlands-stateless/2020/02/e76e11d2-2020-02-qic-oliewinning-bij-de-noordpool.pdf

Hacquebord, L. (1995). In search of *Het Behouden Huys*: A survey of the remains of the house of Willem Barentsz on Novaya Zemlya. *Arctic*, *48*(3), 248–256. https://pubs.aina.ucalgary.ca/arctic/Arctic48-3-248.pdf

Hacquebord, L., & van Leunen, P. (1996). *400 Jaar Willem Barentsz* [400 years of Willem Barentsz]. Flevodruk.

Hacquebord, L. (2001). Three centuries of whaling and walrus hunting in Svalbard and its impact on the Arctic ecosystem. *Environment and History*, *7*(2), 169–185. https://doi.org/10.3197/096734001129342441

Hacquebord, L., & Avango, D. (2009). Settlements in an Arctic resource frontier region. *Arctic Anthropology*, *46*(1–2), 25–39. https://doi.org/10.1353/arc.0.0028

Het Koninklijk Huis (n.d.) *Predicaat Koninklijk aanvragen* [Requesting the Royal Mandate]. Retrieved 7 December 2024, from: https://www.koninklijkhuis.nl/onderwerpen/onderscheidingen/predicaat-koninklijk/aanvragen

de Hoop Scheffer, J.G., Verrijn Stuart, H.M., Gupta, J., Hirsch Ballin, E.M.H., Plooij-van Gorsel, P.C., van Reisen, M.E.H., van Staden, A., Urlings, M.L.M., Voorhoeve, J.J.C., Oostenbrink, T.D.J. (2014). De Toekomst van De Arctische Regio: Samenwerking of Confrontatie? [The future of the Arctic region: Collaboration or confrontation?]. *Adviesraad Internationale Vraagstukken*. https://www.adviesraadinternationalevraagstukken.nl/documenten/publicaties/2014/09/05/de-toekomst-van-de-arctische-regio

Ilulissat Declaration (2008). Arctic Ocean Conference. Ilulissat, Greenland, 27–29 May 2008. https://arcticportal.org/images/stories/pdf/Ilulissat-declaration.pdf

International Tribunal for the Law of the Sea (2013). Press release ITOS/Press 205. *The "Arctic Sunrise" Case* (*Kingdom of the Netherlands v. Russian Federation*). Tribunal orders the release of the Arctic Sunrise and the detained persons upon the posting of a bond. https://www.itlos.org/fileadmin/itlos/documents/press_releases_english/PR_205_E.pdf

de Jong, C. (1972). *Geschiedenis van de oude Nederlandse walvisvaart* [History of old Dutch whale hunt]. [Doctoral Thesis, Tilburg University]. https://pure.uvt.nl/ws/portalfiles/portal/1202359/3955099.pdf

Käpylä, J., & Mikola, H. (2015). *On Arctic exceptionalism: Critical reflections in the light of the Arctic Sunrise case and the crisis in Ukraine* (FIIA Working Paper April 2015, No. 85). The Finnish Institute of International Affairs. https://www.fiia.fi/wp-content/uploads/2017/01/wp85.pdf

Kennedy, J.C. (2021) *Een Beknopte Geschiedenis van Nederland* [A concise history of the Netherlands]. Prometheus.

Keyzer, T. (2021, July 27). *Rutte licht Kamer 'onjuist en onvolledig' in over gascontacten met Rusland* [Rutte provides 'unjust and incomplete' information about gas contracts with Russia to the chamber]. Follow The Money – Platform Voor Onderzoeksjournalistiek. https://www.ftm.nl/artikelen/overheid-overleg-rusland-gas

Kjellén, J. (2022). The Russian northern fleet and the (re)militarisation of the Arctic. *Arctic Review on Law and Politics*, *13*, 34–52. https://arcticreview.no/index.php/arctic/article/view/3338/6317

Mcgee, R. (2020, February 18). *Mapping Russia's Arctic hydrocarbon development scheme*. The Arctic Institute. https://www.thearcticinstitute.org/mapping-russia-arctic-hydrocarbon-development-scheme/

Medusa (2023). *Spitsbergen. Geofysisch onderzoek naar diepte permafrost in 2019 en 2022 SEES* [Svalbard. Geofysical research into depth of permafrost in 2019 and 2022 SEES (Scientific expedition Edgeøya Spitsbergen)]. Presentation for DAC. Retrieved 4 December 2024, from: https://www.dac-netwerk.nl/wp-content/uploads/2023/03/Presentatie-Medusa_kl.pdf

Ministerie van Buitenlandse Zaken (2010). *Beleidskader. Nederland en de Poolgebieden 2011–2015* [Policy Framework. The Netherlands and the Polar Regions 2011–2015]. https://zoek.officielebekendmakingen.nl/blg-213294.pdf

Ministerie van Buitenlandse Zaken (2015) *Nederlandse Polaire Strategie 2016–2020: Samen voor duurzaam* [Dutch Polar strategy 2016–2020: Together for sustainability]. https://zoek.officielebekendmakingen.nl/blg-719818.pdf

Ministerie van Buitenlandse Zaken (2020). *Nederlandse Polaire Strategie 2021–2025: Beslagen ten ijs* [Dutch Polar strategy 2021–2025: Being prepared]. https://open.overheid.nl/documenten/ronl-cd19a1c9-2ddc-4caa-ae89-538cd7e23763/pdf

Nationaal Archief (2024a). *Telegram van Hendrik Herman Dresselhuijs, directeur van Nespico, gericht aan Sjef van Dongen, passagier van het schip Kong Harald, onderweg naar Bergen, Noorwegen* [Telegram from Hendrik Herman Dresselhuijs, director of Nespico, to Sjef van Dongen, passager on the ship Kogn Harald, underway to Bergen, Norway]. https://www.archieven.nl/nl/zoeken?mivast=0&mizig=210&miadt=239&miaet=1&micode=631&minr=32606582&miview=inv2&milang=nl

Nationaal Archief (2024b). *div.nrs. Verlening van medewerking aan financiering en liquidatie van de N.V. Nederlandsche Spitsbergen Compagnie te Rotterdam 1921–1973* [diverse numbers. Provisions of assistance with financing and liquidation of the N.V. Nederlandse Spitsbergen Compagnie in Rotterdam 1921–1973. 2.25.77.28 Inventaris van het archief van de Marx & Co.'s Bank, (1893) 1869–1970 (1988) (De Nederlandsche Bank). https://www.nationaalarchief.nl/onderzoeken/archief/2.25.77.28

Ministry of Foreign Affairs (2021). *Statement by the Netherlands on its involvement in the work of the Arctic Council*. http://hdl.handle.net/11374/2680

Permanent Court of Arbitration (2015). Award of Merit. *The Arctic Sunrise Arbitration (Netherlands v. Russia)* PCA Case No. 2014–02. https://pcacases.com/web/sendAttach/1438

Pompeo, M. (2019). *Speech by Secretary of State of the United States of America*. Arctic Council. http://hdl.handle.net/11374/2409

Project Delta Group (n.d.). *Project Delta Group Foundation*. Retrieved 18 December 2024, from: https://projectdeltagroup.com/

Rijksdienst voor Ondernemend Nederland (2023). *Energiesysteem 2050* [Energy system 2050]. https://www.rvo.nl/onderwerpen/energiesysteem

Rijksoverheid (2021). *Fiche 3: Mededeling EU Arctisch Beleid* [Sheet 3: EU Arctic policy communication]. https://open.overheid.nl/documenten/ronl-1bf93224-98fc-4997-b052-5f761a6423ca/pdf

Royal Wagenborg (n.d.). *Logistical expert under Arctic circumstances*. Royal Wagenborg. Retrieved 4 December 2024, from https://www.wagenborg.com/cases/logistical-expert-under-arctic-circumstances

Rijksoverheid (2022). *Afschrift brief over uitgangspunten samenwerking onderwijs en wetenschap met Russische Federatie en Belarus.* [Copy of letter about principles of cooperation in education and science with the Russian Federation and Belarus]. https://www.rijksoverheid.nl/documenten/brieven/2022/03/04/brief-aan-voorzitters-uitgangspunten-t-b-v-samenwerking-met-de-russische-federatie-en-belarus

Schilder, G. (1984). Development and achievements of Dutch Northern and Arctic cartography in the sixteenth and seventeenth centuries. *Arctic, 37*(4), 493–514. https://doi.org/10.14430/arctic2231

Schokkenbroek, J.C.A. (2008). Dutch whaling and sealing in the seventeenth and eighteenth centuries. In H. Berg, de Jong, J., & W. Koetsenruijter (Eds.), *Trying out: An anatomy of Dutch whaling and sealing in the nineteenth century, 1815–1885* (pp. 26–44). Amsterdam University Press. https://doi.org/10.1515/9789048521104-007

Shell Media Enquiries (2015). *Shell Updates on Alaska Exploration*. https://www.afm.nl/downloadregisterfile.aspx?type=openbaarmaking-voorwetenschap&enc=7Rpj0BBaMD5lzfwUlyQ9TIe+XbKYS1JE7+GVfXY2PxNqAT3NVNKp3QCQcI2WUb5gS/PYmhvg5EA+E7FpgiengZj0NLAMUDbP/0PnUtKH27VA0/CZGu7E4hLGdYYwwWpdu5VmbK9i5W054yqFt5e1PeiF2QAKPaN7uXqJfrRFWzx6YUv9GjqkQr7keap+iF7deTki4IU2j65b6LA4lD9PdyWmfpp5/zqt/h0h+CMc0Nj8XFz/7f/JrbQGdKzCOuMOyCZ5F813XmR0XTjX/7wiuQRynJC3TdrDcJ3zH8VaJQxE8TaEUEx6c7UtmM7IyBgMLuT0W1rlM4ZnTEztD186nQys63VzXJuIGtDajbQ0xp8=

Slingerland, S. (2019, May 21). *Beyond Nord Stream 2: Lessons from the Netherlands.* Clingendael Institute. https://spectator.clingendael.org/nl/publicatie/beyond-nord-stream-2-lessons-netherlands

Teal Jr., J.J. (1951). Europe's northernmost frontier. *Foreign Affairs, 29*(2), 263–275. https://doi.org/10.2307/20030832

Ter Kuile, L. (2018). *Observer report: The Netherlands (1 November 2018)*. Arctic Council. http://hdl.handle.net/11374/3137

Ter Kuile, L. (2021). *Observer review report Reykjavík 2021: The Netherlands* (1 June 2020). Arctic Council. http://hdl.handle.net/11374/3138

van der Togt, T. (2016). Internationaal recht versus harde realpolitik: Hoe MH17 de Nederlands-Russische relatie nog lang zal belasten [International law versus hard realpolitik: How the MH17 will burden the Dutch-Russian relationship for a long time to come]. *Atlantisch Perspectief.* https://www.atlcom.nl/artikel-atlantisch-perspectief/internationaal-recht-versus-harde-realpolitik/

van der Togt, T. (2020). In search of a European Russia strategy. *Atlantisch Perspectief.* https://www.clingendael.org/sites/default/files/2020-03/Analysis_In_Search_of_a_European_Russia_Strategy.pdf

Treaty concerning the Archipelago of Spitsbergen (adopted 9 February 1920, entered into force 14 August 1925) 2 LNTS 7. [1920 Spitsbergen Treaty]

Tweede Kamer der Staten-Generaal (2011). Nieuwe Commissievoorstellen en initiatieven van de lidstaten van de Europese Unie. Fiche 9: Mededeling ontwikkeling EU beleid voor Noordpoolgebied [New Commission proposals and example of the European Union summary. Sheet 9: Communication on the development of EU policy for the Arctic region]. *BRIEF VAN DE STAATSSECRETARIS VAN BUITENLANDSE ZAKEN.* vergaderjaar 2011–2012, 22 112, nr. 1460. https://zoek.officielebekendmakingen.nl/kst-22112-1460.html

United Nations Convention on the Law of the Sea (adopted 10 December 1982, entered into force 16 November 1994) 1833 UNTS 3. [UNCLOS]

Verbond van Verzekeraars (2017, January 19). *Hoe zit het met...negatieve reisadviezen en verzekeren?* [How do negative travel advice and insurance work?]. https://www.verzekeraars.nl/publicaties/actueel/hoe-zit-het-met-negatieve-reisadviezen-en-verzekeren

Watts, J. (1857). *The Dutch at the North pole and the Dutch in Maine: A paper read before the New York historical society.* New York, Printed for the Society.

CHAPTER 8

The South in the North: Interests and Future Challenges for Spain in the Arctic Region

Ana Belén López Tárraga

1 The Arctic: A Region of Growing International Interest

From being an area dedicated to peace and free of geopolitical tensions, as mentioned by the then president of the Soviet Union, Mikhail Gorbachev, in his Murmansk speech in 1987 (Cinelli, 2012, p. 206), the Arctic is one of the places on Earth where the effects of climate change are most visible in a physical and human sense. This is how the current situation in the Arctic, the geographical region north of the Arctic Circle, could be defined at first glance.

From a physical geographic sense, the Arctic is at a critical juncture due to the effects of climate change. According to the latest data from the Intergovernmental Panel on Climate Change (IPCC), the 1.5°C increase in the Earth's average temperature will have its greatest impact on the polar regions by accelerating the melting of permafrost (IPCC, 2023, p. 29). These changes in the region will allow the exploitation of mineral and energy resources and the opening of new commercial shipping and new commercial shipping routes and marine fishing grounds (Dodds & Woodward, 2021, pp. 95–100). From a human geographic sense, mention must be made of the new geopolitical situation that the region has been experiencing since Russia's aggression against Ukraine on 24 February 2022, which has triggered an international military conflict (Torondel, 2022, p. 9).

In this context, not only countries with geographical borders in the Arctic and full membership in the Arctic Council (Finland, Sweden, Norway, Denmark, Iceland, the United States, Canada, and Russia) have interests in the region. Countries that do not have borders in the region, such as China, India, Spain, France, Germany, and Japan, among others, are also seeking to position themselves in the Arctic. The following pages will analyze Spain's interests in this region of the world.

To this end, this chapter will present the main interests that this southern European country has in the region as well as the political and governmental mechanisms it has developed to increase its presence in the Arctic. Next,

 | DOI:10.1163/9789004734685_009

in order to analyze the aforementioned interests, this chapter will also present the results and conclusions obtained from various interviews with members of the Spanish Polar Committee, Spanish representatives at the Arctic Council and in the working groups of the International Arctic Science Committee (IASC).

2 Spain and Its Arctic Interests

The Spanish people and their history are linked to the exploration and conquest of territories in different parts of the planet. The polar areas also have their place in Spanish history and, in the case of the Arctic, the presence of Spanish navigators has been documented since the 16th century with the presence of whalers from Galicia, Cantabria, and the Basque Country. In the same century, Spanish sailors such as Juan Rodríguez Cabrillo and Sebastián Vizcaíno also skirted the coasts of North America, reaching high latitudes in the northern Pacific (Spanish Polar Committee, 2016, p. 7). It would be a century later when explorers such as Alejandro Malaspina and José Bustamante would sail through Arctic waters looking for the Northwest Passage and the possibility of establishing new settlements. In addition, there are documents accrediting the presence of Galician, Cantabrian, and Basque whalers in northern latitudes above Labrador and Newfoundland in the 16th century. While their presence in the waters of Svalbard dates back to the 18th century (Spanish Polar Committee, 2016, p. 8). These historical facts highlight Spain's long-standing interest in the Arctic. Today, the country's interests in the region can be defined as economic, scientific, and political (Morera Castro, 2016, pp. 764–772).

2.1 *Spain and the Arctic: Economic Interests*

From the economic perspective, three interests stand out: the fishing industry, the import of energy and mining resources, and tourism.

As a southern European country, the Mediterranean Sea borders approximately 43% of the length of the Spanish coastline (National Geographic Institute, n.d.). For these reasons, it is not surprising that the diet that bears the same name as the sea, the Mediterranean diet, is the traditional basis of the country's diet. It entails a set of skills, knowledge, and traditions associated with growing, harvesting, gathering, fishing, preserving, processing, and preparing products for consumption. All of this is also the fruit of centuries of exchanges between the different Mediterranean countries, including Spain (Ministry of Culture, n.d.). These food practices are so characteristic and distinctive that, in 2013, the United Nations Educational, Scientific and Cultural Organization (UNESCO) included the Mediterranean diet in the representative list of the Intangible Cultural Heritage of Humanity (UNESCO, 2013).

Among the different foods that make up the Mediterranean diet, fish consumption occupies a fundamental position. So much so that of the ten pillars that make up this diet, the seventh pillar recommends consuming fish in abundance, as its fats, although of animal origin, have properties very similar to those of vegetable fats, which have protective properties against cardiovascular diseases (Ministry of Culture, n.d.). Moreover, in the specific case of Spain, traditional gastronomy has a wide range of dishes featuring cod and salmon, both of which are of northern origin (Mediterranean Diet Foundation n.d.). However, consumption patterns have evolved in recent decades, from purchased salted fish to fish consumed fresh due to the introduction of fridges and freezers in Spanish households and the fact that, due to the frenetic pace of life, less time is available to cook salted fish (Espinosa-Seguí & Sánchez-Hernández, 2013).

Spain's interest in the Arctic is influenced by the presence of fish in its diet, both in the fishing and shipping sectors. In 2021, the per capita consumption of fishery and aquaculture products was 42.98%, placing it in second position behind its neighbour, Portugal (European Market Observatory for Fisheries and Aquaculture Products, 2023, p. 45). Its fishing fleet ranks third in the European Union (EU) in terms of number of vessels with 8,657 (La Moncloa, 2023) and second in terms of tonnage capacity (European Commission, 2022). In addition, the Spanish fleet is the first in terms of catches in Europe, with around 807,697 tonnes of fish in 2022, where the largest volume of fishing, 61%, took place in international waters, followed by 6.5% in EU fishing grounds, and 32% in national waters (La Moncloa, 2023).

This high consumption of fish translates into substantial household expenditure, with Spanish families spending the largest share of their household economy on the purchase of fresh fish (European Market Observatory for Fisheries and Aquaculture Products, 2023, p. 57). The country alone consumed 41% of the total volume of fish consumed in the European Union in 2022. Over the last five years, salmon, hake, sea bass, cod, sardine, and sea bream have been the most consumed species by the Spanish population (European Market Observatory for Fisheries and Aquaculture Products, 2023, pp. 57–86).

In order to safeguard the fishing interests of the various Member States, including Spain, and within the framework of the EU's exclusive competence in the field of fisheries, the Council of the European Union published Regulation (EU) 2022/681 of 28 April 2022 (hereinafter Regulation (EU) 2022/681). This Regulation establishes the fishing opportunities for certain fish stocks and groups of fish stocks in EU waters. It also establishes fishing quotas for Union vessels in certain non-Union waters and in agreement with Norway. Regulation (EU) 2022/681 granted the Spanish fleet almost half of the quota for Arctic cod in Svalbard and the international waters of the Barents Sea, i.e. 49.3% of the 19,636 tonnes available to the EU. This regulation was established after 16 months of formal talks between the EU and Norway.

The importance of the fisheries sector in Spain is aligned with the respect for the environment, the protection of the oceans, and the prevention of biodiversity loss in the high seas. Spain has signed the Agreement under the United Nations Convention on the Law of the Sea on the Conservation and Sustainable Use of Marine Biological Diversity in Areas beyond National Jurisdiction (BBNJ Agreement, 2023). The agreement was signed by the European Union and its Member States on 20 September 2023 in New York, in the framework of the United Nations High-Level Segment and the Spanish rotating presidency of the Council of the European Union (European Commission, 2023). The main objectives of the agreement are the protection of large-scale marine protected areas; the sharing of benefits derived from marine genetic resources; the establishment of clear rules for the conduct of environmental impact assessments; and capacity building and the transfer of marine technology between the different Parties (European Commission, n.d.). In total, as of January 2024, the agreement has been signed by 80 countries, including the 27 countries that make up the EU.

Likewise, from an economic perspective, the mineral and energy resources found in the Arctic are also of interest to Spain. As is the case with many EU States, Spain is an energy-dependent country, which makes the Arctic region a space of possibilities and opportunities (Morera Castro, 2016, p. 765). Additionally, although Spain is currently not heavily dependent on natural resources from the North, it does import almost 10% of its gas from Norway. The increased dependence on Arctic resources by EU Member States, especially from Norway, has been reflected in the increase of the EU spending on gas and oil by 105% in the last decade, from 2012 to 2022 (Eurostat, 2024). This number is expected to increase following Russia's aggression towards Ukraine, which triggered a series of EU sanctions towards Russia that include a disconnection of oil and gas imports by Member States from Russia (Council of the European Union, 2023). In contrast, Spain has

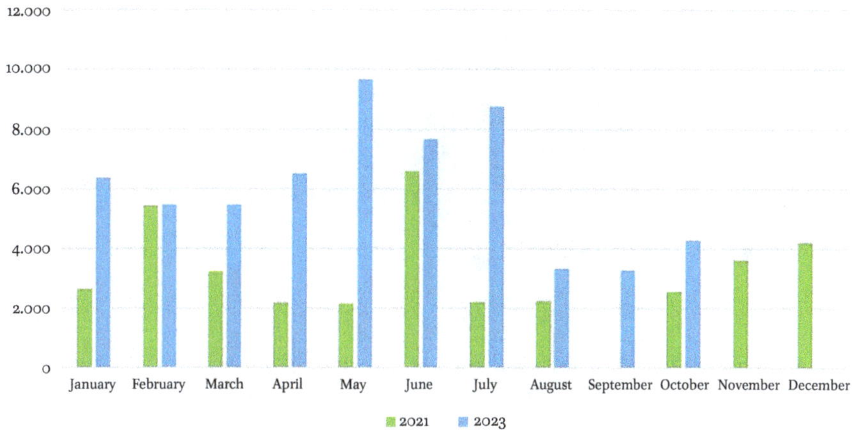

FIGURE 8.1 Evolution of Spain's LNG Imports into Russia in GWh between 2021 and 2023
SOURCE: COMPILED BY AUTHOR BASED ON DATA EXTRACTED FROM WEBSITE OF CORES (HTTPS://WWW.CORES.ES/ES/ESTADISTICAS)

increased its dependence on gas, specifically liquefied natural gas (LNG), as shown in the data from the Corporation of Strategic Reserves of Petroleum Products (CORES) in Figure 8.1.

However, oil and gas are not the only attractive resources in the Arctic. Palladium, diamonds, platinum, cobalt, nickel, tungsten, and zinc are some of the minerals that are yet to be exploited in the region and are of strategic interest (Fisas, 2019, p. 47), as many of them are used to manufacture electronic components. In addition to all these resources, wood, coal, and metals are found in great abundance in Norway, Sweden, and Finland (Adánez & Marino, 2023, pp. 263–265).

Spain's interest in natural resources located in the European Arctic region is reflected in the number of Spanish companies operating there. According to the latest reports prepared by the public entity ICEX Spain Export and Investment (hereinafter ICEX) under the Ministry of Industry, Trade and Tourism, 94 Spanish companies have operated in Finland, Sweden and Norway between 2020 and 2022 (ICEX Spain Export and Investment, 2022). Among the economic activities in which these Spanish companies are mainly engaged are infrastructure development, civil works (rail transport networks) and urban services, the manufacture of industrial machinery, electronic components, automotive and iron and steel, the manufacture of textiles and cellulose, and energy (oil, gas and wind power) (Figure 8.2). These industries require different materials for their development, and the Arctic is one of the places where they can be found.

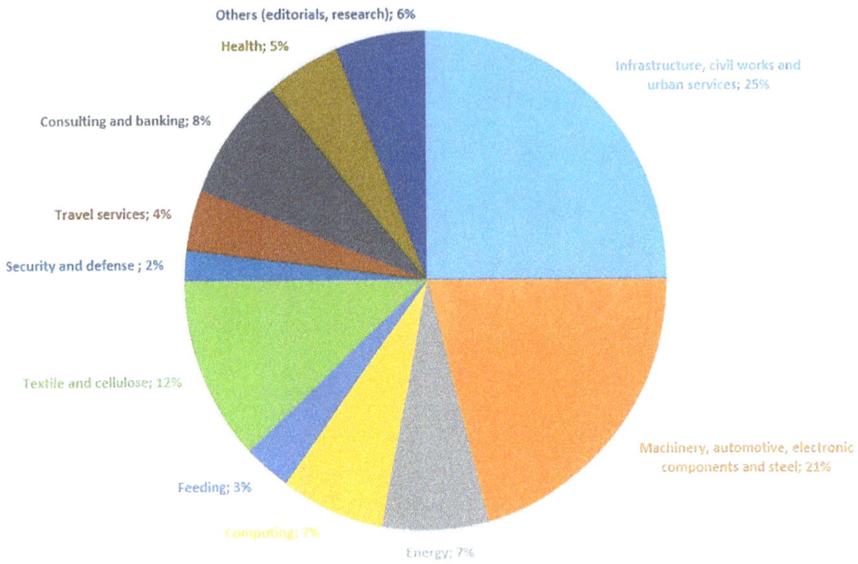

FIGURE 8.2 Main economic activities carried out by Spanish companies in Finland, Sweden, and Norway (2020–2022)
SOURCE: COMPILED BY AUTHOR BASED ON DATA EXTRACTED FROM THE WEBSITE OF THE SPANISH INSTITUTE FOR FOREIGN TRADE (ICEX SPAIN EXPORT AND INVESTMENT)

Within this group of companies, two are particularly noteworthy. Within this group of companies, two stand out. On the one hand, Repsol Exploración S.A., which operates in Norway through its subsidiary Repsol Norge AS. On the other hand, Vilma Oil S.L., which also operates in Norway through its subsidiary Partrederiet VLGC DA (ICEX Spain Export and Investments, 2022). Repsol, started working on Norwegian territory in 2003 in oil and gas exploration and exploitation activities. It is currently extracting oil in the North Sea and the Norwegian Sea. Vilma Oil S.L. has been active since 1996 in oil extraction and trading in more than 25 countries, including Norway (Vilma Oil, n.d.).

Finally, it is worth mentioning the economic activities derived from tourism. Attracted by winter activities (skiing and snowboarding, among others), snowy landscapes and fjords, Spaniards travel to northern Finland, Sweden, and Norway for these activities especially during the winter season. Before COVID-19, Spaniards represented the second largest national group of visitors to the Finnish Lapland (Aguilera Aranda, 2023, p. 131). After the pandemic, the tourism market in northern Finland, Sweden, and Norway is regaining strength and the number of direct flights connecting Spain to northern desti-

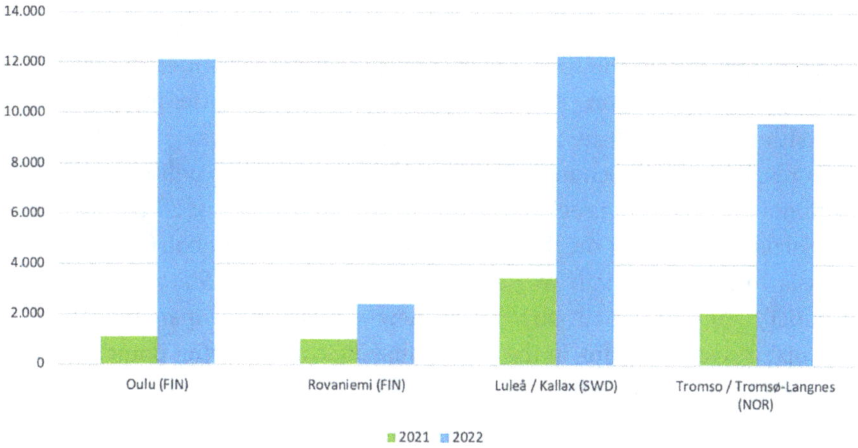

FIGURE 8.3 Evolution of air passengers from Spain to Oulu (Finland), Rovaniemi (Finland), Luleå (Sweden), and Tromsø (Norway) 2021–2022
SOURCE: COMPILED BY AUTHOR BASED ON DATA EXTRACTED FROM AENA'S WEBSITE (AIRPORT OPERATOR)

nations such as Oulu and Rovaniemi in Finland, Luleå in Sweden, and Tromsø in Norway has grown significantly between 2021 and 2022, increasing the number of passengers flying from Spanish airports to these destinations (Aeropuertos Españoles y Navegación Aérea (AENA), n.d.), as can be seen in Figure 8.3.

2.2 *Spain and the Arctic: Political and Institutional Interests*

The economic interests discussed above find their correlative –and sometimes their backing – in political and institutional actions. The polar regions have been of special interest to the Spanish government. At the institutional level, initially, given its special circumstances and characteristics, the Antarctic was the polar region to which Spain turned its attention and in 1982 it joined the 1959 Antarctic Treaty, to which it was admitted as a Consultative Party in 1988. Spain thus sought to contribute to and learn from this space for cooperation and scientific research. Since then, Spain has carried out an annual Antarctic campaign at its two Antarctic scientific bases: the Juan Carlos I base on Livingston Island and the Gabriel de Castilla base on Deception Island, both in the South Shetland archipelago. It also has two oceanographic vessels, the *Hespérides* and the *Sarmiento de Gamboa* (Ministry of Science, Innovation and University, n.d.). With the start of these activities, Spain set up the Spanish Polar Committee in 1998 under the Ministry of Science, Innovation and Universities through the General Secretariat for Research to coordinate Spanish activities in polar areas. Although when the committee was created, Spain did not develop activities in the Arctic, the government coined the term 'polar' to include future activities that could be developed in the region (Real Decreto 852/2020, 22 of septiembre).

With the arrival of the 21st century and the tangible changes in the Arctic as a result of climate change, Spain would materialize its political and institutional interest in the region. At the ministerial meeting of 26 October 2006 in Salekhard (Russia) on the occasion of the change of chairmanship from Russia to Norway, Spain was admitted as an Observer State in the Arctic Council (Arctic Council, 2006). The new status would open the door for Spanish research groups in the Arctic, making this a turning point for Spain in the Arctic. At the same time, Spain's foreign relations in the Arctic began to materialize, as the country was represented in the Arctic Council by a member of the Ministry of Foreign Affairs, European Union and Cooperation and a member of the Spanish Polar Committee, thus creating Spain's Arctic constituency at a political and institutional level. Spain is considered an active observer member due to its high level of participation and work within the different Arctic Council working groups and from different ministries (Aguilera Aranda, 2023, pp. 132–133) (Table 8.1).

Finally, among the political interests, it should be stressed that, as an EU Member State, Spain's actions and interests are aligned with the development of the European Arctic policy (European Commission, 2021) and the development of the EU's Strategic Compass, which seeks to strengthen the EU's security and defence policy from 2022 to 2030, where the Arctic is included. In this area, mention should also be made of Spain's participation as a North Atlantic Treaty Organization (NATO) member in the Trident Juncture manoeuvres held in Norway in 2018 and in the Cold Response exercises held every two years in the same country (Conde Pérez, 2022, p. 139).

2.3 *Spain and the Arctic: Scientific Interests*

Spain's scientific research work is the greatest contribution the country has made in the area since the end of the 20th century. In addition to the economic, political, and institutional interests that can be derived from greater scientific knowledge of the Arctic, Spain is highly committed to the advancement of science and research, especially in the field of climate action (Aguilera Aranda, 2023, p. 131). In this regard, in addition to its participation in the various Arctic Council working groups, as shown in Table 8.1, Spain's work at an international and national level is noteworthy. At the international level, the work carried out in all of working groups of the International Arctic Science Committee (IASC), its involvement in the Association of Polar Early Career Scientists (APECS), its participation in the Arctic Sci-

TABLE 8.1 Participation of the government of Spain in the different Arctic Council Working Groups between 2017–2022

Arctic Council Working Group	Participation of Spain	Ministry/s Government of Spain	Directorate-General or attached body
Emergency Prevention, Preparedness and Response (EPPR)	Participation in plenary meetings since 2018	Ministry of Transport, Mobility and Urban Agenda	–
Protection of the Arctic Marine Environment (PAME)	Participation in plenary meetings since 2018. Interpretation of the Polar Code (meetings).	Ministry of Transport, Mobility and Urban Agenda Ministry of Ecological Transition and Demographic Challenge	Directorate-General for Merchant Shipping
Arctic Contaminants Action Program (ACAP)	Participation in plenary meetings	Ministry of Ecological Transition and Demographic Challenge	–
Conservation of Arctic Flora and Fauna (CAFF)	Participation in plenary meetings. Arctic Migratory Bird Initiative	Ministry of Ecological Transition and Demographic Challenge	–
Arctic Monitoring and Assessment Programme (AMAP)	Participation in plenary meetings. The Spanish Government acted as a reviewer for two of the final reports of the Climate programme. Spain contributed to the 2020 report 'POPs and climate change'.	Ministry of Ecological Transition and Demographic Challenge	State Meteorology Agency (AEMET)
Sustainable Development Working Group (SDWG)	Participation in plenary meetings since 2017	Ministry of Foreign Affairs, Europea n Union and Cooperation	–

SOURCE: COMPILED BY AUTHOR BASED ON DATA EXTRACTED FROM THE ARCTIC COUNCIL'S WEBSITE

ence Ministerial (ASM) meetings, and its contribution to the European Polar Board should be mentioned. At the national level, most notable is the work carried out by researchers at universities, research centres, and foundations.

Within scientific cooperation at the international level, Spain joined IASC in 2009 and currently has two members from different institutions representing the country in each of the five working groups, as well as an active presence on the Council Board. It is very important to emphasize that its participation in IASC is a nexus of union and exchange of knowledge at the highest scientific level due to the fact that it is an organization that has emerged from the scientific community since its beginnings (Quesada del Corral, 2023, pp. 169–171).

IASC works together with APECS, an organization formed by young Polar science researchers. In addition to being a meeting point for people starting their careers, this forum allows them to broaden their academic training and their leadership and communication skills. It is made up of 29 national committees, one for each of the member countries. Accordingly, as a member, Spain holds a national committee gathering young researchers from Spanish universities and research centres (Association of Polar Early Career Scientists, 2024).

Also in the international sphere, ASM meetings, created by President Obama in 2016, stand out as high-level meetings to discuss all scientific issues and ways to collaborate on the Arctic. This forum is an opportunity for non-Arctic countries with scientific interests in the region to collaborate. These meetings are organized between the country holding the rotating chairmanship of the Arctic Council and a non-Arctic country. To date, four meetings have been held, with Spain actively participating in the first three. The fourth meeting was scheduled for 2022 in Paris and was to be organized between Russia, which held the rotating chairmanship of the Arctic Council at the time, and France. After the conflict with Ukraine arose, no Western country participated in the meeting, which was finally held in St. Petersburg with only Chinese and Belarusian scientists present (Quesada del Corral, 2023, pp. 174–175).

Finally, in the international sphere, Spain participates in the European Polar Board, an independent organization exclusively dedicated to the study of and research on the polar regions (Arctic and Antarctic). Spain is represented by the Spanish National Research Council (CSIC) and the Ministry of Science and Innovation (MCIN) (European Polar Board, n.d.). As an example of collaboration, the Barcelona Supercomputing Center is currently coordinating, together with the Arctic Centre of the University of Lapland, one of the projects that were selected by the EU-PolarNet 2 initiative funded by the European Polar Research Programme (EU-PolarNet, n.d.). Among the already completed projects in which Spain has participated is 'Eurofleets 2', where scientists from different research centres dedicated to oceanography and the marine environment worked and contributed to the fleet with a vessel (Eurofleets, n.d.). One of the vessels destined for scientific activities of the Balearic Islands Coastal Observation System (SOCIB), funded by the Spanish Ministry of Science, Innovation and Universities, also took part in the research (Balearic Islands Coastal Observation System, n.d.).

At the national level, the Arctic is a subject of study from the purest sciences to the different disciplines that make up the social sciences. As proof of this, 63 articles have been published between 2022 and 2023 by non-affiliated researchers and researchers currently working in the country's various universities and research centres.[1] In terms of projects, the State Research Agency, which is part of the Spanish Ministry of Science, Innovation and Universities, has financed different initiatives related to science, as can be seen in Table 8.2. The agency has a budget sub-area dedicated exclusively to 'Polar Research', which is included in the area of environmental sciences and technologies (State Research Agency, n.d.).

In addition to the publications and projects mentioned above, it should be noted that the Instituto Francisco De Vitoria of International and European Studies (Universidad Carlos III de Madrid), the Spanish Institute of Strategic Studies (Ministry of Defence) and the Spanish Ministry of Education and Science, the Instituto Universitario de Estudios Europeos Salvador de Madariaga (University of A Coruña), the Centre for Arctic Research (Autonomous University of Barcelona), the International Security Studies Group (University of Granada), the Department of International Law, Ecclesiastical Law and Philosophy of Law (Complutense University of Madrid), and the Departments of Geology and Geography (University of Salamanca) also carry out research on the Arctic.

Finally, mention should be made of the work carried out by non-profit organizations such as foundations. As an example of this, it is worth citing the work carried out by the ECODES Foundation, located in the city of Zaragoza. Since 1992, they have been working towards a society that moves towards a greener, more inclusive and responsible model by influencing

1 To extract this figure, a bibliographic review was carried out in the Web of Science database. The terms 'Arctic' and 'Ártico' were entered and filtered by language (English and Spanish), affiliation (universities and research centres) and date (2022 and 2023).

TABLE 8.2 List of Arctic-related projects funded by the Spanish State Research Agency (2016–2025)

Project	Institution	Thematic area	Period
Biodiversity, three-dimensional organization, functioning and interdependency in cryptogamic covers of arid and polar regions	National Museum of Natural Sciences	Natural Resources	2016–2019
Polar viruses and climate change	Severo Ochoa Centre for Molecular Biology	Biology and Biomedicine	2015
Arctic rank preservers of symmetric matrices and cybersecurity	Institute of Physical and Information Technologies "Leonardo Torres Quevedo".	Chemical Science and Technologies	2017–2018
Ecology and management of the invasive snow crab: Predicting expansion, impacts and sustainability in the Arctic under climate change (EISA)	Institute of Marine Sciences	Natural Resources	2019–2022
Aerosol Emissions in Polar Environments Under Change	Institute of Marine Sciences	Natural Resources	2020–2023
Structure and Dynamics of Hydrothermal Systems in Polar Volcanic Calderas (Hydrocal)	Barcelona Institute of Geosciences	Natural Resources	2021–2023
Effects of Community Assembly Processes for Trophic Network Structures in the High Arctic: Implications for Understanding the Ecological Consequences of Climate Change	Joint Institute for Biodiversity Research	Chemical Science and Technologies	2020–2023
Ecogenomics and Evolution of Key Polar Uncultured Prokaryotes	Institute of Marine Sciences	Natural Resources	2021–2024
Advances on Monitoring the Sea Ice Thickness and Snow Depth, Ocean Dynamics, and Freshwater Content in the Arctic Using Remote Sensing Data	Institute of Marine Sciences	Natural Resources	2022–2025

SOURCE: COMPILED BY AUTHOR BASED ON DATA EXTRACTED FROM THE STATE RESEARCH AGENCY'S WEBSITE

public policies and providing scientific data. Specifically, their work on the Arctic focuses on the prohibition of heavy fuels used by maritime transport.

3 The Spanish Polar Strategy

Spain's interests in the polar regions was reflected in 2016 with the publication of the document *Guidelines for a Spanish Polar Strategy* (Spanish Polar Committee, 2016), which reviews the relationship Spain has had and continues to have with the polar areas, the necessary reasons for developing a strategy, and the geostrategic aspects of both regions. The text ends with a series of proposals for action based on scientific, logistical, and sectoral grounds.

3.1 *Why Is It Necessary?*

The first nuance that can be seen in this document is that Spain treats both polar regions in the same way, despite their physical, biological, geographical, human, and legal differences. On the other hand, it does point out that work and experience has always been more present in the Antarctic due to the presence of Spanish infrastructures on the ground and the seniority of the Spanish National Antarctic Research Programme, which was established back in 1988 (Spanish Polar Committee, 2016, p. 1).

Climate change and the related environmental impacts in both polar regions have increased the interests for these regions with regard to its ecological, social, political, geostrategic, and economic aspects (Spanish Polar Committee, 2016, p. 9). In this regard, Spain emphasizes this point in the document concerning the reasons in the scientific sphere as the basis for progress and underlines the promotion and support that Spain gives to scientific research, a fact noted in the previous section. For Spain, this knowledge is fundamental for forecasting the future and helping local populations (both Arctic and non-Arctic) to improve their resilience to global changes (Spanish Polar Committee, 2016, p. 11).

As regards geostrategic aspects, the strategy stresses that Spain's participation in polar affairs must be a matter of State and therefore must participate with all its civil and military means. In this sense, Spain, as a member of NATO, is already actively involved in defence matters, as also pointed out in the previous paragraph. At institutional level, Spain has ratified different legal instruments promoting the preservation of the environment. Some of these instruments are the 1980 Convention on Future Multilateral Co-Operation in North-East Atlantic Fisheries (NEAFC) through the European

Union, the 1992 Convention for the Protection of the Marine Environment of the North-East Atlantic (OSPAR Convention), the International Maritime Organization's (IMO) 1973 International Convention for the Prevention of Pollution from Ships (MARPOL) and 2014/2015 International Code for Ships Operating in Polar Waters (Polar Code), the 1982 United Nations Convention on the Law of the Sea (UNCLOS), and the 1992 Convention on Biological Diversity (CBD) (Comité Polar Español, pp. 12–14).

3.2 *How to Act?*

Based on the aforementioned premises, Spain stresses that it must occupy a prominent place on the polar scene and proposes a series of lines of action of a scientific, logistical, and sectoral nature (Spanish Polar Committee, 2016, pp. 17–34).

From the scientific point of view, it assumes that in order to make progress in the fight against the adverse effects of climate change, scientific advances in the knowledge of the terrestrial environment and the global oceans are essential. Among the priority lines of work that Spain has set itself in the scientific field, one is to improve knowledge of the functioning of polar atmospheres and their interactions with the climate and the oceans, ice variations, terrestrial geology, the adaptive capacity of organisms, and anthropogenic effects. In the specific case of the Arctic, Spain is committed to developing concrete actions to study the impacts of climate change on resident populations, natural resources, and economic activities (Spanish Polar Committee, 2016, pp. 18–21).

The strategy states that Spain prioritizes polar research because of its high internationalization and socio-economic interest. The specific lines of action on which the country proposes to work in scientific matters are geographic mobility, establishing relationships that allow the development of research activities in this field with a greater level of impact in the Arctic, where Spain does not have its own infrastructures; scientific cooperation between Spanish groups and groups from other countries; providing continuity and managing historical series of observations with a budget that is independent of research projects; promoting and enhancing the value of the National Polar Data Centre; encouraging participation in international forums through a strategy to foster continuous participation; to promote the coordination, communication, and dissemination of Spanish polar activity; and to foster new opportunities for young polar researchers, since the integration of young people into this field is taking place at a very low rate (Spanish Polar Committee, 2016, pp. 21–26).

The second of the priorities that Spain describes in its strategy is related to logistics, that is, the infrastructures that the country has in the Arctic, as well as the resources that it can participate in and make available. (Spanish Polar Committee, 2016, p. 26). The priorities for Spain in the Arctic in the short and medium term (2016–2025) include facilitating access for Spanish researchers to land-based facilities, making all the necessary agreements with countries and institutions that have infrastructures on the ground, and developing oceanographic campaigns (Spanish Polar Committee, 2016, p. 27).

The third line is in harmony with the economic activities derived from the exploitation of the natural reserves available in the Polar areas, fishing, and navigation. Spain stresses that all these actions must be carried out in a sustainable and environmentally friendly manner, as well as ensuring the maintenance of living conditions for local populations, fauna, and flora. This section also mentions that attention should be paid to the development of the Arctic Economic Council (Spanish Polar Committee, 2016, pp. 27–29). Spain focuses its guidelines on two activities along these lines: fishing resources and trans-Arctic navigation (Spanish Polar Committee, 2016, pp. 29–37).

Spain reflects the fact that the deficit of fishery resources in both the country and the European Union is low. However, any action taken will always be in line with the decisions taken by the EU, which has exclusive competence over fisheries matters. As a consequence of this aspect, Spain must show its support for the creation of marine protected areas, the development of the EU's Arctic Policy, and must continue to provide information on Spanish fisheries within the framework of scientific monitoring bodies in the polar regions (Spanish Polar Committee, 2016, pp. 29–31).

In relation to trans-Arctic shipping, the strategy mentions that it is of great interest in Spain. Although Spain is aware that these routes present difficulties because they are not navigable all year round and have extreme weather conditions. In relation to navigability, the Spanish Polar Strategy describes that the effects of the opening of the Arctic routes will have a greater effect on the Atlantic ports than on the Mediterranean ports due to their proximity; the savings in distance by using the Northern Sea Route above Russia would lead to the opening of a permanent trade route that would compete with the classic navigation routes; although the opening of new routes would favour the reduction of greenhouse gas emissions by shortening distances, there is the possibility of a rebound effect as the flow of transactions increases (Spanish Polar Committee, 2016, pp. 31–37).

No reference is made to deadlines or possible approximate dates by which the Spanish Polar Strategy will be issued. As of late 2024, there are still no news in this regard.

3.3 *Where Is Spain Heading in the Arctic?*

Since Spain published the guidelines for the development of its polar strategy in 2016, the country has not taken any further steps to advance and translate this roadmap into an official strategy, as other non-Arctic European countries, such as France or Germany, have done. Despite this, the Spanish Polar Committee, as well as the researchers representing Spain in international scientific organizations, have continued their work. In order to identify possible next steps during the first quarter of 2023, five interviews were conducted by the author. Four of them were with Spanish representatives in IASC working groups: Carlos Toledano, Spanish representative in the atmospheric working group; Jaime Otero and Carolina Gabarro, representatives in the cryosphere working group; and Ana Manero, representative in the Social and Human Sciences research working group. The fifth interview was with the executive secretary of the Spanish Polar Committee and one of Spain's representatives on the Arctic Council, Antonio Quesada del Corral.

The interviews were conducted via email and consisted of questions related to each researcher's field of work. The questionnaire addressed to the IASC representatives working on issues related to environmental sciences was aimed at finding out what specific aspect of their field related to the Arctic they are working on in their research and within the IASC, the economic resources they have to carry out this activity, and the prospects for the future. The interview with the representative of the group dedicated to Social and Human Sciences, Ana Manero, in addition to the aforementioned issues, included questions on future prospects related to Spain's action at the institutional level in the Arctic. Finally, the interview with Antonio Quesada del Corral, given the roles he holds, focused more on the institutional actions carried out by the Spanish Polar Committee.

The following is an analysis of the interviews and a brief discussion of the results. As the interviewees are all people with a scientific profile, the analysis starts from a scientific point of view.

Spain's scientific interest in the Arctic has been a reality for decades. This is a unanimous affirmation by all those interviewed, although most of the research has been carried out in the Antarctic region. This fact can be explained by historical reasons: in the 1980s, in order to join the Antarctic Treaty, one of the requirements for consultative membership was to have scientific activity in the field. Since then, the Polar research programme has been in place without interruption. This is in addition to the presence of Spanish-owned infrastructures in the area. However, Spanish scientific research in the Arctic region has been carried out since the 1960s, as in the case of the atmosphere field, where Spain is working in the long term on measures to mitigate the effects of atmospheric pollution.

Funding for scientific activities comes mainly from the Spanish Research Agency, which has a specific section dedicated to Polar Research, for which the different researchers periodically compete every three years in order to carry out their research. The budget earmarked by Spain for scientific activities in the Polar areas is not equitable, with most of it going to research in the Antarctic. In the 2023/2024 campaign, 75% of the Polar Research budget was allocated to this region (Agencia Estatal de Investigación, 2023). Again, the reason for this is the country's infrastructure in the region. It should also be mentioned that this budget sub-area is dedicated to environmental sciences and technologies, leaving aside social sciences. Researchers in these areas who wish to develop projects related to the poles have to apply to their thematic area and not to a specific sub-area dedicated to Polar Research. Thus, within the State Research Agency, there is an unequal budgetary designation in the funding of the different scientific branches.

In addition, Polar science, especially in the Arctic, has an indisputably collaborative character. Since the 1990s, when the forums and institutions related to scientific research in the Arctic were being created, which Spain has joined, Spanish scientists have been able to work in the Arctic more effectively. The researchers interviewed stated that the organizations in which they are working on various projects, such as IASC, are responsible for covering their expenses. In addition, Spain continues to work on agreements with other countries that have infrastructure in the Arctic to share facilities and projects. Despite this scientific cooperation, which has recently been disrupted by Russia's aggression against Ukraine, there are clear differences between the resources allocated to the Arctic and the Antarctic. According to the Antarctic Treaty, the Antarctic is a zone dedicated to science and Article IV of the 1959 Antarctic Treaty, among other things, freezes the territorial claims of all States that have made territorial claims. In the Arctic, on the other hand, the sovereignty, sovereign rights, and jurisdiction of the eight Arctic States prevail over much of the region, except in the high seas areas of the Arctic Ocean. This prevents non-Arctic States from having an equal say in the development of science and knowledge in most of the Arctic. This is particularly true in the case of the EU, which has not yet been able to join the Arctic Council for political reasons. Additionally, EU Member States that are observers to the Arctic Council, such as Spain, have not been able to mediate or influence in the organization's inclusion (Quesada del Corral, 2023, p. 181).

Within the scientific field, one of the statements made by interviewees is that Spain does not have a specific plan describing the lines of research it wishes to focus on. On the contrary, each researcher approaches projects according to his or her own lines of interest and specialization. This can mean that the scientific research being developed in these regions does not correspond to the needs that Spain as a country may have or need to develop in order to meet its strategic interests. The research aligned with Spain's strategic interests would not be carried out at the national level due to the lack of specific strategic guidelines, nor at the international level due to the participation of scientists and researchers in projects that are specific to their lines of research, which are mainly of interest to them within organizations such as IASC.

Among the different economic aspects in which Spain has an interest in the Arctic, fishing is the economic activity most reflected by those interviewed. The Svalbard archipelago is one of the fishing regions from which cod is harvested. The 1920 Treaty of Svalbard, of which Spain is a Party since 1925, recognizes Norway's sovereignty over Svalbard, but recognizes the right of equal access to the resources of the Contracting Parties (Svalbard Treaty, Arts. 1–3). Thus, the EU, which has exclusive competence over the fisheries of the different Member States that make up the EU, periodically negotiates the fishing quotas to which Member States' vessels may have access, with Spain currently having the largest quota, as discussed above. In addition to looking after its interests in fishing matters, Spain is a country that is very involved in legislative proposals for the protection of marine areas in the Arctic and North Atlantic, as well as closely following all European and international legislation, the interviewees explain. As an example of this, the interviewees cite the adoption of the 2018 Agreement to Prevent Unregulated High Seas Fisheries in the Central Arctic Ocean (CAOFA), the renewal of the partnership with Greenland on sustainable fishing in 2021 (Official Journal of the European Union, 2021), or the signing of the BBNJ Agreement in 2023.

Finally, mention should be made of the international dimension, where Spain is a very active country, as reflected in the interview with the representative of the Spanish Polar Committee in the Arctic Council, Antonio Quesada del Corral. He maintains that Spain's participation in the Arctic

Council's working groups is diverse and active, a point made clear in the previous section. This participation is also reflected in the development of the European policy on the Arctic, where Spain has participated very actively in the latest official documents issued by the European Commission, making constructive comments on the text.

4 Conclusions: How Spain's Relationship with the Arctic Could Be Articulated in the Future

After what has been explained in these pages, it can be affirmed that Spain, despite not being a country that is very close geographically to the polar regions, does have a great interest in these regions. This is especially true of the Arctic for a number of reasons related to economics, politics, and science. In fact, it is these three areas that are the focus of Spain's Polar strategy. A document that Spain must translate into an official strategy in the short term. This would enable the country to attain greater influence and transparency in the international sphere.

Spain has a great deal of polar scientific activity. However, this activity remains diluted and is limited to the specific fields of each individual researcher. It is, therefore, necessary for the country's Arctic policy to define specific lines of action to act as a guiding thread for future research. This will make it possible to organize and concentrate the diversity of studies that currently exist and to focus on the scientific needs of the moment, thus unifying the forces of all Spanish scientists who have the Arctic as an object of study.

At the institutional level, Spain, as an EU Member State, and given its active status in the various working groups of the Arctic Council, could be an actor that could mediate between the EU and the Arctic Council in the future. This could lead to the European Union becoming an observer member in the short term.

Finally, it should be noted that in order to be able to analyze Spain's role at the institutional level, it is necessary to further extend the interviews with decision-makers. This is a line of work and analysis that the author intends to continue in the future in order to complete this work. Therefore, although science is of great relevance for Spain in Arctic matters, there are important issues related to economic activities that could not be analyzed and discussed due to the lack of interviews with actors in the sector.

Bibliography

Adánez Sanjuán, P., & Marino, E. (2023). Recursos minerales y energéticos y su industria [Industry, mineral resources, and energy in the Arctic]. *Cuadernos de Estrategia, 218*, 235–296. https://www.defensa.gob.es/ceseden/-/cuaderno-de-estrategia-218

Aeropuertos Españoles y Navegación Aérea (AENA) (n.d.). *Estadísticas de tráfico aéreo* [Air traffic statistics]. AENA. Retrieved 1 December 2024, from: https://www.aena.es/es/estadisticas/inicio.html

Agencia Estatal de Investigación (2023). *Thematic areas*. Retrieved 1 December 2024, from: https://www.aei.gob.es/en/thematic-areas/thematic-areas

Agreement to Prevent Unregulated High Seas Fisheries in the Central Arctic Ocean (adopted 3 October 2018, entered into force 25 June 2021). https://www.mofa.go.jp/files/000449233.pdf

Aguilera Aranda, F. (2023). El Ártico y las relaciones internacionales [The Arctic and international relations]. *Cuadernos de Estrategia, 218*, 107–156. https://www.defensa.gob.es/ceseden/-/cuaderno-de-estrategia-218

Antarctic Treaty (adopted 1 December 1959, entered into force 23 June 1961) 402 UNTS 71.

Association of Polar Early Career Scientists (2024). *National committees*. Retrieved 1 December 2024, from: https://apecs.is/who-we-are/national-committees.html

Balearic Islands Coastal Observation System (2024). *Facilities*. Retrieved 1 December 2024, from: https://www.socib.es/en/icts-socib-facilities

BBNJ Agreement (2023). Agreement under the United Nations Convention on the Law of the Sea on the Conservation and Sustainable Use of Marine Biological Diversity of Areas beyond National Jurisdiction (adopted 19 June 2023). https://treaties.un.org/pages/ViewDetails.aspx?src=TREATY&mtdsg_no=XXI-10&chapter=21&clang=_en

Cinelli, C. (2012). *El Ártico ante el derecho del mar contemporáneo* [The Arctic in contemporary law of the sea]. Tirant lo Blanch.

Conde Pérez, E. (2023). Derecho, geopolítica y sociedades árticas [Arctic law, geopolitics and societies]. *Cuadernos de Estrategia, 218*, 17–50. https://www.defensa.gob.es/ceseden/-/cuaderno-de-estrategia-218

CORES (2024). *Estadísticas* [Satistical data]. CORES. Retrieved 1 December 2024, from: https://www.cores.es/es/estadisticas

Council of the European Union (2023). *EU response to Russia's war of aggression against Ukraine*. Council of the European Union. Retrieved 1 December 2024, from: https://www.consilium.europa.eu/en/policies/eu-response-ukraine-invasion/

Dodds, K., & Woodward, J. (2021). *The Arctic: A very short introduction.* Oxford University Press.

Espinosa Seguí, A., & Sánchez Hernández, J.L. (2013). El mercado español del bacalao en salazón: Une aproximación regional desde la geografía de la convenciones [The Spanish salted cod market: a regional approach from the geography of conventions]. *Estudios Geográficos, 74*(275), 439–467. https://doi.org/10.3989/estgeogr.201316

European Commission (n.d.). *Protecting the ocean, time for action.* Retrieved from: https://oceans-and-fisheries.ec.europa.eu/ocean/international-ocean-governance/protecting-ocean-time-action_en

European Commission (2021). *Joint communication to the European Parliament, the Council, the European Economic and Social Committee and the Committee of the Regions "A stronger EU engagement for a peaceful, sustainable and prosperous Arctic".* Brussels 13.10.2021 JOIN (2021) 27 final. https://eur-lex.europa.eu/legal-content/EN/TXT/?uri=CELEX%3A52021JC0027

European Commission (2022). *Facts and figures on the common fisheries policy: Basic statistical data – 2022.* Retrieved 1 December 2024, from: https://oceans-and-fisheries.ec.europa.eu/facts-and-figures/facts-and-figures-common-fisheries-policy_en

European Commission (2023a). *A win for the ocean: High seas treaty signed at United Nations. News Announcement.* Retrieved 1 December 2024, from: https://oceans-and-fisheries.ec.europa.eu/news/win-ocean-high-seas-treaty-signed-united-nations-2023-09-20_en#:~:text=Once%20ratified%2C%20the%20High%20Seas,30%25%20of%20the%20planet%20by

European Market Observatory for Fisheries and Aquaculture Products (2023). *The EU fish market: 2023 edition. Highlights the EU in the world market supply consumption import-export landings in the EU aquaculture.* Retrieved 1 December 2024, from: https://eumofa.eu/documents/20124/35668/EFM2023_EN.pdf/95612366-79d2-a4d1-218b-8089c8e7508c?t=1699541180521

Eurofleets (2024). *Data management.* Eurofleets. Retrieved 1 December 2024, from: https://www.eurofleets.eu/project-information/partners/

European Polar Board (n.d.). *Membership.* European Polar Board. Retrieved 1 December 2024, from: https://www.europeanpolarboard.org/about-us/membership/

EU-PolarNet. (n.d.). *Call for services results.* EU-PolarNet. Retrieved 1 December 2024, from: https://eu-polarnet.eu/services-arcticxchange/

Eurostat (2024). *Database (environment and energy).* Retrieved 1 December 2024, from: https://ec.europa.eu/eurostat/data/database

ICEX Spain Export and Investments (2022). *Análisis del comercio exterior español* [Analysis of the foreign trade of Spain]. ICEX Spain Export and Investments. Retrieved from: https://informesestadisticos-est.icex.es/InformesComerciales/para metros_multiselect.jsp?TipoInforme=2

IPCC (2023). Summary for policymakers. In The Core Writing Team, H. Lee, & J. Romero (Eds.), *Climate change 2023: Synthesis report. A report of the intergovernmental panel on climate change* (pp. 1–34). IPCC. https://www.ipcc.ch/report/ar6/syr/downloads/report/IPCC_AR6_SYR_SPM.pdf

La Moncloa (2023, December 12). *Planas: Spain achieves the best quota of the 21st century for southern hake and increases quotas in monkfish, Cornish sole and southern horse mackerel.* Retrieved 1 December 2024, from: https://www.lamon cloa.gob.es/lang/en/gobierno/news/paginas/2023/20231212_eu-agriculture-fisheri es-council.aspx#:~:text=The%20Spanish%20fleet%20is%20the,international%20 waters%20(495%2C520%20tonnes)

Manfredi, D. (2001). *Alessandro Malaspina. A biography.* Alexandro Malaspina Research Centre, Malaspina University College.

Mediterranean Diet Foundation (n.d.). *What's the mediterranean diet?* Retrieved 1 December 2024, from: https://dietamediterranea.com/en/nutrition/

Ministry of Agriculture, Fisheries and Food (28 April 2022). *La Unión Europea y Noruega cierran un acuerdo sobre la cuota del bacalao ártico en aguas de Svalbard para el año 2022 que garantiza la actividad a la flota española* [The European Union and Norway reach an agreement on the Arctic cod quota in Svalbard waters for 2022 that guarantees activity for the Spanish fleet]. Ministry of Agriculture, Fisheries and Food. Retrieved 1 December 2024, from: https://www.ma pa.gob.es/fr/prensa/ultimas-noticias/la-uni%C3%B3n-europea-y-noruega-cierran -un-acuerdo-sobre-la-cuota-del-bacalao-%C3%A1rtico-en-aguas-de-svalbard-para -el-a%C3%B1o-2022-que-garantiza-la-actividad/tcm:36-618869#:~:text=La%20flo ta%20espa%C3%B1ola%20dispondr%C3%A1%20de,aguas%20internacionales% 20del%20mar%20de

Ministry of Science, Innovation and University (n.d.). *Oceanographic vessels.* Retrieved 1 December 2024, from: https://www.ciencia.gob.es/en/Organismos-y-Ce ntros/Comite-Polar-Espanol/Buques-Oceanograficos.html

Ministry of Culture (n.d.). *La dieta Mediterránea* [*The Mediterranean diet*]. Retrieved 1 December 2024, from: https://www.cultura.gob.es/cultura/areas/patrimonio/ mc/patrimonio-inmaterial/elementos-declarados/internacionales/dieta-mediter ranea.html

Ministry of Economy, Trade and Business (2024). *ICEX: Perfil de la empresa exportadora* [ICEX: Exporting company profile]. Retrieved 1 December 2024, from: https://informesestadisticos-est.icex.es/InformesComerciales/default.jsp?TipoIn forme=1

Morera Castro, M. (2016). Los intereses de España en el Ártico [Spain's interest in the Arctic]. *Bie3: Boletín IEEE*, 2, 761–792.

National Geographic Institute (n.d.). *Datos geográfico y toponimia* [Geographical data and toponymy]. National Geographic Institute. Retrieved 1 December 2024, from: https://www.ign.es/web/ane-datos-geograficos/-/datos-geograficos/datosGenerales?tipoBusqueda=longCosta

Quesada del Corral, A. (2023). Ciencia en colaboración en el Ártico [Collaborative science in the Arctic]. *Cuadernos de Estrategia, 218*, 157–184. https://www.defensa.gob.es/ceseden/-/cuaderno-de-estrategia-218

Official Journal of the European Union (2021). *Sustainable fisheries partnership agreement between the European Union, of the one part, and the Government of Greenland and the Government of Denmark, of the other part.* L 175/3. https://eur-lex.europa.eu/legal-content/EN/TXT/?uri=CELEX%3A22021A0518%2801%29

Real Decreto 852/2020, de 22 de septiembre, por el que se regula la composición y el funcionamiento del Comité Polar Español [Royal order 852/2020 of 22 September regulating the composition and operation of the Spanish Polar Committee]. Boletín Oficial del Estado, 16 de octubre de 2020. Retrieved 1 December 2024, from: https://www.boe.es/buscar/doc.php?id=BOE-A-2020-12360

Regulation (EU) 2022/681 of 28 April 2022 amending Regulation (EU) 2022/109 fixing for 2022 the fishing opportunities for certain fish stocks and groups of fish stocks applicable in Union waters and for Union fishing vessels in certain non-Union waters. Official Journal of the European Union, No L 126/2 of 29 April 2022. https://eur-lex.europa.eu/legal-content/EN/TXT/?uri=CELEX%3A32022R0681

Spanish Polar Committee (2016). *Guidelines for a Spanish Polar strategy.* Retrieved 1 December 2024, from: https://www.ciencia.gob.es/InfoGeneralPortal/documento/ef4fc9c3-10c3-444c-8f56-b6e6a76cb550

State Research Agency (n.d.). *Convocatorias* [Call for proposals]. State Research Agency. Retrieved 1 December 2024, from: https://www.aei.gob.es/convocatorias/buscador-convocatorias?status=1

Treaty concerning the Archipelago of Spitsbergen (adopted 9 February 1920, entered into force 14 August 1925) 2 LNTS 7. [1920 Svalbard Treaty]

Torondel Lara, M. (2022). Nuevos escenarios en el Ártico el cambio climático y la guerra de Ucrania [New scenarios in the Arctic: Climate change and the war in Ukraine]. *bie3: Boletín IEEE*, *28*, 654–664.

UNESCO (2013). Decision of the intergovernmental committee: 8.COM 8.10. Retrieved from: https://ich.unesco.org/en/decisions/8.COM/8.10

Vilma Oil (n.d.). *About us.* https://vilmaoil.com/

Index

www.ingramcontent.com/pod-product-compliance
Lightning Source LLC
Chambersburg PA
CBHW071247230926
51849CB00001B/253
9789004734678